Linux Installation and Getting Started

Version 2.2.2, 11 February 1995.

This book is an installation and new-user guide for the Linux system, meant for UNIX novices and gurus alike. Contained herein is information on how to obtain Linux, installation of the software, a beginning tutorial for new UNIX users, and an introduction to system administration. It is meant to be general enough to be applicable to any distribution of the Linux software.

Contents

Preface

"You are in a maze of twisty little passages, all alike."

Before you looms one of the most complex and utterly intimidating systems ever written. Linux, the free UNIX clone for the personal computer, produced by a mishmash team of UNIX gurus, hackers, and the occasional loon. The system itself reflects this complex heritage, and although the development of Linux may appear to be a disorganized volunteer effort, the system is powerful, fast, and free. It is a true 32-bit operating system solution.

My own experiences with Linux began several years ago, when I sat down to figure out how to install the only "distribution" available at the time—a couple of diskettes made available by H.J. Lu. I downloaded a slew of files and read pages upon pages of loosely-organized installation notes. Somehow, I managed to install this basic system and get everything working together. This was long before you could buy the Linux software on CD-ROM from worldwide distributors; before, in fact, Linux even knew how to access a CD-ROM drive. This was before XFree86, before Emacs, before commercial software support, and before Linux became a true rival to MS-DOS, Microsoft Windows, and OS/2 in the personal computer market.

You hold in your very hands the map and guidebook to the world of Linux. It is my hope that this book will help you to get rolling with what I consider to be the fastest, most powerful operating system for the personal computer. Setting up your own Linux system can be a great deal of fun—so grab a cup of coffee, sit back, and read on.

Grab a cup for me, too, while you're at it. I've been up hacking Linux for days.

Audience

This book is for any personal computer user who wants to install and use Linux on their system. We assume that you have basic knowledge about personal computers and operating systems such as MS-DOS. No previous knowledge about Linux or UNIX is assumed.

Despite this, we strongly suggest that UNIX novices invest in one of the many good UNIX books out there. Several of them are listed in Appendix A.

Organization

This book contains the following chapters.

Chapter 1, *Introduction to Linux*, gives a general introduction to what Linux is, what it can do for you, and what is required to run it on your system. It also provides helpful hints for getting help and reducing overall stress.

Chapter 2, *Obtaining and Installing Linux*, explains how to obtain the Linux software, as well as how to install it—from repartitioning your drive, creating filesystems, and loading the software on the system. It contains instructions meant to be general for any distribution of Linux, and relies on the documentation provided for your particular release to fill in any gaps.

Chapter 3, *Linux Tutorial*, is a complete introduction to using the Linux system for UNIX novices. If you have previous UNIX experience, most of this material should be familiar.

Chapter 4, *System Administration*, introduces many of the important concepts of system administration under Linux. This will also be of interest to UNIX system administrators who want to know about the Linux-specific issues of running a system.

Chapter 5, *Advanced Features*, introduces the reader to a number of advanced features supported by Linux, such as the X Window System and TCP/IP networking. A complete guide to configuring XFree86-3.1 is included.

Appendix A, *Sources of Linux Information*, is a listing of other sources of information about Linux, including newsgroups, mailing lists, online documents, and books.

Appendix B, *Linux Vendor List*, provides a short list of software vendors offering Linux software and services.

Appendix C, *FTP Tutorial and Site List*, is a tutorial for downloading files from the Internet with FTP. This appendix also includes a listing of FTP archive sites which carry Linux software.

Appendix D, *Linux BBS List*, is a listing of bulletin board systems worldwide which carry Linux software. Because most Linux users are do not have access to the Internet, it is important that information on BBS systems becomes available.

Appendix E, *The GNU General Public License*, contains a copy of the GNU GPL, the license agreement under which Linux is distributed. It is very important that Linux users understand the GPL; many disagreements over the terms of the GPL have been raised in recent months.

Acknowledgments

This book has been long in the making, and many people are responsible for the outcome. In particular, I would like to thank Larry Greenfield and Karl Fogel for their work on the first version of Chapter 3, and to Lars Wirzenius for his work on Chapter 4. Thanks to Michael K. Johnson for his assistance with the LDP and the LaTeX conventions used in this manual, and to Ed Chi, who sent me a printed copy of the book for edition.

Thanks to Melinda A. McBride at SSC, Inc., who did an excellent job completing the index for Chapters 3, 4, and 5. I would also like to thank Andy Oram, Lar Kaufman, and Bill Hahn at O'Reilly and Associates for their assistance with the Linux Documentation Project.

Thanks to Linux Systems Labs, Morse Telecommunications, Yggdrasil Computing, and others for their support of the Linux Documentation Project through sales of this book and other works.

Much thanks to the many activists, including (in no particular order) Linus Torvalds, Donald Becker, Alan Cox, Remy Card, Ted T'so, H.J. Lu, Ross Biro, Drew Eckhardt, Ed Carp, Eric Youngdale, Fred van Kempen, Steven Tweedie, and a score of others, for devoting so much time and energy to this project, and without whom there wouldn't be anything to write a book about.

Special thanks to the myriad of readers who have sent their helpful comments and corrections. There are far too many to list here. Who needs a spell checker, when you have an audience?

Matt Welsh
13 January 1994

Credits and Legalese

The Linux Documentation Project is a loose team of writers, proofreaders, and editors who are working on a set of definitive Linux manuals. The overall coordinator of the project is Matt Welsh, aided by Lars Wirzenius and Michael K. Johnson.

This manual is but one in a set of several being distributed by the Linux Documentation Project, including a Linux User's Guide, System Administrator's Guide, and Kernel Hacker's Guide. These manuals are all available in LaTeX source format and Postscript output for anonymous FTP from sunsite.unc.edu, in the directory /pub/Linux/docs/LDP.

We encourage anyone with a penchant for writing or editing to join us in improving Linux documentation. If you have Internet e-mail access, you can join the DOC channel of the Linux-Activists mailing list by sending mail to

   linux-activists-request@niksula.hut.fi

with the line

    X-Mn-Admin: join DOC

as the first line of the message body.

Feel free to get in touch with the author and coordinator of this manual if you have questions, postcards, money, or ideas. Matt Welsh can be reached via Internet e-mail at **mdw@sunsite.unc.edu**, and in real life at

205 Gray Street
Wilson, N.C. 27896
U.S.A.

UNIX is a trademark of X/Open.

Linux is not a trademark, and has no connection to UNIX™ or X/Open.

The X Window System is a trademark of the Massachusetts Institute of Technology.

MS-DOS and Microsoft Windows are trademarks of Microsoft, Inc.

Printed in Canada

Exceptions to these rules may be granted for academic purposes: Write to Matt Welsh, at the above address, or email **mdw@sunsite.unc.edu**, and ask. These restrictions are here to protect us as authors, not to restrict you as educators and learners.

The author encourages distributors of Linux software in any medium to use the book as an installation and new user guide. Given the copyright above, you are free to print and distribute copies of this book with your software. You may either distribute this book free of charge, or for profit. If doing so, you may wish to include a short "installation supplement" for your release.

The author would like to know of any plans to publish and distribute this book commercially. In this way, we can ensure that you are kept up-to-date with new revisions. And, should a new version be right around the corner, you might wish to delay your publication of the book until it is available.

If you are distributing this book commercially, donations, royalties, and/or printed copies are greatly appreciated by the author. Contributing in this way shows your support for free software and the Linux Documentation Project.

All source code in *Linux Installation and Getting Started* is placed under the GNU General Public License. See Appendix E for a copy of the GNU "GPL."

Documentation Conventions

These conventions should be obvious, but we'll include them here for the pedantic.

Bold Used to mark **new concepts**, **WARNINGS**, and **keywords** in a language.

italics Used for *emphasis* in text, and occasionally for quotes or introductions at the beginning of a section. Also used to indicate commands for the user to type when showing screen interaction (see below).

⟨*slanted*⟩ Used to mark **meta-variables** in the text, especially in representations of the command line. For example,

ls -l ⟨*foo*⟩

where ⟨*foo*⟩ would "stand for" a filename, such as **/bin/cp**.

`Typewriter` Used to represent screen interaction, as in

```
$ ls –l /bin/cp
-rwxr-xr-x  1 root     wheel    12104 Sep 25 15:53 /bin/cp
```

Also used for code examples, whether it is C code, a shell script, or something else, and to display general files, such as configuration files. When necessary for clarity's sake, these examples or figures will be enclosed in thin boxes.

| Key |

Represents a key to press. You will often see it in this form:

Press | return | to continue.

◇   A diamond in the margin, like a black diamond on a ski hill, marks "danger" or "caution." Read paragraphs marked this way carefully.

Chapter 1

Introduction to Linux

Linux is quite possibly the most important achievement of free software since the original *Space War*, or, more recently, Emacs. It has developed into the operating system for businesses, education, and personal productivity. Linux is no longer just for UNIX wizards who sit for hours in front of the glowing console (although we assure you that quite a number of users fall into this category). This book will help you get the most out of it.

Linux (pronounced with a short *i*, as in *LIH-nucks*) is a clone of the UNIX operating system that runs on Intel 80386 and 80486 computers. It supports a wide range of software, from TeX to X Windows to the GNU C/C++ compiler to TCP/IP. It's a versatile, bona fide implementation of UNIX, freely distributed by the terms of the GNU General Public License (see Appendix E).

Linux can turn any 386 or 486 PC into a workstation. It will give you the full power of UNIX at your fingertips. Businesses are installing Linux on entire networks of machines, using the operating system to manage financial and hospital records, a distributed user computing environment, telecommunications, and more. Universities worldwide are using Linux for teaching courses on operating systems programming and design. And, of course, computing enthusiasts everywhere are using Linux at home, for programming, productivity, and all-around hacking.

What makes Linux so different is that it is a *free* implementation of UNIX. It was and still is developed by a group of volunteers, primarily on the Internet, exchanging code, reporting bugs, and fixing problems in an open-ended environment. Anyone is welcome to join in the Linux development effort: all it takes is interest in hacking a free UNIX clone and some kind of programming know-how. The book that you hold in your hands is your tour guide.

1.1   About This Book

This book is an installation and entry-level guide to the Linux system. The purpose is to get new users up and running with the system by consolodating as much important material as possible into one book. Instead of covering many of the volatile technical details, those things which tend to change with rapid development, we give you enough background to find out more on your own.

Linux is not difficult to install and use. However, as with any implementation of UNIX, there is often some black magic involved to get everything working correctly. We hope that this book will get you on the Linux tourbus and show you how groovy this operating system can be.

In this book, we cover the following topics.

- What is Linux? The design and philosophy of this unique operating system, and what it can do for you.

- All of the details of what is needed to run Linux, including suggestions on what kind of hardware configuration is recommended for a complete system.

- How to obtain and install Linux. There are many distributions of the Linux software. We present a general discussion of Linux software distributions, how to obtain them, and generic instructions for installing the software (which should be applicable to any distribution).

  This edition also contains specific instructions for the Slackware distribution of Linux.

- A brief introductory UNIX tutorial, for those users who have never had experience with UNIX before. This tutorial should, hopefully, provide enough material for complete novices to have enough basic know-how to find their way around the system.

- An introduction to systems administration with Linux. This covers the most important tasks that new Linux administrators will need to be familiar with, such as creating users, managing filesystems, and so forth.

- Information on configuring more advanced aspects of Linux, such as the X Window System, networking with TCP/IP and SLIP, and the setup of electronic mail and news systems.

This book is for the personal computer user wishing to get started with Linux. We don't assume previous UNIX experience, but do expect novices to refer to other materials along the way. For those unfamiliar with UNIX, a list of useful sources of information is given in Appendix A. In general, this book is meant to be read along with another book on basic UNIX concepts.

1.2   A Brief History of Linux

UNIX is one of the most popular operating systems worldwide because of its large support base and distribution. It was originally developed as a multitasking system for minicomputers and mainframes in the mid-1970's, but has since grown to become one of the most widely used operating systems anywhere, despite its sometimes confusing interface and lack of central standardization.

The real reason for UNIX's popularity? Many hackers feel that UNIX is the Right Thing—the One True Operating System. Hence, the development of Linux by an expanding group of UNIX hackers who want to get their hands dirty with their own system.

Versions of UNIX exist for many systems—ranging from personal computers to supercomputers such as the Cray Y-MP. Most versions of UNIX for personal computers are quite expensive and cumbersome. At the time of this writing, a one-machine version of AT&T's System V for the 386 runs at about US$1500.

Linux is a freely distributable version of UNIX developed primarily by Linus Torvalds [1] at the University of Helsinki in Finland. Linux was developed with the help of many UNIX programmers and wizards across the Internet, allowing anyone with enough know-how and gumption the ability to develop and change the system. The Linux kernel uses no code from AT&T or any other proprietary source, and much of the software available for Linux is developed by the GNU project at the Free Software Foundation in Cambridge, Massachusetts. However, programmers all over the world have contributed to the growing pool of Linux software.

Linux was originally developed as a hobby project by Linus Torvalds. It was inspired by Minix, a small UNIX system developed by Andy Tanenbaum, and the first discussions about Linux were on the USENET newsgroup `comp.os.minix`. These discussions were concerned mostly with the development of a small, academic UNIX system for Minix users who wanted more.

The very early development of Linux was mostly dealing with the task-switching features of the 80386 protected-mode interface, all written in assembly code. Linus writes,

> "After that it was plain sailing: hairy coding still, but I had some devices, and debugging was easier. I started using C at this stage, and it certainly speeds up developement. This is also when I start to get serious about my megalomaniac ideas to make 'a better Minix than Minix'. I was hoping I'd be able to recompile `gcc` under Linux some day...
>
> "Two months for basic setup, but then only slightly longer until I had a disk-driver (seriously buggy, but it happened to work on my machine) and a small filesystem. That was about when I made 0.01 available [around late August of 1991]: it wasn't pretty, it had no floppy driver, and it couldn't do much anything.

---

[1] `torvalds@kruuna.helsinki.fi`.

I don't think anybody ever compiled that version. But by then I was hooked,
and didn't want to stop until I could chuck out Minix."

No announcement was ever made for Linux version 0.01. The 0.01 sources weren't even
executable: they contained only the bare rudiments of the kernel source, and assumed that
you had access to a Minix machine to compile and play with them.

On 5 October 1991, Linus announced the first "official" version of Linux, version 0.02.
At this point, Linus was able to run `bash` (the GNU Bourne Again Shell) and `gcc` (the
GNU C compiler), but not very much else was working. Again, this was intended as a
hacker's system. The primary focus was kernel development—none of the issues of user
support, documentation, distribution, and so on had even been addressed. Today, the
Linux community still seems to treat these ergonomic issues as secondary to the "real
programming"—kernel development.

Linus wrote in `comp.os.minix`,

> "Do you pine for the nice days of Minix-1.1, when men were men and wrote
> their own device drivers? Are you without a nice project and just dying to cut
> your teeth on a OS you can try to modify for your needs? Are you finding it
> frustrating when everything works on Minix? No more all-nighters to get a nifty
> program working? Then this post might be just for you.
>
> "As I mentioned a month ago, I'm working on a free version of a Minix-
> lookalike for AT-386 computers. It has finally reached the stage where it's even
> usable (though may not be depending on what you want), and I am willing
> to put out the sources for wider distribution. It is just version 0.02...but I've
> successfully run `bash`, `gcc`, `gnu-make`, `gnu-sed`, `compress`, etc. under it."

After version 0.03, Linus bumped the version number up to 0.10, as more people started
to work on the system. After several further revisions, Linus increased the version number to
0.95, to reflect his expectation that the system was ready for an "official" release very soon.
(Generally, software is not assigned the version number 1.0 until it is theoretically complete
or bug-free.) This was in March of 1992. Almost a year and a half later, in late December
of 1993, the Linux kernel was still at version 0.99.pl14—asymptotically approaching 1.0. As
of the time of this writing, the current kernel version is 1.1 patchlevel 52, and 1.2 is right
around the corner.

Today, Linux is a complete UNIX clone, capable of running X Windows, TCP/IP, Emacs,
UUCP, mail and news software, you name it. Almost all of the major free software packages
have been ported to Linux, and commercial software is becoming available. Much more
hardware is supported than in original versions of the kernel. Many people have executed
benchmarks on 80486 Linux systems and found them comparable with mid-range workstations from Sun Microsystems and Digital Equipment Corporation. Who would have ever
guessed that this "little" UNIX clone would have grown up to take on the entire world of
personal computing?

1.3 System Features

Linux supports most of the features found in other implementations of UNIX, plus quite a few that aren't found elsewhere. This section is a nickel tour of the Linux kernel features.

Linux is a complete multitasking, multiuser operating system (just like all other versions of UNIX). This means that many users can be logged into the same machine at once, running multiple programs simultaneously.

The Linux system is mostly compatible with a number of UNIX standards (inasmuch as UNIX has standards) on the source level, including IEEE POSIX.1, System V, and BSD features. It was developed with source portability in mind: therefore, you are most likely to find commonly-used features in the Linux system which are shared across multiple implementations. A great deal of free UNIX software available on the Internet and elsewhere compiles on Linux out of the box. In addition, all source code for the Linux system, including the kernel, device drivers, libraries, user programs, and development tools, is freely distributable.

Other specific internal features of Linux include POSIX job control (used by shells such as `csh` and `bash`), pseudoterminals (`pty` devices), and support for national or customized keyboards using dynamically-loadable keyboard drivers. Linux also supports **virtual consoles**, which allow you to switch between multiple login sessions from the system console in text mode. Users of the "`screen`" program will find the Linux virtual console implementation familiar.

The kernel is able to emulate 387-FPU instructions itself, so that systems without a math coprocessor can run programs that require floating-point math instructions.

Linux supports various filesystem types for storing data. Various filesystems, such as the *ext2fs* filesystem, have been developed specifically for Linux. Other filesystem types, such as the Minix-1 and Xenix filesystems, are also supported. The MS-DOS filesystem has been implemented as well, allowing you to access MS-DOS files on hard drive or floppy directly. The ISO 9660 CD-ROM filesystem type, which reads all standard formats of CD-ROMs, is also supported. We'll talk more about filesystems in Chapters 2 and 4.

Linux provides a complete implementation of TCP/IP networking. This includes device drivers for many popular Ethernet cards, SLIP (Serial Line Internet Protocol, allowing you to access a TCP/IP network via a serial connection), PLIP (Parallel Line Internet Protocol), PPP (Point-to-Point Protocol), NFS (Network File System), and so on. The complete range of TCP/IP clients and services is supported, such as FTP, `telnet`, NNTP, and SMTP. We'll talk more about networking in Chapter 5.

The Linux kernel is developed to use the special protected-mode features of the Intel 80386 and 80486 processors. In particular, Linux makes use of the protected-mode descriptor-based memory management paradigm and many of the other advanced features of these processors. Anyone familiar with 80386 protected-mode programming knows that this chip was designed for a multitasking system such as UNIX (or, actually, Multics). Linux exploits this functionality.

The Linux kernel supports demand-paged loaded executables. That is, only those segments of a program which are actually used are read into memory from disk. Also, copy-on-write pages are shared among executables, meaning that if several instances of a program are running at once, they will share pages in physical memory, reducing overall memory usage.

In order to increase the amount of available memory, Linux also implements disk paging: that is, up to 256 megabytes of "swap space"[2] can be allocated on disk. When the system requires more physical memory, it will swap out inactive pages to disk, thus allowing you to run larger applications and support more users at once. However, swap is no substitute for physical RAM—it is much slower due to drive access latency times.

The kernel also implements a unified memory pool for user programs and disk cache. In this way, all free memory is used for caching, and the cache is reduced when running large programs.

Executables use dynamically linked shared libraries, meaning that executables share common library code in a single library file found on disk, not unlike the SunOS shared library mechanism. This allows executable files to occupy much less space on disk, especially those that use many library functions. There are also statically-linked libraries for those who wish to use object debugging or maintain "complete" executables without the need for shared libraries to be in place. Linux shared libraries are dynamically linked at run-time, allowing the programmer to replace modules of the libraries with their own routines.

To facilitate debugging, the Linux kernel does core dumps for post-mortem analysis. Using a core dump and an executable linked with debugging support, it is possible to determine what caused a program to crash.

1.4   Software Features

In this section, we'll introduce you to many of the software applications available for Linux, and talk about a number of common computing tasks. After all, the most important part of the system is the wide range of software available for it. The fact that most of this software is freely distributable is even more impressive.

1.4.1   Basic commands and utilities

Virtually every utility that you would expect to find on standard implementations of UNIX has been ported to Linux. This includes basic commands such as `ls`, `awk`, `tr`, `sed`, `bc`, `more`,

---

[2]Swap space is inappropriately named: entire processes are not swapped, but rather individual pages. Of course, in many cases entire processes will be swapped out, but this is not neccessarily always the case.

and so on. You name it, Linux has it. Therefore, you can expect your familiar working environment on other UNIX systems to be duplicated on Linux. All of the standard commands and utilities are there. (Novice Linux users should see Chapter 3 for an introduction to these basic UNIX commands.)

Many text editors are available, including **vi**, **ex**, **pico**, **jove**, as well as GNU Emacs and variants such as Lucid Emacs (which incorporates extensions for use under X Windows) and **joe**. Whatever text editor you're accustomed to using has more than likely been ported to Linux.

The choice of a text editor is an interesting one. Many UNIX users still use "simple" editors such as **vi** (in fact, the author wrote this book using **vi** under Linux). However, **vi** has many limitations, due to its age, and more modern (and complex) editors such as Emacs are gaining popularity. Emacs supports a complete LISP-based macro language and interpreter, a powerful command syntax, and other fun-filled extensions. Emacs macro packages exist to allow you to read electronic mail and news, edit the contents of directories, and even engage in an artificially intelligent psychotherapy session (indispensible for stressed-out Linux hackers).

One interesting note is that most of the basic Linux utilities are GNU software. These GNU utilities support advanced features not found in the standard versions from BSD or AT&T. For example, GNU's version of the **vi** editor, **elvis**, includes a structured macro language which differs from the original AT&T implementation. However, the GNU utilities strive to remain compatible with their BSD and System V counterparts. Many people consider the GNU versions of these programs superior to the originals.

The most important utility to many users is the **shell**. The shell is a program which reads and executes commands from the user. In addition, many shells provide features such as **job control** (allowing the user to manage several running processes at once—not as Orwellian as it sounds), input and output redirection, and a command language for writing **shell scripts**. A shell script is a file containing a program in the shell command language, analogous to a "batch file" under MS-DOS.

There are many types of shells available for Linux. The most important difference between shells is the command language. For example, the **C Shell** (**csh**) uses a command language somewhat like the C programming language. The classic **Bourne Shell** uses a different command language. One's choice of a shell is often based on the command language that it provides. The shell that you use defines, to some extent, your working environment under Linux.

No matter what shell you're accustomed to, some version of it has probably been ported to Linux. The most popular shell is the GNU Bourne Again Shell (**bash**), a Bourne shell variant which includes many advanced features, such as job control, command history, command and filename completion, an Emacs-like interface for editing the command line, and powerful extensions to the standard Bourne shell language. Another popular shell is **tcsh**, a version of the C Shell with advanced functionality similar to that found in **bash**. Other shells include **zsh**, a small Bourne-like shell; the Korn shell (**ksh**); BSD's **ash**; and **rc**, the

Plan 9 shell.

What's so important about these basic utilities? Linux gives you the unique opportunity to tailor a custom system to your needs. For example, if you're the only person who uses your system, and you prefer to exclusively use the `vi` editor, and `bash` as your shell, there's no reason to install other editors or shells. The "do it yourself" attitude is prevalent among Linux hackers and users.

1.4.2   Text processing and word processing

Almost every computer user has a need for some kind of document preparation system. (How many computer enthusiasts do you know who still use pen and paper? Not many, we'll wager.) In the PC world, *word processing* is the norm: it involves editing and manipulating text (often in a "What-You-See-Is-What-You-Get" environment) and producing printed copies of the text, complete with figures, tables, and other garnishes.

In the UNIX world, *text processing* is much more common, which is quite different than the classical concept of word processing. With a text processing system, text is entered by the author using a "typesetting language", which describes how the text should be formatted. Instead of entering the text within a special word processing environment, the source may be modified with any text editor such as `vi` or Emacs. Once the source text (in the typesetting language) is complete, the user formats the text with a separate program, which converts the source to a format suitable for printing. This is somewhat analogous to programming in a language such as C, and "compiling" the document into a printable form.

There are many text processing systems available for Linux. One is `groff`, the GNU version of the classic `nroff` text formatter originally developed by Bell Labs and still used on many UNIX systems worldwide. Another modern text processing system is TeX, developed by Donald Knuth of computer science fame. Dialects of TeX, such as LaTeX, are also available.

Text processors such as TeX and `groff` differ mostly in the syntax of their formatting languages. The choice of one formatting system over another is also based upon what utilities are available to satisfy your needs, as well as personal taste.

For example, some people consider the `groff` formatting language to be a bit obscure, so they use TeX, which is more readable by humans. However, `groff` is capable of producing plain ASCII output, viewable on a terminal, while TeX is intended primarily for output to a printing device. However, various programs exist to produce plain ASCII from TeX-formatted documents, or to convert TeX to `groff`, for example.

Another text processing system is `texinfo`, an extension to TeX used for software documentation by the Free Software Foundation. `texinfo` is capable of producing a printed document, or an online-browsable hypertext "Info" document from a single source file. Info files are the main format of documentation used by GNU software such as Emacs.

Text processors are used widely in the computing community for producing papers, theses, magazine articles, and books (in fact, this book was produced using LaTeX). The ability to process the source language as a plain text file opens the door to many extensions to the text processor itself. Because source documents are not stored in an obscure format, readable only by a particular word processor, programmers are able to write parsers and translators for the formatting language, extending the system.

What does such a formatting language look like? In general, the formatting language source consists mostly of the text itself, along with "control codes" to produce a particular effect, such as changing fonts, setting margins, creating lists, and so on.

As an example, take the following text:

> Mr. Torvalds:
>
> We are very upset with your current plans to implement *post-hypnotic suggestion* in the **Linux** terminal driver code. We feel this way for three reasons:
>
> 1. Planting subliminal messages in the terminal driver is not only immoral, it is a waste of time;
> 2. It has been proven that "post-hypnotic suggestions" are ineffective when used upon unsuspecting UNIX hackers;
> 3. We have already implemented high-voltage electric shocks, as a security measure, in the code for `login`.
>
> We hope you will reconsider.

This text would appear in the LaTeX formatting language as the following:

```
\begin{quote}
Mr. Torvalds:

We are very upset with your current plans to implement {\em post-hypnotic
suggestion\/} in the {\bf Linux} terminal driver code. We feel this
way for three reasons:
\begin{enumerate}
\item Planting subliminal messages in the kernel driver is not only
        immoral, it is a waste of time;
\item It has been proven that ``post-hypnotic suggestions'' are ineffective
        when used upon unsuspecting UNIX hackers;
\item We have already implemented high-voltage electric shocks, as a
        security measure, in the code for {\tt login}.
\end{enumerate}
We hope you will reconsider.
\end{quote}
```

The author enters the above "source" text using any text editor, and generates the formatted output by processing the source with LaTeX. At first glance, the typesetting language may appear to be obscure, but it's actually quite easy to learn. Using a text processing system enforces typographical standards when writing. For example, all enumerated lists within a document will look the same, unless the author modifies the definition of the enumerated list "environment". The primary goal is to allow the author to concentrate on writing the actual text, instead of worrying about typesetting conventions.

WYSIWYG word processors are attractive for many reasons; they provide a powerful (and sometimes complex) visual interface for editing the document. However, this interface is inherently limited to those aspects of text layout which are accessible to the user. For example, many word processors provide a special "format language" for producing complicated expressions such as mathematical formulae. This is identical text processing, albeit on a much smaller scale.

The subtle benefit of text processing is that the system allows you to specify exactly what you mean. Also, text processing systems allow you to edit the source text with any text editor, and the source is easily converted to other formats. The tradeoff for this flexibility and power is the lack of a WYSIWYG interface.

Many users of word processors are used to seeing the formatted text as they edit it. On the other hand, when writing with a text processor, one generally does not worry about how the text will appear when formatted. The writer learns to expect how the text should look from the formatting commands used in the source.

There are programs which allow you to view the formatted document on a graphics display before printing. For example, the **xdvi** program displays a "device independent" file generated by the TeX system under the X Windows environment. Other software applications, such as **xfig**, provide a WYSIWYG graphics interface for drawing figures and diagrams, which are subsequently converted to the text processing language for inclusion in your document.

Admittedly, text processors such as **nroff** were around long before word processing was available. However, many people still prefer to use text processing, because it is more versatile and independent of a graphics environment. In either case, the **idoc** word processor is also available for Linux, and before long we expect to see commercial word processors becoming available as well. If you absolutely don't want to give up word processing for text processing, you can always run MS-DOS, or some other operating system, in addition to Linux.

There are many other text-processing-related utilities available. The powerful META-FONT system, used for designing fonts for TeX, is included with the Linux port of TeX. Other programs include **ispell**, an interactive spell checker and corrector; **makeindex**, used for generating indicies in LaTeX documents; as well as many **groff** and TeX-based macro packages for formatting many types of documents and mathematical texts. Conversion programs to translate between TeX or **groff** source to a myriad of other formats are available.

1.4.3 Programming languages and utilities

Linux provides a complete UNIX programming environment, including all of the standard libraries, programming tools, compilers, and debuggers that you would expect to find on other UNIX systems. Within the UNIX software development world, applications and systems programming is usually done in C or C++. The standard C and C++ compiler for Linux is GNU's **gcc**, which is an advanced, modern compiler supporting many options. It is also capable of compiling C++ (including AT&T 3.0 features) as well as Objective-C, another object-oriented dialect of C.

Besides C and C++, many other compiled and interpreted programming languages have been ported to Linux, such as Smalltalk, FORTRAN, Pascal, LISP, Scheme, and Ada (if you're masochistic enough to program in Ada—we're not going to stop you). In addition, various assemblers for writing protected-mode 80386 code are available, as are UNIX hacking favorites such as Perl (the script language to end all script languages) and Tcl/Tk (a shell-like command processing system including support for developing simple X Windows applications).

The advanced **gdb** debugger has been ported, which allows you to step through a program to find bugs, or examine the cause for a crash using a core dump. **gprof**, a profiling utility, will give you performance statistics for your program, letting you know where your program is spending most of its time executing. The Emacs text editor provides an interactive editing and compilation environment for various programming languages. Other tools include GNU **make** and **imake**, used to manage compilation of large applications; and RCS, a system for source locking and revision control.

Linux implements dynamically-linked shared libraries, which allow binaries to be much smaller as the subroutine code is linked at run-time. These DLL libraries also allow the applications programmer to override function definitions with their own code. For example, if a programmer wished to write her own version of the **malloc()** library routine, the linker would use the programmer's new routine instead of the one found in the libraries.

Linux is ideal for developing UNIX applications. It provides a modern programming environment with all of the bells and whistles. Various standards such as POSIX.1 are supported, allowing software written for Linux to be easily ported to other systems. Professional UNIX programmers and system administrators can use Linux to develop software at home, and then transfer the software to UNIX systems at work. This not only can save a great deal of time and money, but will also let you work in the comfort of your own home.[3] Computer Science students can use Linux to learn UNIX programming and to explore other aspects of the system, such as kernel architecture.

With Linux, not only do you have access to the complete set of libraries and programming utilities, but you also have the complete kernel and library source code at your fingertips.

---

[3] The author uses his Linux system to develop and test X Windows applications at home, which can be directly compiled on workstations elsewhere.

1.4.4   The X Window System

The X Window System is the standard graphics interface for UNIX machines. It is a powerful environment supporting many applications. Using X Windows, the user can have multiple terminal windows on the screen at once, each one containing a different login session. A pointing device such as a mouse is often used with the X interface, although it isn't required.

Many X-specific applications have been written, such as games, graphics utilities, programming and documentation tools, and so on. With Linux and X, your system is a bona fide workstation. Coupled with TCP/IP networking, you can even display X applications running on other machines on your Linux display, as is possible with other systems running X.

The X Window System was originally developed at MIT, and is freely distributable. However, may commercial vendors have distributed proprietary enhancements to the original X Windows software. The version of X Windows available for Linux is known as XFree86, a port of X11R5 made freely distributable for 80386-based UNIX systems such as Linux. XFree86 supports a wide range of video hardware, including VGA, Super VGA, and a number of accelerated video adaptors. This is a complete distribution of the X Windows software, containing the X server itself, many applications and utilities, programming libraries, and documentation.

Standard X applications include `xterm` (a terminal emulator used for most text-based applications within an X window); `xdm` (the X Session Manager, which handles logins); `xclock` (a simple clock display); `xman` (an X-based man page reader), and more. The many X applications available for Linux are too numerous to mention here, but the base XFree86 distribution includes the "standard" applications found in the original MIT release. Many others are available separately, and theoretically any application written for X Windows should compile cleanly under Linux.

The look and feel of the X Windows interface is controlled to a large extent by the **window manager**. This friendly program is in charge of the placement of windows, the user interface for resizing, iconifying, and moving windows, the appearance of window frames, and so on. The standard XFree86 distribution includes `twm`, the classic MIT window manager, although more advanced window managers such as the Open Look Virtual Window Manager (`olvwm`) are available as well. One window manager that is popular among Linux users is `fvwm`. This is a small window manager, requiring less than half of the memory used by `twm`. It provides a 3-D appearance for windows, as well a virtual desktop—if the user moves the mouse to the edge of the screen, the entire desktop is shifted as if the display were much larger than it actually is. `fvwm` is greatly customizable, and allows all functions to be accessed from the keyboard as well as the mouse. Many Linux distributions use `fvwm` as the standard window manager.

The XFree86 distribution contains programming libraries and include files for those wily programmers who wish to develop X applications. Various widget sets, such as Athena, Open Look, and Xaw3D are supported. All of the standard fonts, bitmaps, man pages, and documentation are included. PEX (a programming interface for 3-D graphics) is also supported.

Many X applications programmers use the proprietary Motif widget set for development. Several vendors sell single and multiple-user licenses for a binary version of Motif for Linux. Because Motif itself is relatively expensive, not many Linux users own it. However, binaries statically linked with Motif routines may be freely distributed. Therefore, if you write a program using Motif and wish to distribute it freely, you may provide a binary so that users without Motif can use the program.

The only major caveats with X Windows are the hardware and memory requirements. A 386 with 4 megabytes of RAM is capable of running X, but 8 megabytes or more of physical RAM are needed to use it comfortably. A faster processor is nice to have as well, but having enough physical RAM is much more important. In addition, to achieve really slick video performance, an accelerated video card (such as a local bus S3-chipset card) is strongly recommended. Performance ratings in excess of 140,000 xstones have been acheived with Linux and XFree86. With sufficient hardware, you'll find that running X and Linux is as fast, or faster, than running X on other UNIX workstations.

In Chapter 5 we'll discuss how to install and use X on your system.

1.4.5 Networking

Interested in communicating with the world? Yes? No? Maybe? Linux supports the two primary networking protocols for UNIX systems: **TCP/IP** and **UUCP**. TCP/IP (Transmission Control Protocol/Internet Protocol, for acronym aficionados) is the set of networking paradigms that allow systems all over the world to communicate on a single network known as the Internet. With Linux, TCP/IP, and a connection to the network, you can communicate with users and machines across the Internet via electronic mail, USENET news, file transfers with FTP, and more. There are many Linux systems currently on the Internet.

Most TCP/IP networks use Ethernet as the physical network transport. Linux supports many popular Ethernet cards and interfaces for personal computers, including the D-Link pocket Ethernet adaptor for laptops.

However, because not everyone has an Ethernet drop at home, Linux also supports **SLIP** (Serial Line Internet Protocol), which allows you to connect to the Internet via modem. In order to use SLIP, you'll need to have access to a SLIP server, a machine connected to the network which allows dial-in access. Many businesses and universities provide such SLIP servers. In fact, if your Linux system has an Ethernet connection as well as a modem, you can configure it as a SLIP server for other hosts.

NFS (Network File System) allows your system to seamlessly share files with other machines on the network. FTP (File Transfer Protocol) allows you to transfer files between other machines. Other applications include **sendmail**, a system for sending and receiving electronic mail using the SMTP protocol; NNTP-based electronic news systems such as C-

News and INN; `telnet`, `rlogin`, and `rsh`, which allow you to login and execute commands on other machines on the network; and `finger`, which allows you to get information on other Internet users. There are literally tons of TCP/IP-based applications and protocols out there.

The full range of mail and news readers are available for Linux, such as `elm`, `pine`, `rn`, `nn`, and `tin`. Whatever your preference, you can configure your Linux system to send and receive electronic mail and news from all over the world.

If you have experience with TCP/IP applications on other UNIX systems, Linux will be very familiar to you. The system provides a standard socket programming interface, so virtually any program which uses TCP/IP can be ported to Linux. The Linux X server also supports TCP/IP, allowing you to display applications running on other systems on your Linux display.

In Chapter 5 we'll discuss configuration and setup of TCP/IP, including SLIP, for Linux.

UUCP (UNIX-to-UNIX Copy) is an older mechanism used to transfer files, electronic mail, and electronic news between UNIX machines. Classically, UUCP machines connected to each other over the phone lines via modem, but UUCP is able to transport over a TCP/IP network as well. If you do not have access to a TCP/IP network or a SLIP server, you can configure your system to send and receive files and electronic mail using UUCP. See Chapter 5 for more information.

1.4.6   Telecommunications and BBS software

If you have a modem, you will be able to communicate with other machines using one of the telecommunications packages available for Linux. Many people use telecommunications software to access bulletin board systems (BBSs), as well as commercial online services such as Prodigy, CompuServe, and America On-Line. Other people use their modems to connect to a UNIX system at work or school. You can even use your modem and Linux system to send and receive facsimiles. Telecommunications software under Linux is very similar to that found under MS-DOS or other operating systems. Anyone who has ever used a telecommunications package will find the Linux equivalent familiar.

One of the most popular communications packages for Linux is Seyon, an X application providing a customizable, ergonomic interface, with built-in support for various file transfer protocols such as Kermit, ZModem, and so on. Other telecommunications programs include C-Kermit, `pcomm`, and `minicom`. These are similar to communications programs found on other operating systems, and are quite easy to use.

If you do not have access to a SLIP server (see the previous section), you can use `term` to multiplex your serial line. `term` will allow you to open multiple login sessions over the modem connection to a remote machine. `term` will also allow you to redirect X client connections to your local X server, through the serial line, allowing you to display remote X applications on your Linux system. Another software package, KA9Q, implements a similar

SLIP-like interface.

Running a bulletin board system (BBS) is a favorite hobby (and means of income) for many people. Linux supports a wide range of BBS software, most of which is more powerful than what is available for other operating systems. With a phone line, a modem, and Linux, you can turn your system into a BBS, providing dial-in access to your system to users worldwide. BBS software for Linux includes XBBS and the UniBoard BBS packages.

Most BBS software locks the user into a menu-based system where only certain functions and applications are available. An alternative to BBS access is full UNIX access, which would allow users to dial into your system and login as a regular user. While this would require a fair amount of maintenance on the part of the system administrator, it can be done, and providing public UNIX access from your Linux system is not difficult to do. Along with a TCP/IP network, you can provide electronic mail and news access to users on your system.

If you do not have access to a TCP/IP network or UUCP feed, Linux will also allow you to communicate with a number of BBS networks, such as FidoNet, with which you can exchange electronic news and mail via the phone line. More information on telecommunications and BBS software under Linux can be found in Chapter 5.

1.4.7 Interfacing with MS-DOS

Various utilities exist to interface with the world of MS-DOS. The most well-known application is the Linux MS-DOS Emulator, which allows you to run many MS-DOS applications directly from Linux. Although Linux and MS-DOS are completely different operating systems, the 80386 protected-mode environment allows certain tasks to behave as if they were running in 8086-emulation mode, as MS-DOS applications do.

The MS-DOS emulator is still under development, yet many popular applications run under it. Understandably, however, MS-DOS applications which use bizarre or esoteric features of the system may never be supported, because it is only an emulator. For example, you wouldn't expect to be able to run any programs which use 80386 protected-mode features, such as Microsoft Windows (in 386 enhanced mode, that is).

Applications which run successfully under the Linux MS-DOS Emulator include 4DOS (a command interpreter), Foxpro 2.0, Harvard Graphics, MathCad, Stacker 3.1, Turbo Assembler, Turbo C/C++, Turbo Pascal, Microsoft Windows 3.0 (in *real* mode), and WordPerfect 5.1. Standard MS-DOS commands and utilities (such as `PKZIP`, and so on) work with the emulator as well.

The MS-DOS Emulator is meant mostly as an ad hoc solution for those people who need MS-DOS only for a few applications, but use Linux for everything else. It's not meant to be a complete implementation of MS-DOS. Of course, if the Emulator doesn't satisfy your needs, you can always run MS-DOS as well as Linux on the same system. Using the LILO boot loader, you can specify at boot time which operating system to start. Linux can coexist with other operating systems, such as OS/2, as well.

Linux provides a seamless interface for transferring files between Linux and MS-DOS. You can mount an MS-DOS partition or floppy under Linux, and directly access MS-DOS files as you would any other.

Currently under development is a project known as **WINE**—a Microsoft Windows emulator for the X Window System under Linux. Once WINE is complete, users will be able to run MS-Windows applications directly from Linux. This is similar to the proprietary WABI Windows emulator from Sun Microsystems. At the time of this writing, WINE is still in the early stages of development, but the outlook is good.

In Chapter 5 we'll talk about the MS-DOS tools available for Linux.

1.4.8 Other applications

A host of miscellany is available for Linux, as one would expect from such a hodgepodge operating system. Linux's primary focus is currently for personal UNIX computing, but this is rapidly changing. Business and scientific software is expanding, and commercial software vendors are beginning to contribute to the growing pool of applications.

Several relational databases are available for Linux, including Postgres, Ingres, and Mbase. These are full-featured, professional client/server database applications similar to those found on other UNIX platforms. `/rdb`, a commercial database system, is available as well.

Scientific computing applications include FELT (a finite element analysis tool); `gnuplot` (a plotting and data analysis application); Octave (a symbolic mathematics package, similar to MATLAB); `xspread` (a spreadsheet calculator); `xfractint`, an X-based port of the popular Fractint fractal generator; `xlispstat` (a statistics package), and more. Other applications include Spice (a circuit design and analysis tool) and Khoros (an image/digital signal processing and visualization system).

Of course, there are many more such applications which have been, and can be, ported to run on Linux. Whatever your field, porting UNIX-based applications to Linux should be quite straightforward. Linux provides a complete UNIX programming interface, sufficient to serve as the base for any scientific application.

As with any operating system, Linux has its share of games. These include classic text-based dungeon games such as Nethack and Moria; MUDs (multi-user dungeons, which allow many users to interact in a text-based adventure) such as DikuMUD and TinyMUD; as well as a slew of X games such as `xtetris`, `netrek`, and `Xboard` (the X11 version of `gnuchess`). The popular shoot-em-up arcade-style *Doom* has also been ported to Linux.

For audiophiles, Linux has support for various sound cards and related software, such as CDplayer (a program which can control a CD-ROM drive as a conventional CD player, surprisingly enough), MIDI sequencers and editors (allowing you to compose music for playback through a synthesizer or other MIDI-controlled instrument), and sound editors for digitized sounds.

Can't find the application you're looking for? The Linux Software Map, described in Appendix A, contains a list of many software packages which have been written and ported to Linux. While this list is far from complete, it contains a great deal of software. Another way to find Linux applications is to look at the **INDEX** files found on Linux FTP sites, if you have Internet access. Just by poking around you'll find a great deal of software just waiting to be played with.

If you absolutely can't find what you need, you can always attempt to port the application from another platform to Linux. Most freely distributable UNIX-based software will compile on Linux with few problems. Or, if all else fails, you can write the application yourself. If it's a commercial application you're looking for, there may be a free "clone" available. Or, you can encourage the software company to consider releasing a Linux binary version. Several individuals have contacted software companies, asking them to port their applications to Linux, and have met with various degrees of success.

1.5 About Linux's Copyright

Linux is covered by what is known as the GNU *General Public License, or GPL*. The GPL was developed for the GNU project by the Free Software Foundataion. It makes a number of provisions for the distribution and modification of "free software". "Free" in this sense refers to freedom, not just cost. The GPL has always been subject to misinterpretation, and we hope that this summary will help you to understand the extent and goals of the GPL and its effect on Linux. A complete copy of the GPL is included in Appendix E.

Originally, Linus Torvalds released Linux under a license more restrictive than the GPL, which allowed the software to be freely distributed and modified, but prevented any money changing hands for its distribution and use. On the other hand, the GPL allows people to sell and make profit from free software, but does not allow them to restrict the right for others to distribute the software in any way.

First, it should be explained that "free software" covered by the GPL is *not* in the public domain. Public domain software is software which is not copyrighted, and is literally owned by the public. Software covered by the GPL, on the other hand, is copyrighted to the author or authors. This means that the software is protected by standard international copyright laws, and that the author of the software is legally defined. Just because the software may be freely distributed does not mean that it is in the public domain.

GPL-licensed software is also not "shareware". Generally, "shareware" software is owned and copyrighted by the author, but the author requires users to send in money for its use after distribution. On the other hand, software covered by the GPL may be distributed and used free of charge.

The GPL also allows people to take and modify free software, and distribute their own versions of the software. However, any derived works from GPL software must also be covered by the GPL. In other words, a company could not take Linux, modify it, and sell it under a restrictive license. If any software is derived from Linux, that software must be covered by the GPL as well.

The GPL allows free software to be distributed and used free of charge. However, it also allows a person or organization to distribute GPL software for a fee, and even to make a profit from its sale and distribution. However, in selling GPL software, the distributor cannot take those rights away from the purchaser; that is, if you purchase GPL software from some source, you may distribute the software for free, or sell it yourself as well.

This might sound like a contradiction at first. Why sell software for profit when the GPL allows anyone to obtain it for free? As an example, let's say that some company decided to bundle a large amount of free software on a CD-ROM and distribute it. That company would need to charge for the overhead of producing and distributing the CD-ROM, and the company may even decide to make profit from the sales of software. This is allowed by the GPL.

Organizations which sell free software must follow certain restrictions set forth in the GPL. First, they cannot restrict the rights of users who purchase the software. This means that if you buy a CD-ROM of GPL software, you can copy and distribute that CD-ROM free of charge, or resell it yourself. Secondly, distributors must make it obvious to users that the software is indeed covered by the GPL. Thirdly, distributors must provide, free of charge, the complete source code for the software being distributed. This will allow anyone who purchases GPL software to make modifications of that software.

Allowing a company to distribute and sell free software is a very good thing. Not everyone has access to the Internet to download software, such as Linux, for free. The GPL allows companies to sell and distribute software to those people who do not have free (cost-wise) access to the software. For example, many organizations sell Linux on diskette, tape, or CD-ROM via mail order, and make profit from these sales. The developers of Linux may never see any of this profit; that is the understanding that is reached between the developer and the distributor when software is licensed by the GPL. In other words, Linus knew that companies may wish to sell Linux, and that he may not see a penny of the profits from those sales.

In the free software world, the important issue is not money. The goal of free software is always to develop and distribute fantastic software and to allow anyone to obtain and use it. In the next section, we'll discuss how this applies to the development of Linux.

1.6   The Design and Philosophy of Linux

When new users encounter Linux, they often have a few misconceptions and false expectations of the system. Linux is a unique operating system, and it is important to understand its philosophy and design in order to use it effectively. Time enough for a soapbox. Even if you are an aged UNIX guru, what follows is probably of interest to you.

In commercial UNIX development houses, the entire system is developed with a rigorous policy of quality assurance, source and revision control systems, documentation, and bug reporting and resolution. Developers are not allowed to add features or to change key sections of code on a whim: they must validate the change as a response to a bug report and consequently "check in" all changes to the source control system, so that the changes can be backed out if necessary. Each developer is assigned one or more parts of the system code, and only that developer may alter those sections of the code while it is "checked out".

Internally, the quality assurance department runs rigorous regression test suites on each new pass of the operating system, and reports any bugs. It is the responsibility of the developers to fix these bugs as reported. A complicated system of statistical analysis is employed to ensure that a certain percentage of bugs are fixed before the next release, and that the operating system as a whole passes certain release criteria.

In all, the process used by commercial UNIX developers to maintain and support their code is very complicated, and quite reasonably so. The company must have quantitative proof that the next revision of the operating system is ready to be shipped; hence, the gathering and analysis of statistics about the operating system's performance. It is a big job to develop a commercial UNIX system, often large enough to employ hundreds (if not thousands) of programmers, testers, documentors, and administrative personel. Of course, no two commercial UNIX vendors are alike, but you get the general picture.

With Linux, you can throw out the entire concept of organized development, source control systems, structured bug reporting, or statistical analysis. Linux is, and more than likely always will be, a hacker's operating system.[4]

Linux is primarily developed as a group effort by volunteers on the Internet from all over the world. Across the Internet and beyond, anyone with enough know-how has the opportunity to aid in developing and debugging the kernel, porting new software, writing documentation, or helping new users. There is no single organization responsible for developing the system. For the most part, the Linux community communicates via various mailing lists and USENET newsgroups. A number of conventions have sprung up around the development effort: for example, anyone wishing to have their code included in the "official" kernel should mail it to Linus Torvalds, which he will test and include in the kernel (as long as it doesn't break things or go against the overall design of the system, he will more than likely include it).

The system itself is designed with a very open-ended, feature-minded approach. While recently the number of new features and critical changes to the system have diminished, the general rule is that a new version of the kernel will be released about every few months (sometimes even more frequently than this). Of course, this is a very rough figure: it depends on a several factors including the number of bugs to be fixed, the amount of feedback from users testing pre-release versions of the code, and the amount of sleep that Linus has had this week.

---

[4] What I mean by "hacker" is a feverishly dedicated programmer, a person who enjoys exploiting computers and generally doing interesting things with them. This is in contrast to the common denotation of "hacker" as a computer wrongdoer or outlaw.

Let it suffice to say that not every single bug has been fixed, and not every problem ironed out between releases. As long as the system appears to be free of critical or oft-manifesting bugs, it is considered "stable" and new revisions will be released. The thrust behind Linux development is not an effort to release perfect, bug-free code: it is to develop a free implementation of UNIX. Linux is *for* the developers, more than anyone else.

Anyone who has a new feature or software application to add to the system generally makes it available in an "alpha" stage—that is, a stage for testing by those brave or unwary users who want to bash out problems with the initial code. Because the Linux community is largely based on the Internet, alpha software is usually uploaded to one or more of the various Linux FTP sites (see Appendix C) and a message posted to one of the Linux USENET newsgroups about how to get and test the code. Users who download and test alpha software can then mail results, bug fixes, or questions to the author.

After the initial problems in the alpha code have been fixed, the code enters a "beta" stage, in which it is usually considered stable but not complete (that is, it works, but not all of the features may be present). Otherwise, it may go directly to a "final" stage in which the software is considered complete and usable. For kernel code, once it is complete the developer may ask Linus to include it in the standard kernel, or as an optional add-on feature to the kernel.

Keep in mind that these are only conventions—not rules. Some people feel so confident with their software that they don't need to release an alpha or test version. It is always up to the developer to make these decisions.

You might be amazed that such a nonstructured system of volunteers, programming and debugging a complete UNIX system, could get anything done at all. As it turns out, it is one of the most efficient and motivated development efforts ever employed. The entire Linux kernel was written *from scratch*, without employing any code from proprietary sources. A great deal of work was put forth by volunteers to port all of the free software under the sun to the Linux system. Libraries were written and ported, filesystems developed, and hardware drivers written for many popular devices.

The Linux software is generally released as a *distribution*, which is a set of pre-packaged software making up an entire system. It would be quite difficult for most users to build a complete system from the ground up, starting with the kernel, adding utilities, and installing all of the necessary software by hand. Instead, there are a number of software distributions including everything that you need to install and run a complete system. Again, there is no standard distribution—there are many, each with their own advantages and disadvantages. We'll talk more about the various available Linux distributions in Section 2.1.

Despite the completeness of the Linux software, you will still need a bit of UNIX know-how to install and run a complete system. No distribution of Linux is completely bug-free, so you may be required to fix small problems by hand after installation. Running a UNIX system is not an easy task, not even for commercial versions of UNIX. If you're serious about Linux, bear in mind that it will take a considerable amount of effort and attention on your part to keep the system running and take care of things: this is true of *any* UNIX system, and Linux is no exception. Because of the diversity of the Linux community and the many needs which the software is attempting to meet, not eveything can be taken care of for you all of the time.

1.6.1 Hints for UNIX novices

Installing and using your own Linux system does not require a great deal of background in UNIX. In fact, many UNIX novices successfully install Linux on their systems. This is a worthwhile learning experience, but keep in mind that it can be very frustrating to some. If you're lucky, you will be able to install and start using your Linux system without any UNIX background. However, once you are ready to delve into the more complex tasks of running Linux—installing new software, recompiling the kernel, and so forth—having background knowledge in UNIX is going to be a necessity.

Fortunately, by running your own Linux system you will be able to learn the essentials of UNIX necessary for these tasks. This book contains a good deal of information to help you get started—Chapter 3 is a tutorial covering UNIX basics, and Chapter 4 contains information on Linux system administration. You may wish to read these chapters before you attempt to install Linux at all—the information contained therein will prove to be invaluable should you run into problems.

Nobody can expect to go from being a UNIX novice to a UNIX system administrator overnight. No implementation of UNIX is expected to run trouble- and maintenance-free. You must be aptly prepared for the journey which lies ahead. Otherwise, if you're new to UNIX, you may very well become overly frustrated with the system.

1.6.2 Hints for UNIX gurus

Even those people with years of UNIX programming and systems administration experience may need assistance before they are able to pick up and install Linux. There are still aspects of the system that UNIX wizards will need to be familiar with before diving in. For one thing, Linux is not a commercial UNIX system. It does not attempt to uphold the same standards as other UNIX systems you have may have come across. To be more specific, while stability is an important factor in the development of Linux, it is not the *only* factor.

More important, perhaps, is functionality. In many cases, new code will make it into the standard kernel even though it is still buggy and not functionally complete. The assumption is that it is more important to release code which users can test and use than delay a release until it is "complete". As an example, WINE (the Microsoft Windows Emulator for Linux) had an "official" alpha release before it was completely tested. In this way, the Linux community at large had a chance to work with the code, test it, and help develop it, while those who found the alpha code "good enough" for their needs could use it. Commercial UNIX vendors rarely, if ever, release software in this manner.

If you have been a UNIX systems administrator for more than a decade, and have used every commercial UNIX system under the Sun (no pun intended), Linux may take some getting used to. The system is very modern and dynamic. A new kernel release is made approximately every few months. New software is constantly being released. One day your system may be completely up-to-date with the current trend, and the next day the same system is considered to be in the Stone Age.

With all of this dynamic activity, how can you be expected to keep up with the ever-changing Linux world? For the most part, it is best to upgrade incrementally; that is, upgrade only those parts of the system that *need* upgrading, and then only when you think an upgrade is necessary. For example, if you never use Emacs, there is little reason to continuously install every new release of Emacs on your system. Furthermore, even if you are an avid Emacs user, there is usually no reason to upgrade it unless you find that some feature is missing that is in the next release. There is little or no reason to always be on top of the newest version of software.

We hope that Linux will meet or exceed your expectations of a homebrew UNIX system. At the very core of Linux is the spirit of free software, of constant development and growth. The Linux community favors expansion over stability, and that is a difficult concept to swallow for many people, especially those so steeped in the world of commercial UNIX. You cannot expect Linux to be perfect; nothing ever is in the free software world. However, we believe that Linux really is as complete and useful as any other implementation of UNIX.

1.7   Differences Between Linux and Other Operating Systems

It is important to understand the differences between Linux and other operating systems, such as MS-DOS, OS/2, and other implementations of UNIX for the personal computer. First of all, it should be made clear that Linux will coexist happily with other operating systems on the same machine: that is, you can run MS-DOS and OS/2 along with Linux on the same system without problems. There are even ways to interact between the various operating systems, as we'll see.

1.7.1   Why use Linux?

Why use Linux instead of a well-known, well-tested, and well-documented commercial operating system? We could give you a thousand reasons. One of the most important, however, is that Linux is an excellent choice for personal UNIX computing. If you're a UNIX software developer, why use MS-DOS at home? Linux will allow you to develop and test UNIX software on your PC, including database and X Windows applications. If you're a student, chances are that your university computing systems run UNIX. With Linux, you can run your own UNIX system and tailor it to your own needs. Installing and running Linux is also an excellent way to learn UNIX if you don't have access to other UNIX machines.

But let's not lose sight. Linux isn't just for personal UNIX users. It is robust and complete enough to handle large tasks, as well as distributed computing needs. Many businesses—especially small ones—are moving to Linux in lieu of other UNIX-based workstation environments. Universities are finding Linux to be perfect for teaching courses in operating systems design. Larger commercial software vendors are starting to realize the opportunities that a free operating system can provide.

The following sections should point out the most important differences between Linux and other operating systems. We hope that you'll find that Linux can meet your computing needs, or (at least) enhance your current computing environment. Keep in mind that they best way to get a taste for Linux is just to try it out—you needn't even install a complete system to get a feel for it. In Chapter 2, we'll show you how.

1.7.2   Linux vs. MS-DOS

It's not uncommon to run both Linux and MS-DOS on the same system. Many Linux users rely on MS-DOS for applications such as word processing. While Linux provides its own analogues for these applications (for example, TEX), there are various reasons why a particular user would want to run MS-DOS as well as Linux. If your entire dissertation is written using WordPerfect for MS-DOS, you may not be able to easily convert it to TEX or some other format. There are many commercial applications for MS-DOS which aren't available for Linux, and there's no reason why you can't use both.

As you might know, MS-DOS does not fully utilize the functionality of the 80386 and 80486 processors. On the other hand, Linux runs completely in the processor's protected mode, and exploits all of the features of the processor. You can directly access all of your available memory (and beyond, using virtual RAM). Linux provides a complete UNIX interface not available under MS-DOS—developing and porting UNIX applications under Linux is easily done, while under MS-DOS you are limited to a small subset of the UNIX programming functionality. Because Linux is a true UNIX system, you do not have these limitations.

We could debate the pros and cons of MS-DOS and Linux for pages on end. However, let it suffice to say that Linux and MS-DOS are completely different entities. MS-DOS is inexpensive (compared to other commercial operating systems), and has a strong foothold in the PC computing world. No other operating system for the PC has reached the level of popularity of MS-DOS—largely because the cost of these other operating systems is unapproachable to most personal computer users. Very few PC users can imagine spending $1000 or more on the operating system alone. Linux, however, is free, and you finally have the chance to decide.

We will allow you to make your own judgments of Linux and MS-DOS based on your expectations and needs. Linux is not for everybody. If you have always wanted to run a complete UNIX system at home, without the high cost of other UNIX implementations for the PC, Linux may be what you're looking for.

There are tools available to allow you to interact between Linux and MS-DOS. For example, it is easy to access MS-DOS files from Linux. There is also an MS-DOS emulator available, which allows you to run many popular MS-DOS applications. A Microsoft Windows emulator is currently under development.

1.7.3   Linux vs. The Other Guys

A number of other advanced operating systems are on the rise in the PC world. Specifically, IBM's OS/2 and Microsoft's Windows NT are becoming very popular as more users move away from MS-DOS.

Both OS/2 and Windows NT are full multitasking operating systems, much like Linux. Technically, OS/2, Windows NT, and Linux are quite similar: they support roughly the same features in terms of user interface, networking, security, and so forth. However, the real difference between Linux and The Other Guys is the fact that Linux is a version of UNIX, and hence benefits from the contributions of the UNIX community at large.

What makes UNIX so important? Not only is it the most popular operating system for multiuser machines, it is also the foundation for the majority of the free software world. If you have access to the Internet, nearly all of the free software available there is written specifically for UNIX systems. (The Internet itself is largely UNIX-based.)

There are many implementations of UNIX, from many vendors, and no single organization is responsible for distribution. There is a large push in the UNIX community for standardization in the form of open systems, but no single corporation controls this design. Hence, any vendor (or, as it turns out, any hacker) may implement these standards in an implementation of UNIX.

OS/2 and Windows NT, on the other hand, are proprietary systems. The interface and design are controlled by a single corporation, and only that corporation may implement that design. (Don't expect to see a free version of OS/2 anytime in the near future.) In one sense, this kind of organization is beneficial: it sets a strict standard for the programming and user interface unlike that found even in the open systems community. OS/2 is OS/2 wherever you go—the same holds for Windows NT.

However, the UNIX interface is constantly developing and changing. Several organizations are attempting to standardize the programming model, but the task is very difficult. Linux, in particular, is mostly compliant with the POSIX.1 standard for the UNIX programming interface. As time goes on, it is expected that the system will adhere to other such standards, but standardization is not the primary issue in the Linux development community.

1.7.4 Other implementations of UNIX

There are several other implementations of UNIX for the 80386 and 80486. The 80386 architecture lends itself to the UNIX design, and a number of vendors have taken advantage of this.

Feature-wise, other implementations of UNIX for the PC are quite similar to Linux. You will see that almost all commercial versions of UNIX support roughly the same software, programming environment, and networking features. However, there are some strong differences between Linux and commercial versions of UNIX.

First of all, Linux supports a different range of hardware from commercial implementations. In general, Linux supports the most well-known hardware devices, but support is still limited to that hardware which developers actually have access to. However, commercial UNIX vendors generally have a wider support base, and tend to support more hardware, although Linux is not far behind. We'll cover the hardware requirements for Linux in Section 1.8.

Secondly, commercial implementations of UNIX usually come bundled with a complete set of documentation as well as user support from the vendor. In contrast, most of the documentation for Linux is limited to documents available on the Internet—and books such as this one. In Section 1.9 we'll list sources of Linux documentation and other information.

As far as stability and robustness are concerned, many users have reported that Linux is at least as stable as commercial UNIX systems. Linux is still under development, and certain features (such TCP/IP networking) are less stable but improve as time goes by.

The most important factor to consider for many users is price. The Linux software is free, if you have access to the Internet (or another computer network) and can download it. If you do not have access to such a network, you may need to purchase it via mail order on diskette, tape, or CD-ROM (see Appendix B). Of course, you may copy Linux from a friend who may already have the software, or share the cost of purchasing it with someone else. If you are planning to install Linux on a large number of machines, you need only purchase a single copy of the software—Linux is not distributed on a "single machine" license.

The value of commercial UNIX implementations should not be demeaned: along with the price of the software itself, one usually pays for documentation, support, and assurance of quality. These are very important factors for large institutions, but personal computer users may not require these benefits. In any case, many businesses and universities are finding that running Linux on a lab of inexpensive personal computers is preferrable to running a commercial version of UNIX in a lab of workstations. Linux can provide the functionality of a workstation on PC hardware at a fraction of the cost.

As a "real-world" example of Linux's use within the computing community, Linux systems have travelled the high seas of the North Pacific, managing telecommunications and data analysis for an oceanographic research vessel. Linux systems are being used at research stations in Antarctica. As a more mundane example, perhaps, several hospitals are using Linux to maintain patient records. It is proving to be as reliable and useful as other implementations of UNIX.

There are other free or inexpensive implementations of UNIX for the 386 and 486. One of the most well-known is 386BSD, an implementation and port of BSD UNIX for the 386. 386BSD is comparable to Linux in many ways, but which one is "better" depends on your own personal needs and expectations. The only strong distinction that we can make is that Linux is developed openly (where any volunteer can aid in the development process), while 386BSD is developed within a closed team of programmers who maintain the system. Because of this, serious philosophical and design differences exist between the two projects. The goals of the two projects are entirely different: the goal of Linux is to develop a complete UNIX system from scratch (and have a lot of fun in the process), and the goal of 386BSD is in part to modify the existing BSD code for use on the 386.

NetBSD is another port of the BSD NET/2 distribution to a number of machines, including the 386. NetBSD has a slightly more open development structure, and is comparable to 386BSD in many respects.

Another project of note is HURD, an effort by the Free Software Foundation to develop and distribute a free version of UNIX for many platforms. Contact the Free Software Foundation (the address is given in Appendix E) for more information about this project. At the time of this writing, HURD is still in early stages of development.

Other inexpensive versions of UNIX exist as well, such as Coherent (available for about $99) and Minix (an academic but useful UNIX clone upon which early development of Linux was based). Some of these implementations are of mostly academic interest, while others are full-fledged systems for real productivity. Needless to say, however, many personal UNIX users are moving to Linux.

1.8   Hardware Requirements

Now you must be convinced of how wonderful Linux is, and all of the great things that it can do for you. However, before you rush out and install the software, you need to be aware of the hardware requirements and limitations that Linux has.

Keep in mind that Linux was developed by its users. This means, for the most part, that the hardware which is supported by Linux is only the hardware which the users and developers actually have access to. As it turns out, most of the popular hardware and peripherals for 80386/80486 systems are supported (in fact, Linux supports more hardware than some commercial implementations of UNIX). However, some of the more obscure and esoteric devices aren't supported yet. As time goes on, a wider range of hardware is supported, so if your favorite devices aren't listed here, chances are that support for them is forthcoming.

Another drawback for hardware support under Linux is that many companies have decided to keep the hardware interface proprietary. The upshot of this is that volunteer Linux developers simply can't write drivers for those devices (if they could, those drivers would be owned by the company that owned the interface, which would violate the GPL). The companies that maintain proprietary interfaces write their own drivers for operating systems such as MS-DOS and Microsoft Windows; the end user (that's you) never needs to know about the interface. Unfortunately, this does not allow Linux developers to write drivers for those devices.

There is very little that can be done about the situation. In some cases, programmers have attempted to write hackish drivers based on assumptions about the interface. In other cases, developers will work with the company in question and attempt to obtain information about the device interface, with varying degrees of success.

In the following sections, we'll attempt to summarize the hardware requirements for Linux. The Linux *Hardware HOWTO* (see Section 1.9) contains a more complete listing of hardware supported by Linux.

Disclaimer: a good deal of hardware support for Linux is currently in the development stage. Some distributions may or may not support these experimental features. This section primarily lists hardware which has been supported for some time and is known to be stable. When in doubt, consult the documentation for the distribution of Linux you are using (see Section 2.1 for more information on Linux distributions).

1.8.1 Motherboard and CPU requirements

Linux currently supports systems with an Intel 80386, 80486, or Pentium CPU. This includes all variations on this CPU type, such as the 386SX, 486SX, 486DX, and 486DX2. Non-Intel "clones", such as AMD and Cyrix processors, work with Linux as well.

If you have a 80386 or 80486SX, you may also wish to use a math coprocessor, although one isn't required (the Linux kernel can do FPU emulation if you do not have a math coprocessor). All standard FPU couplings are supported, such as IIT, Cyrix FasMath, and Intel coprocessors.

The system motherboard must use ISA or EISA bus architecture. These terms define how the system interfaces with peripherals and other components on the main bus. Most systems sold today are either ISA or EISA bus. IBM's MicroChannel (MCA) bus, found on machines such as the IBM PS/2, is not currently supported.

Systems which use a local bus architecture (for faster video and disk access) are supported as well. It is suggested that you have a standard local bus architecture such as the VESA Local Bus ("VLB").

1.8.2 Memory requirements

Linux requires very little memory to run compared to other advanced operating systems. You should have at the very least 2 megabytes of RAM; however, it is strongly suggested that you have 4 megabytes. The more memory you have, the faster the system will run.

Linux can support the full 32-bit address range of the 386/486; in other words, it will utilize all of your RAM automatically.

Linux will run happily with only 4 megabytes of RAM, including all of the bells and whistles such as X Windows, Emacs, and so on. However, having more memory is almost as important as having a faster processor. 8 megabytes is more than enough for personal use; 16 megabytes or more may be needed if you are expecting a heavy user load on the system.

Most Linux users allocate a portion of their hard drive as swap space, which is used as virtual RAM. Even if you have a great deal of physical RAM in your machine, you may wish to use swap space. While swap space is no replacement for actual physical RAM, it can allow your system to run larger applications by swapping out inactive portions of code to disk. The amount of swap space that you should allocate depends on several factors; we'll come back to this question in Section 2.2.3.

1.8.3   Hard drive controller requirements

You do not need to have a hard drive to run Linux; you can run a minimal system completely from floppy. However, this is slow and very limited, and many users have access to hard drive storage anyway. You must have an AT-standard (16-bit) controller. There is support in the kernel for XT-standard (8 bit) controllers; however, most controllers used today are AT-standard. Linux should support all MFM, RLL, and IDE controllers. Most, but not all, ESDI controllers are supported—only those which do ST506 hardware emulation.

The general rule for non-SCSI hard drive and floppy controllers is that if you can access the drive from MS-DOS or another operating system, you should be able to access it from Linux.

Linux also supports a number of popular SCSI drive controllers, although support for SCSI is more limited because of the wide range of controller interface standards. Supported SCSI controllers include the Adaptec AHA1542B, AHA1542C, AHA1742A (BIOS version 1.34), AHA1522, AHA1740, AHA1740 (SCSI-2 controller, BIOS 1.34 in Enhanced mode); Future Domain 1680, TMC-850, TMC-950; Seagate ST-02; UltraStor SCSI; Western Digital WD7000FASST. Clones which are based on these cards should work as well.

1.8.4   Hard drive space requirements

Of course, to install Linux, you'll need to have some amount of free space on your hard drive. Linux will support multiple hard drives in the same machine; you can allocate space for Linux across multiple drives if necessary.

The *amount* of hard drive space that you will require depends greatly on your needs and the amount of software that you're installing. Linux is relatively small as UNIX implementations go; you could run a complete system in 10 to 20 megabytes of space on your drive.

However, if you want to have room for expansion, and for larger packages such as X Windows, you will need more space. If you plan to allow multiple users to use the machine, you will need to allocate storage for their files.

Also, unless you have a large amount of physical RAM (16 megabytes or more), you will more than likely want to allocate swap space, to be used as virtual RAM. We will discuss all of the details of installing and using swap space in Section 2.2.3.

Each distribution of Linux usually comes with some literature that should help you to gauge the precise amount of required storage depending on the amount of software you plan to install. You can run a minimal system with less than 20 megabytes; a complete system with all of the bells and whistles in 80 megabytes or less; and a very large system with room for many users and space for future expansion in the range of 100-150 megabytes. Again, these figures are meant only as a ballpark approximation; you will have to look at your own needs and goals in order to determine your specific storage requirements.

1.8.5 Monitor and video adapator requirements

Linux supports all standard Hercules, CGA, EGA, VGA, IBM monochrome, and Super VGA video cards and monitors for the default text-based interface. In general, if the video card and monitor coupling works under another operating system such as MS-DOS, it should work fine with Linux. Original IBM CGA cards suffer from "snow" under Linux, which is not pleasant to use.

Graphical environments such as the X Window System have video hardware requirements of their own. Instead of listing these requirements here, we relegate the discussion to Section 5.1.1. In short, to run the X Window System on your Linux machine, you will need one of the video cards listed in that section.

1.8.6 Miscellaneous hardware

The above sections described the hardware which is required to run a Linux system. However, most users have a number of "optional" devices such as tape and CD-ROM storage, sound boards, and so on, and are interested in whether or not this hardware is supported by Linux. Read on.

1.8.6.1 Mice and other pointing devices

For the most part, you will only be using a mouse under a graphical environment such as the X Window System. However, several Linux applications not associated with a graphics environment do make use of the mouse.

Linux supports all standard serial mice, including Logitech, MM series, Mouseman, Microsoft (2-button) and Mouse Systems (3-button). Linux also supports Microsoft, Logitech, and ATIXL busmice. The PS/2 mouse interface is supported as well.

All other pointing devices, such as trackballs, which emulate the above mice, should work as well.

1.8.6.2   CD-ROM storage

Almost all CD-ROM drives use the SCSI interface. As long as you have a SCSI adaptor supported by Linux, then your CD-ROM drive should work. A number of CD-ROM drives have been verified to work under Linux, including the NEC CDR-74, Sony CDU-541, and Texel DM-3024. The Sony internal CDU-31a and the Mistsumi CD-ROM drives are supported by Linux as well.

Linux supports the standard ISO-9660 filesystem for CD-ROMs.

1.8.6.3   Tape drives

There are several types of tape drives available on the market. Most of them use the SCSI interface, all of which should be supported by Linux. Among the verified SCSI tape drives are the Sankyo CP150SE; Tandberg 3600; Wangtek 5525ES, 5150ES, and 5099EN with the PC36 adaptor. Other QIC-02 drives should be supported as well.

Drivers are currently under development for various other tape devices, such as Colorado drives which hang off of the floppy controller.

1.8.6.4   Printers

Linux supports the complete range of parallel printers. If you are able to access your printer via the parallel port from MS-DOS or another operating system, you should be able to access it from Linux as well. The Linux printing software consists of the UNIX standard `lp` and `lpr` software. This software also allows you to print remotely via the network, if you have one available.

1.8.6.5   Modems

As with printer support, Linux supports the full range of serial modems, both internal and external. There is a great deal of telecommunications software available for Linux, including Kermit, `pcomm`, `minicom`, and Seyon. If your modem is accessible from another operating system on the same machine, you should be able to access it from Linux with no difficulty.

1.8.7   Ethernet cards

Many popular Ethernet cards and LAN adaptors are supported by Linux. These include:

- 3com 3c503, 3c503/16

- Novell NE1000, NE2000

- Western Digital WD8003, WD8013

- Hewlett Packard HP27245, HP27247, HP27250

- D-Link DE-600

The following clones are reported to work:

- LANNET LEC-45

- Alta Combo

- Artisoft LANtastic AE-2

- Asante Etherpak 2001/2003,

- D-Link Ethernet II

- LTC E-NET/16 P/N 8300-200-002

- Network Solutions HE-203,

- SVEC 4 Dimension Ethernet

- 4-Dimension FD0490 EtherBoard 16

Clones which are compatible with any of the above cards should work as well.

1.9 Sources of Linux Information

As you have probably guessed, there are many sources of information about Linux available apart from this book. In particular, there are a number of books, not specific to Linux but rather about UNIX in general, that will be of importance, especially to those readers without previous UNIX experience. If you are new to the UNIX world, we seriously suggest that you take the time to peruse one of these books before you attempt to brave the jungles of Linux. Specifically, the book *Learning the UNIX Operating System*, by Grace Todino and John Strang, is a good place to start.

Many of the following sources of information are available online in some electronic form. That is, you must have access to an online network, such as the Internet, USENET, or Fidonet, in order to access the information contained therein. If you do not have online access to any of this material, you might be able to find someone kind enough to give you hardcopies of the documents in question. Read on.

1.9.1   Online documents

If you have access to the Internet, there are many Linux documents available via anonymous FTP from archive sites all over the world. If you do not have direct Internet access, these documents may still be available to you: many Linux distributions on CD-ROM contain all of the documents mentioned here. Also, they are distributed on many other networks, such as Fidonet and CompuServe. If you are able to send mail to Internet sites, you may be able to retrieve these files using one of the `ftpmail` servers which will electronically mail you the documents or files from FTP archive sites. See Appendix C for more information on using `ftpmail`.

There is a great number of FTP archive sites which carry Linux software and related documents. A list of well-known Linux archive sites is given in Appendix C. In order to reduce network traffic, you should always use the FTP site which is geographically (network-wise) closest to you.

Appendix A contains a listing of some of the Linux documents which are available via anonymous FTP. The filenames will differ depending on the archive site in question; most sites keep Linux-related documents in the `docs` subdirectory of their Linux archive space. For example, on the FTP site `sunsite.unc.edu`, Linux files are stored in the directory `/pub/Linux`, with Linux-related documentation being found in `/pub/Linux/docs`.

Examples of available online documents are the *Linux FAQ*, a collection of frequently asked questions about Linux; the Linux *HOWTO* documents, each describing a specific aspect of the system—including the *Installation HOWTO*, the *Printing HOWTO*, and the *Ethernet HOWTO*; and, the Linux META-FAQ, a list of other sources of Linux information on the Internet.

Most of these documents are also regularly posted to one or more Linux-related USENET newsgroups; see Section 1.9.4 below.

1.9.2   Linux on the World Wide Web

The Linux Documentation Home Page is available for World Wide Web users at the URL

```
http://sunsite.unc.edu/mdw/linux.html
```

This page contains many HOWTOs and other documents in HTML format, as well as pointers to other sites of interest to Linux users.

1.9.3   Books and other published works

At this time, there are few published works specifically about Linux. Most noteworthy are the books from the Linux Documentation Project, a project carried out over the Internet to write and distribute a bona fide set of "manuals" for Linux. These manuals are analogues to the documentation sets available with commercial versions of UNIX: they cover everything from installing Linux, to using and running the system, programming, networking, kernel development, and more.

The Linux Documentation Project manuals are available via anonymous FTP from the Internet, as well as via mail order from several sources. Appendix A lists the manuals which are available and covers means of obtaining them in detail.

There are not many books specifically about Linux currently available. However, there are a large number of books about UNIX in general which are certainly applicable to Linux— as far as using and programming the system is concerned, Linux does not differ greatly from other implementations of UNIX. In short, almost everything you want to know about using and programming Linux can be found in sources meant for a general UNIX audience. In fact, this book is meant to be complemented by the large library of UNIX books currently available; here, we present the most important Linux-specific details and hope that you will look to other sources for more in-depth information.

Armed with a number of good books about using UNIX, as well as the book you hold in your hands, you should be able to tackle just about anything. Appendix A includes a list of highly-recommended UNIX books, both for UNIX newcomers and UNIX wizards alike.

There is also a monthly magazine about Linux, called the *Linux Journal*. It is distributed worldwide, and is an excellent way to keep in touch with the many goings-on in the Linux community—especially if you do not have access to USENET news (see below). See Appendix A for information on subscribing to the *Linux Journal*.

1.9.4 USENET newsgroups

USENET is a worldwide electronic news and discussion forum with a heavy contingent of so-called "newsgroups"—discussion areas devoted to a particular topic. Much of the development of Linux has been done over the waves of the Internet and USENET, and not suprisingly there are a number of USENET newsgroups available for discussions about Linux.

The original Linux newsgroup was `alt.os.linux`, and was created to move some of the discussions about Linux out of `comp.os.minix` and the various mailing lists. Soon, the traffic on `alt.os.linux` grew to be large enough that a newsgroup in the `comp` hierarchy was warranted; a vote was taken in February of 1992, and `comp.os.linux` was created.

`comp.os.linux` quickly became one of the most popular (and loudest) USENET groups; more popular than any other `comp.os` group. In December of 1992, a vote was taken to split the newsgroup in order to reduce traffic; only `comp.os.linux.announce` passed this vote. In July of 1993, the group was finally split into the new hierarchy. Almost 2000 people voted in the `comp.os.linux` reorganization, making it one of the largest USENET Call For Votes ever.

If you do not have direct USENET access, but are able to send and receive electronic mail from the Internet, there are mail-to-news gateways available for each of the newsgroups below.

`comp.os.linux.announce`

>   `comp.os.linux.announce` is a moderated newsgroup for announcements and important postings about the Linux system (such as bug reports, important patches to software, and so on). If you read any Linux newsgroups at all, read this one. Often, the important postings in this group are not crossposted to other groups. This group also contains many periodic postings about Linux, including many of the online documents described in the last section and listed in Appendix A.

>   Postings to this newsgroup must be approved by the moderators, Matt Welsh and Lars Wirzenius. If you wish to submit and article to this group, in most cases you can simply post the article as you normally would (using `Pnews` or whatever posting software that you have available); the news software will automatically forward the article to the moderators for approval. However, if your news system is not set up correctly, you may need to mail the article directly; the submission address is `linux-announce@tc.cornell.edu`.

>   The rest of the Linux newsgroups listed below are unmoderated.

`comp.os.linux.help`

>   This is the most popular Linux newsgroup. It is for questions and answers about using, setting up, or otherwise running a Linux system. If you are having problems with Linux, you may post to this newsgroup, and hopefully receive a reply from someone who might be able to help. However, it is strongly suggested that you read all of the available Linux documentation before posting questions to this newsgroup.

`comp.os.linux.admin`

>   This newsgroup is for questions and discussion about running a Linux system, most commonly in an active, multi-user environment. Any discussion about administrative issues of Linux (such as packaging software, making backups, handling users, and so on) is welcome here.

`comp.os.linux.development`

>   This is a newsgroup for discussions about development of the Linux system. All issues related to kernel and system software development should be discussed here. For example, if you are writing a kernel driver and need help with certain aspects of the programming, this would be the place to ask. This newsgroup is also for discussions about the direction and goals behind the Linux development effort, as described (somewhat) in Section 1.6.

It should be noted that this newsgroup is not (technically) for discussions about development of software *for* Linux, but rather for discussions of development *of* Linux. That is, issues dealing with applications programming under Linux should be discussed in another Linux newsgroup; `comp.os.linux.development` is about developing the Linux system itself, including the kernel, system libraries, and so on.

`comp.os.linux.misc`

This newsgroup is for all discussion which doesn't quite fit into the other available Linux groups. In particular, advocacy wars (the incessant "Linux versus Windows NT" thread, for example), should be waged here, as opposed to in the technical Linux groups. Any nontechnical or metadiscourse about the Linux system should remain in `comp.os.linux.misc`.

It should be noted that the newsgroup `comp.os.linux`, which was originally the only Linux group, has been superseded by the new hierarchy of groups. If you have access to `comp.os.linux`, but not to the newer Linux groups listed above, encourage your news administrator to create the new groups on your system.

1.9.5 Internet mailing lists

If you have access to Internet electronic mail, you can participate in a number of mailing lists even if you do not have USENET access. Note that if you are not directly on the Internet, you can join one of these mailing lists as long as you are able to exchange electronic mail with the Internet (for example, UUCP, FidoNET, CompuServe, and other networks all have access to Internet mail).

The "Linux Activists" mailing list is primarily for Linux developers and people interested in aiding the development process. This is a "multi-channel" mailing list, in which you join one or more "channels" based on your particular interests. Some of the available channels include: **NORMAL**, for general Linux-related issues; **KERNEL**, for kernel development; **GCC**, for discussions relating to the `gcc` compiler and library development; **NET**, for discussions about the TCP/IP networking code; **DOC**, for issues relating to writing and distributing Linux documentation; and more.

For more information about the Linux Activists mailing list, send mail to

`linux-activists@niksula.hut.fi`

You will receive a list of currently available channels, including information on how to subscribe and unsubscribe to particular channels on the list.

Quite a few special-purpose mailing lists about and for Linux exist as well. The best way to find out about these is to watch the Linux USENET newsgroups for announcements, as well as to read the list of publicly-available mailing lists, periodically posted to the USENET group `news.answers`.

1.10 Getting Help

You will undoubtedly require some degree of assistance during your adventures in the Linux world. Even the most wizardly of UNIX wizards occasionally is stumped by some quirk or feature of Linux, and it's important to know how and where to find help when you need it.

The primary means of getting help in the Linux world are via Internet mailing lists and USENET newsgroups, as discussed in Section 1.9. If you don't have online access to these sources, you might be able to find comparable Linux discussion forums on other online services, such as on local BBS's, CompuServe, and so on.

A number of businesses are providing commercial support for Linux. This will allow you to pay a "subscription fee" which will allow you to call the consultants for help with your Linux problems. Appendix B contains a list of Linux vendors, some of which provide commercial support. However, if you have access to USENET and Internet mail, you may find the free support found there to be just as useful.

Keeping the following suggestions in mind will greatly improve your experiences with Linux and will guarantee you more success in finding help to your problems.

Consult all available documentation... first! The first thing you should do when encountering a problem is consult the various sources of information listed in Section 1.9 and Appendix A. These documents were laboriously written for people like you—people who need help with the Linux system. Even books written for UNIX in general are applicable to Linux, and you should take advantage of them. More than likely, you will find the answer to your problems somewhere in this documentation, as impossible as it may seem.

If you have access to USENET news or any of the Linux-related mailing lists, be sure to actually *read* the information there before posting for help with your problem. Many times, solutions to common problems are not easy to find in documentation, and instead are well-covered in the newsgroups and mailing lists devoted to Linux. If you only post to these groups, and don't actually read them, you are asking for trouble.

Learn to appreciate self-maintenance. In most cases, it is preferable to do as much independent research and investigation into the problem as possible before seeking outside help. After all, you asked for it, by running Linux in the first place! Remember that Linux is all about hacking and fixing problems yourself. It is not a commercial operating system, nor does it try to look like one. Hacking won't kill you. In fact, it will teach you a great deal about the system to investigate and solve problems yourself—maybe even enough to one day call yourself a Linux guru. Learn to appreciate the value of hacking the system, and how to fix problems yourself. You can't expect to run a complete, homebrew Linux system without some degree of handiwork.

Remain calm. It is vital to refrain from getting frustrated with the system, at all costs. Nothing is earned by taking an axe—or worse, a powerful electromagnet—to your Linux system in a fit of anger. The authors have found that a large punching bag or similar inanimate object is a wonderful way to relieve the occasional stress attack. As Linux matures and distributions become more reliable, we hope that this problem will go away. However, even commercial UNIX implementations can be tricky at times. When all else fails, sit back, take a few deep breaths, and go after the problem again when you feel relaxed. Your mind and conscience will be clearer.

Refrain from posting spuriously. Many people make the mistake of posting or mailing messages pleading for help prematurely. When encountering a problem, do not—we repeat, do *not*—rush immediately to your nearest terminal and post a message to one of the Linux USENET newsgroups. Often, you will catch your own mistake five minutes later and find yourself in the curious situation of defending your own sanity in a public forum. Before posting anything any of the Linux mailing lists or newsgroups, first attempt to resolve the problem yourself and be absolutely certain what the problem is. Does your system not respond when switched on? Perhaps the machine is unplugged.

If you do post for help, make it worthwhile. If all else fails, you may wish to post a message for help in any of the number of electronic forums dedicated to Linux, such as USENET newsgroups and mailing lists. When posting, remember that the people reading your post are not there to help you. The network is not your personal consulting service. Therefore, it is important to remain as polite, terse, and informative as possible.

How can one accomplish this? First, you should include as much (relevant) information about your system and your problem as possible. Posting the simple request, "I cannot seem to get e-mail to work" will probably get you nowhere unless you include information on your system, what software you are using, what you have attempted to do so far and what the results were. When including technical information, it is usually a good idea to include general information on the version(s) of your software (Linux kernel version, for example), as well as a brief summary of your hardware configuration. However, don't overdo it—including information on the brand and type of monitor that you have probably is irrelevant if you're trying to configure networking software.

Secondly, remember that you need to make some attempt—however feeble—at solving your problem before you go to the Net. If you have never attempted to set up electronic mail, for instance, and first decide to ask folks on the Net how to go about doing it, you are making a big mistake. There are a number of documents available (see the Section 1.9) on how to get started with many common tasks under Linux. The idea is to get as far along as possible on your own and *then* ask for help if and when you get stuck.

Also remember that the people reading your message, however helpful, may occasionally get frustrated by seeing the same problem over and over again. Be sure to actually read the Linux newsgroups and mailing lists before posting your problems. Many times, the solution to your problem has been discussed repeatedly, and all that's required to find it is to browse the current messages.

Lastly, when posting to electronic newsgroups and mailing lists, try to be as polite as possible. It is much more effective and worthwhile to be polite, direct, and informative—more people will be willing to help you if you master a humble tone. To be sure, the flame war is an art form across many forms of electronic communication, but don't allow that to preoccupy your and other people's time. Save the network undue wear and tear by keeping bandwidth as low as possible, and by paying as much attention to other sources of information which are available to you. The network is an excellent way to get help with your Linux problems—but it is important to know how to use the network *effectively*.

Chapter 2

Obtaining and Installing Linux

In this chapter, we'll describe how to obtain the Linux software, in the form of one of the various pre-packaged distributions, and how to install the distribution that you choose.

As we have mentioned, there is no single "official" distribution of the Linux software; there are, in fact, many distributions, each of which serves a particular purpose and set of goals. These distributions are available via anonymous FTP from the Internet, on BBS systems worldwide, and via mail on diskette, tape, and CD-ROM.

Here, we present a general overview of the installation process. Each distribution has its own specific installation instructions, but armed with the concepts presented here you should be able to feel your way through any installation. Appendix A lists sources of information for installation instructions and other help, if you're at a total loss.

This book contains additional sections detailing the Slackware distribution of Linux.

2.1 Distributions of Linux

Because Linux is free software, no single organization or entity is responsible for releasing and distributing the software. Therefore, anyone is free to put together and distribute the Linux software, as long as the restrictions in the GPL are observed. The upshot of this is that there are many distributions of Linux, available via anonymous FTP or via mail order.

You are now faced with the task of deciding upon a particular distribution of Linux which suits your needs. Not all distributions are alike. Many of them come with just about all of the software you'd need to run a complete system—and then some. Other Linux distributions are "small" distributions intended for users without copious amounts of diskspace. Many distributions contain only the core Linux software, and you are expected to install larger software packages, such as the X Window System, yourself. (In Chapter 4

39

we'll show you how.)

The Linux *Distribution HOWTO* (see Appendix A) contains a list of Linux distributions available via the Internet as well as mail order. Appendix B also lists contact addresses for a number of Linux mail-order vendors. If you purchased this book in printed the form, the publisher should also be able to provide you with a Linux distribution or tell you who can.

How can you decide among all of these distributions? If you have access to USENET news, or another computer conferencing system, you might want to ask there for personal opinions from people who have installed Linux. Even better, if you know someone who has installed Linux, ask them for help and advice. There are many factors to consider when choosing a distribution, however, everyone's needs and opinions are different. In actuality, most of the popular Linux distributions contain roughly the same set of software, so the distribution that you select is more or less arbitrary.

This book contains information on installing the popular Slackware and Slackware Pro distributions of Linux.

2.1.1   Getting Linux from the Internet

If you have access to the Internet, the easiest way to obtain Linux is via anonymous FTP.[1] Appendix C lists a number of FTP archive sites which carry Linux software. One of these is `sunsite.unc.edu`, and the various Linux distributions can be found in the directory

```
/pub/Linux/distributions
```

there.

Many distributions are released via anonymous FTP as a set of disk images. That is, the distribution consists of a set of files, and each file contains the binary image of a floppy. In order to copy the contents of the image file onto the floppy, you can use the `RAWRITE.EXE` program under MS-DOS. This program copies, block-for-block, the contents of a file to a floppy, without regard for disk format.[2]

`RAWRITE.EXE` is available on the various Linux FTP sites, including `sunsite.unc.edu` in the directory

```
/pub/Linux/system/Install/rawrite
```

---

[1] If you do not have direct Internet access, you can obtain Linux via the `ftpmail` service, provided that you have the ability to exchange e-mail with the Internet. See Appendix C for details.

[2] If you have access to a UNIX workstation with a floppy drive, you can also use the `dd` command to copy the file image directly to the floppy. A command such as "dd of=/dev/rfd0 if=foo bs=18k" will "raw write" the contents of the file `foo` to the floppy device on a Sun workstation. Consult your local UNIX gurus for more information on your system's floppy devices and the use of `dd`.

Therefore, in many cases, you simply download the set of diskette images, and use `RAWRITE.EXE` with each image in turn to create a set of diskettes. You boot from the so-called "boot diskette" and you're ready to roll. The software is usually installed directly from the floppies, although some distributions allow you to install from an MS-DOS partition on your hard drive. Some distributions allow you to install over a TCP/IP network. The documentation for each distribution should describe these installation methods if they are available.

Other Linux distributions are installed from a set of MS-DOS format floppies. For example, the Slackware distribution of Linux requires only the boot and root diskettes to be created using `RAWRITE.EXE`. The rest of the diskettes are copied to MS-DOS format diskettes using the MS-DOS `COPY` command. The system installs the software directly from the MS-DOS floppies. This saves you the trouble of having to use `RAWRITE.EXE` for many image files, although it requires you to have access to an MS-DOS system to create the diskettes.

Each distribution of Linux available via anonymous FTP should include a `README` file describing how to download and prepare the diskettes for installation. Be sure to read all of the available documentation for the release that you are using.

When downloading the Linux software, be sure to use *binary* mode for all file transfers (with most FTP clients, the command "`binary`" enables this mode).

See Section 2.1.4, below, for information on obtaining the Slackware distribution from the Internet.

2.1.2   Getting Linux from other online sources

If you have access to another computer network such as CompuServe or Prodigy, there may be a means to download the Linux software from these sources. In addition, many bulletin board (BBS) systems carry Linux software. A list of Linux BBS sites is given in Appendix D. Not all Linux distributions are available from these computer networks, however—many of them, especially the various CD-ROM distributions, are only available via mail order.

2.1.3   Getting Linux via mail order

If you don't have Internet or BBS access, many Linux distributions are available via mail order on diskette, tape, or CD-ROM. Appendix B lists a number of these distributors. Many of them accept credit cards as well as international orders, so if you're not in the United States or Canada you still should be able to obtain Linux in this way.

Linux is free software, although distributors are allowed by the GPL to charge a fee for it. Therefore, ordering Linux via mail order might cost you between US$30 and US$150, depending on the distribution. However, if you know someone who has already purchased or downloaded a release of Linux, you are free to borrow or copy their software for your own use. Linux distributors are not allowed to restrict the license or redistribution of the software in any way. If you are thinking about installing an entire lab of machines with Linux, for example, you only need to purchase a single copy of one of the distributions, which can be used to install all of the machines.

2.1.4   Getting Slackware

Slackware is a popular distribution of Linux maintained by Patrick Volkerding.[3] It is easy to install and fairly complete, and may be obtained both from the Internet as well as on CD-ROM from a number of vendors (see Appendix B).

The Slackware distribution consists of a number of "disk sets", each one containing a particular type of software (for example, the **d** disk set contains development tools such as the **gcc** compiler, and the **x** disk set contains the X Window System software). You can elect to install whatever disk sets you like, and can install new ones later.

The version of Slackware described here is 2.0.0, of 25 June 1994. Installation of later versions of Slackware should be very similar to the information given here.

2.1.4.1   Slackware disk sets

Unfortunately, Slackware does not maintain a complete list of diskspace requirements for each disk set. You need at least 7 megabytes to install just the "**A**" series of disks; a very rough estimate of the required diskspace would be 2 or 2.5 megabytes per disk.

The following disk sets are available:

A   The base system. Enough to get up and running and have elvis and comm programs available. Based around the 1.0.9 Linux kernel, and the new filesystem standard (FSSTND).

These disks are known to fit on 1.2M disks, although the rest of Slackware won't. If you have only a 1.2M floppy, you can still install the base system, download other disks you want and install them from your hard drive.

AP   Various applications and add ons, such as the manual pages, **groff**, **ispell** (GNU and international versions), **term**, **joe**, **jove**, **ghostscript**, **sc**, **bc**, and the quota patches.

D   Program development. GCC/G++/Objective C 2.5.8, **make** (GNU and BSD), **byacc** and GNU **bison**, **flex**, the 4.5.26 C libraries, **gdb**, kernel source for 1.0.9, **SVGAlib**, **ncurses**, **clisp**, **f2c**, **p2c**, **m4**, **perl**, **rcs**.

E   GNU Emacs 19.25.

---

[3]Patrick Volkerding can be reached on the Internet at **volkerdi@mhd1.moorhead.msus.edu**.

F   A collection of FAQs and other documentation.

I   Info pages for GNU software. Documentation for various programs readable by `info` or Emacs.

N   Networking. TCP/IP, UUCP, `mailx`, `dip`, `deliver`, `elm`, `pine`, `smail`, `cnews`, `nn`, `tin`, `trn`.

OOP   Object Oriented Programming. GNU Smalltalk 1.1.1, and the Smalltalk Interface to X (STIX).

Q   Alpha kernel source and images (currently contains Linux 1.1.18).

TCL   Tcl, Tk, TclX, blt, itcl.

Y   Games. The BSD games collection, and Tetris for terminals.

X   The base XFree86 2.1.1 system, with `libXpm`, `fvwm` 1.20, and `xlock` added.

XAP   X applications: X11 `ghostscript`, `libgr13`, `seyon`, `workman`, `xfilemanager`, `xv` 3.01, GNU `chess` and `xboard`, `xfm` 1.2, `ghostview`, and various X games.

XD   X11 program development. X11 libraries, server linkkit, PEX support.

XV   Xview 3.2 release 5. XView libraries, and the Open Look virtual and non-virtual window managers.

IV   Interviews libraries, include files, and the `doc` and `idraw` apps.

OI   ParcPlace's Object Builder 2.0 and Object Interface Library 4.0, generously made available for Linux developers according to the terms in the "copying" notice found in these directories. Note that these only work with `libc`-4.4.4, but a new version may be released once `gcc` 2.5.9 is available.

T   The TeX and LaTeX text formatting systems.

You must get the "A" disk set; the rest are optional. We suggest installing the A, AP, and D sets, as well as the X set if you plan to run the X Window System.

2.1.4.2   Getting Slackware from the Internet

The Slackware release of Linux may be found on any number of FTP sites worldwide. Appendix C lists several of the Linux FTP sites; we suggest that you try to find the software on the FTP site nearest you, to reduce net traffic. However, two of the major Linux FTP archives are `sunsite.unc.edu` and `tsx-11.mit.edu`.

The Slackware release may be found at least on the following sites:

- `sunsite.unc.edu:/pub/Linux/distributions/slackware`

- `tsx-11.mit.edu:/pub/linux/packages/slackware`

- `ftp.cdrom.com:/pub/linux/slackware`

`ftp.cdrom.com` is Slackware's home site.

2.1.4.2.1   Downloading the files   You should download the following files using FTP. Be sure to use binary mode when transferring. Appendix C contains a complete tutorial on using FTP.

- The various **README** files, as well as **SLACKWARE_FAQ**. Be sure to read these files before attempting to install the software, to get any updates or changes to this document.

- A bootdisk image. This is a file that you will write to a floppy to create the Slackware boot disk. If you have a 1.44 megabyte boot floppy (3.5"), look in the directory **bootdsks.144**. If you have a 1.2 megabyte boot floppy (5.25"), look in the directory **bootdsks.12**.

  You need one of the following bootdisk files.

  - **bare.gz**. This is a boot floppy that has only IDE hard drive drivers. (No SCSI, CD-ROM, or networking support.) Use this if you only have an IDE hard drive controller and aren't going to be installing over the network or from CD-ROM.
  - **cdu31a.gz**. Contains IDE, SCSI, and the Sony CDU31A/33A driver.
  - **mitsumi.gz**. Contains IDE, SCSI, and the Mitsumi CD-ROM driver.
  - **modern.gz**. An experimental boot disk with a newer kernel, and all drivers except those for network cards and the Sony 535 CD-ROM.
  - **net.gz**. Contains IDE and network drivers.
  - **sbpcd.gz**. Contains IDE, SCSI, and SoundBlaster Pro/Panasonic CD-ROM drivers.
  - **scsi.gz**. Contains IDE, SCSI, and SCSI CD-ROM drivers.
  - **scsinet.gz**. Contains IDE, SCSI, SCSI CD-ROM, and network drivers.
  - **sony535.gz**. Contains IDE, SCSI, and Sony 535/531 CD-ROM drivers.
  - **xt.gz**. Contains IDE and XT hard drive drivers.

  You need only *one* of the above bootdisk images, depending on the hardware that you have in your system.

  The issue here is that some hardware drivers conflict with each other in strange ways, and instead of attempting to debug hardware problems on your system it's easier to use a boot floppy image with only certain drivers enabled. Most users should try `scsi.gz` or `bare.gz`.

- A rootdisk image. This is a file that you will write to a floppy to create the Slackware installation disk. As with the bootdisk image, look in **rootdsks.144** or **rootdsks.12** depending on the type of boot floppy drive that you have.

  You need one of the following files:

  - **color144.gz**. The menu-based color installation disk for 1.44 megabyte drives. Most users should use this rootdisk.

  - **umsds144.gz**. A version of the **color144** disk for installing with the UMSDOS filesystem, which allows you to install Linux onto a directory of an MS-DOS filesystem. This installation method is not discussed in detail here, but it will prevent you from having to repartition your drive. More on this later.

  - **tty144.gz**. The terminal-based installation disk for 1.44 megabyte drives. If **color144.gz** doesn't work for you, try **tty144.gz** instead.

  - **colrlite.gz**. The menu-based color installation disk for 1.2 megabyte drives.

  - **umsds12.gz**. A version of the **colrlite** disk for installing with the UMSDOS filesystem. See the description of **umsds144.gz**, above.

  - **tty12.gz**. The terminal-based installation disk for 1.2 megabyte drives. Use this rootdisk if you have a 1.2 megabyte boot floppy and **colrlite.gz** doesn't work for you.

  Again, you need only *one* of the above rootdisk images, depending on the type of boot floppy drive that you have.

- **GZIP.EXE**. This is an MS-DOS executable of the **gzip** compression program used to compress the boot and rootdisk files (the **.gz** extension on the filenames indicates this). This can be found in the **install** directory.

- **RAWRITE.EXE**. This is an MS-DOS program that will write the contents of a file (such as the boot and rootdisk images) directly to a floppy, without regard to format. You will use **RAWRITE.EXE** to create the boot and root floppies. This can be found in the **install** directory as well.

  You only need **RAWRITE.EXE** and **GZIP.EXE** if you plan to create the boot and root floppies from an MS-DOS system. If you have access to a UNIX workstation with a floppy drive instead, you can create the floppies from there, using the **dd** command. See the man page for **dd** and ask your local UNIX administrators for assistance.

- The files in the directories **slakware/a1**, **slakware/a2**, and **slakware/a3**. These files make up the "A" disk set of the Slackware distribution. They are required. Later, you will copy these files to MS-DOS floppies for installation (or, you can install from your hard drive). Therefore, when you download these files, keep them in separate directories; don't mix the **a1** files with the **a2** files, and so on.

  Be sure that you get the files without periods in the filenames as well. That is, within FTP, use the command "**mget ***" instead of "**mget *.***".

- The files in the directories **ap1**, **ap2**, etc., depending on what disk sets you are installing. For example, if you are installing the "**X**" disk series, get the files in the directories **x1** through **x5**. As with the "**A**" disk set, above, be sure to keep the files in separate directories when you download them.

2.1.4.3   Getting Slackware on CD-ROM

Slackware is also available on CD-ROM. Most Slackware CD-ROMs simply contain a copy of the files as they appear on the FTP archive sites, as described above. Therefore, if you have a Slackware CD-ROM, you have all of the files that you need.

You will have to create a boot and root floppy from the files on the CD-ROM. See Section 2.1.4.2.1, above, for a discussion on the available boot and root disk images.

First, decide which boot and root disk images you will use. They should all be on the CD-ROM. Below, we will describe how to create these floppies.

2.1.4.4   Installation methods

Slackware provides several different means of installing the software. The most popular is installing from an MS-DOS partition on your hard drive; another is to install from a set of MS-DOS floppies created from the disk sets that you downloaded.

If you have Slackware on a CD-ROM, you can install the files directly from there. The Slackware Pro distribution, from Morse Telecommunications, allows you to install Slackware so that many files are accessed directly on the CD-ROM. This can save a great deal of space on your hard drive, with the tradeoff that running certain applications will be slower.

2.1.4.4.1   Creating the boot and root floppies   You must create floppies from the bootdisk and rootdisk images that you downloaded (or have on CD-ROM), no matter what type of installation you will be doing.

On an MS-DOS system, you must uncompress the bootdisk and rootdisk images using **GZIP.EXE**. For example, if you're using the **bare.gz** bootdisk image, issue the MS-DOS command:

```
C:\> GZIP -D BARE.GZ
```

which will uncompress **bare.gz** and leave you with the file **bare**. If you are installing from CD-ROM, you can copy the bootdisk image (such as **bare.gz**) to you hard drive, and run **GZIP.EXE** from the CD-ROM to uncompress it.

You must similarly uncompress the rootdisk image. For example, if you are using the rootdisk **color144.gz**, issue the command:

```
C:\> GZIP -D COLOR144.GZ
```

which will uncompress the file and leave you with **color144**.

Next, you must have two *high-density* MS-DOS formatted floppies. (They must be of the same type; that is, if your boot floppy drive is a 3.5" drive, both floppies must be high-density 3.5" disks.) You will use **RAWRITE.EXE** to write the boot and rootdisk images to the floppies.

Issue the command:

```
C:\> RAWRITE
```

Answer the prompts for the name of the file to write (such as **bare**, or **color144**) and the floppy to write it to (such as **A:**). **RAWRITE** will copy the file, block-by-block, directly to the floppy. Also use **RAWRITE** for the root disk image. When you're done, you'll have two floppies: one containing the boot disk, the other containing the root disk. Note that these two floppies will no longer be readable by MS-DOS (they are "Linux format" floppies, in some sense).

Be sure that you're using brand-new, error-free floppies. The floppies must have no bad blocks on them.

Note that you do not need to be running MS-DOS in order to install Slackware. However, running MS-DOS makes it easier to create the boot and root floppies, and it makes it easier to install the software (as you can install directly from an MS-DOS partition on your system). If you are not running MS-DOS on your system, you can use someone else's MS-DOS system just to create the floppies, and install from there.

It is not necessary to use **GZIP.EXE** and **RAWRITE.EXE** under MS-DOS to create the boot and root floppies, either. You can use the **gzip** and **dd** commands on a UNIX system to do the same job. (For this, you will need a UNIX workstation with a floppy drive, of course.) For example, on a Sun workstation with the floppy drive on device **/dev/rfd0**, you can use the commands:

```
$ gunzip bare.gz
$ dd if=bare of=/dev/rfd0 obs=18k
```

You must provide the appropriate block size argument (the **obs** argument) on some workstations (e.g., Suns) or this will fail. If you have problems the man page for **dd** will be instructive.

2.1.4.4.2 Preparing for installation from hard drive If you're planning on installing the Slackware software directly from the hard drive (which is often faster and more reliable than a floppy installation), you will need an MS-DOS partition on the system that you're installing Slackware to.

Note: If you plan to install Slackware from an MS-DOS partition, that partition must NOT be compressed with DoubleSpace, Stacker, or any other MS-DOS drive compression utility. Linux currently cannot read DoubleSpace/Stacker MS-DOS partitions directly. (You can access them via the MS-DOS Emulator, but that is not an option when installing the Linux software.)

To prepare for hard drive installation, simply create a directory on the hard drive to store the Slackware files. For example,

```
C:\> MKDIR SLACKWAR
```

will create the directory `C:\SLACKWAR` to hold the Slackware files. Under this directory, you should create subdirectories `A1`, `A2`, and so on, for each disk set that you downloaded, using the `MKDIR` command. All of the files from the `A1` disk should go into the directory `SLACKWAR\A1`, and so forth.

2.1.4.4.3 Preparing for floppy installation

If you wish to install Slackware from floppies instead of the hard drive, you'll need to have one blank, MS-DOS formatted floppy for each Slackware disk that you downloaded. These disks must be high-density format.

The **A** disk set (disks **A1** through **A3**) may be either 3.5" or 5.25" floppies. However, the rest of the disk sets must be 3.5" disks. Therefore, if you only have a 5.25" floppy drive, you'll need to borrow a 3.5" drive from someone in order to install disk sets other than **A**. (Or, you can install from the hard drive, as explained in the previous section.)

To make the disks, simply copy the files from each Slackware directory onto an MS-DOS formatted floppy, using the MS-DOS `COPY` command. As so:

```
C:\> COPY A1\*.* A:
```

will copy the contents of the **A1** disk to the floppy in drive **A:**. You should repeat this for each disk that you downloaded.

You do *not* need to modify or uncompress the files on the disks in any way; you merely need to copy them to MS-DOS floppies. The Slackware installation procedure takes care of uncompressing the files for you.

2.1.4.4.4 Preparing for CD-ROM installation

If you have Slackware on a CD-ROM, you are ready to install the software once you have created the boot and root floppies. The software will be installed directly from CD.

2.2 Preparing to Install Linux

After you have obtained a distribution of Linux, you're ready to prepare your system for installation. This takes a certain degree of planning, especially if you're already running other operating systems. In the following sections we'll describe how to plan for the Linux installation.

2.2.1 Installation overview

While each release of Linux is different, in general the method used to install the software is as follows:

1. **Repartition your hard drive(s).** If you have other operating systems already installed, you will need to *repartition* the drives in order to allocate space for Linux. This is discussed in Section 2.2.4, below.

2. **Boot the Linux installation media.** Each distribution of Linux has some kind of installation media—usually a "boot floppy"—which is used to install the software. Booting this media will either present you with some kind of installation program, which will step you through the Linux installation, or allow you to install the software by hand.

3. **Create Linux partitions.** After repartitioning to allocate space for Linux, you create Linux partitions on that empty space. This is accomplished with the Linux `fdisk` program, covered in Section 2.3.3.

4. **Create filesystems and swap space.** At this point, you will create one or more *filesystems*, used to store files, on the newly-created partitions. In addition, if you plan to use swap space, you will create the swap space on one of your Linux partitions. This is covered in Sections 2.3.4 and 2.3.5.

5. **Install the software on the new filesystems.** Finally, you will install the Linux software on your newly-created filesystems. After this, it's smooth sailing—if all goes well. This is covered in Section 2.3.6. Later, in Section 2.5, we describe what to do if anything goes wrong.

Many distributions of Linux provide an installation program which will step you through the installation process, and automate one or more of the above steps for you. Keep in mind throughout this chapter that any number of the above steps may be automated for you, depending on the distribution.

The Slackware distribution of Linux, covered in this book, only requires you to repartition your drive, using `fdisk`, and use the `setup` program to accomplish the other steps.

Important hint: While preparing to install Linux, the best advice that we can give is to *take notes* during the entire procedure. Write down everything that you do, everything that you type, and everything that you see that might be out of the ordinary. The idea here is simple: if (or when!) you run into trouble, you want to be able to retrace your steps and find out what went wrong. Installing Linux isn't difficult, but there are many details to remember. You want to have a record of all of these details so that you can experiment with other methods if something goes wrong. Also, keeping a notebook of your Linux installation experience is useful when you want to ask other people for help, for example, when posting a message to one of the Linux-related USENET groups. Your notebook is also something that you'll want to show to your grandchildren someday.[4]

2.2.2   Repartitioning concepts

In general, hard drives are divided into *partitions*, where a single partition is devoted to a single operating system. For example, on one hard drive, you may have several separate partitions—one devoted to, say, MS-DOS, another to OS/2, and another to Linux.

If you already have other software installed on your system, you may need to resize those partitions in order to free up space for Linux. You will then create one or more Linux partitions on the resulting free space for storing the Linux software and swap space. We call this process *repartitioning*.

Many MS-DOS systems utilize a single partition inhabiting the entire drive. To MS-DOS, this partition is known as `C:`. If you have more than one partition, MS-DOS names them `D:`, `E:`, and so on. In a way, each partition acts like a separate hard drive.

On the first sector of the disk is a **master boot record** along with a **partition table**. The boot record (as the name implies) is used to boot the system. The partition table contains information about the locations and sizes of your partitions.

There are three kinds of partitions: **primary**, **extended**, and **logical**. Of these, primary partitions are used most often. However, because of a limit in the size of the partition table, you can only have four primary partitions on any given drive.

The way around this four-partition limit is to use an extended partition. An extended partition doesn't hold any data by itself; instead, it acts as a "container" for logical partitions. Therefore, you could create one extended partition, covering the entire drive, and within it create many logical partitions. However, you may have only one extended partition per drive.

2.2.3   Linux partition requirements

Before we explain how to repartition your drives, you need to have an idea of how much space you will be allocating for Linux. We will be discussing how to create these partitions later, in Section 2.3.3.

---

[4]The author shamefully admits that he kept a notebook of all of his tribulations with Linux for the first few months of working with the system. It is now gathering dust on his bookshelf.

On UNIX systems, files are stored on a **filesystem**, which is essentially a section of the hard drive (or other medium, such as CD-ROM or diskette) formatted to hold files. Each filesystem is associated with a specific part of the directory tree; for example, on many systems, there is a filesystem for all of the files in the directory **/usr**, another for **/tmp**, and so on. The **root filesystem** is the primary filesystem, which corresponds to the topmost directory, **/**.

Under Linux, each filesystem lives on a separate partition on the hard drive. For instance, if you have a filesystem for **/** and another for **/usr**, you will need two partitions to hold the two filesystems.

Before you install Linux, you will need to prepare filesystems for storing the Linux software. You must have at least one filesystem (the root filesystem), and therefore one partition, allocated to Linux. Many Linux users opt to store all of their files on the root filesystem, which is in most cases easier to manage than several filesystems and partitions.

However, you may create multiple filesystems for Linux if you wish—for example, you may want to use separate filesystems for **/usr** and **/home**. Those readers with UNIX system administration experience will know how to use multiple filesystems creatively. In Chapter 4 we discuss the use of multiple partitions and filesystems.

Why use more than one filesystem? The most commonly stated reason is safety; if, for some reason, one of your filesystems is damaged, the others will (usually) be unharmed. On the other hand, if you store all of your files on the root filesystem, and for some reason the filesystem is damaged, then you may lose all of your files in one fell swoop. This is, however, rather uncommon; if you backup the system regularly you should be quite safe.[5]

Another reason to use multiple filesystems is to divvy up storage between multiple hard drives. If you have, say, 40 megabytes free on one hard drive, and 50 megabytes free on another, you might want to create a 40-megabyte root filesystem on the first drive and a 50-megabyte **/usr** filesystem on the other. Currently it is not possible for a single filesystem to span multiple drives; if your free hard drive storage is fragmented between drives you will need to use multiple filesystems to utilize it all.

In summary, Linux requires at least one partition, for the root filesystem. If you wish to create multiple filesystems, you will need a separate partition for each additional filesystem. Some distributions of Linux automatically create partitions and filesystems for you, so you may not need to worry about these issues at all.

Another issue to consider when planning your partitions is swap space. If you wish to use swap space with Linux, you have two options. The first is to use a *swap file* which exists on one of your Linux filesystems. You will create the swap file for use as virtual RAM after you install the software. The second option is to create a *swap partition*, an individual partition to be used only as swap space. Most people use a swap partition instead of a swap file.

---

[5] The author uses a single 200-megabyte filesystem for all of his Linux files, and hasn't had any problems (so far).

A single swap file or partition may be up to 16 megabytes in size. If you wish to use more than 16 megabytes of swap, you can create multiple swap partitions or files—up to eight in all. For example, if you need 32 megabytes of swap, you can create two 16-megabyte swap partitions.

Setting up a swap partition is covered in Section 2.3.4, and setting up a swap file in Chapter 4.

Therefore, in general, you will create at least two partitions for Linux: one for use as the root filesystem, and the other for use as swap space. There are, of course, many variations on the above, but this is the minimal setup. You are not required to use swap space with Linux, but if you have less than 16 megabytes of physical RAM it is strongly suggested that you do.

Of course, you need to be aware of how much *space* these partitions will require. The size of your Linux filesystems (containing the software itself) depends greatly on how much software you're installing and what distribution of Linux you are using. Hopefully, the documentation that came with your distribution will give you an approximation of the space requirements. A small Linux system can use 20 megabytes or less; a larger system anywhere from 80 to 100 megabytes, or more. Keep in mind that in addition to the space required by the software itself, you need to allocate extra space for user directories, room for future expansion, and so forth.

The size of your swap partition (should you elect to use one) depends on how much virtual RAM you require. A rule of thumb is to use a swap partition that is twice the space of your physical RAM; for example, if you have 4 megabytes of physical RAM, an 8-megabyte swap partition should suffice. Of course, this is mere speculation—the actual amount of swap space that you require depends on the software which you will be running. If you have a great deal of physical RAM (say, sixteen megabytes or more), you may not wish to use swap space at all.

Important note: Because of BIOS limitations, it is usually not possible to boot from partitions using cylinders numbered over 1023. Therefore, when setting aside space for Linux, keep in mind that you may not want to use a partition in the >1023-cylinder range for your Linux root filesystem. Linux can still *use* partitions with cylinders numbered over 1023, however, you may not be able to *boot* Linux from such a partition. This advice may seem premature, but it is important to know while planning your drive layout.

If you absolutely must use a partition with cylinders numbered over 1023 for your Linux root filesystem, you can always boot Linux from floppy. This is not so bad, actually—it only takes a few seconds longer to boot than from the hard drive. At any rate, it's always an option.

2.2.4   Repartitioning your drives

In this section, we'll describe how to resize your current partitions (if any) to make space for Linux. If you are installing Linux on a "clean" hard drive, you can skip this section and proceed to Section 2.3, below.

The usual way to resize an existing partition is to delete it (thus destroying all of the data on that partition) and recreate it. Before repartitioning your drives, *backup your system*. After resizing the partitions, you can reinstall your original software from the backup. However, there are several programs available for MS-DOS which are able to resize partitions nondestructively. One of these is known as "FIPS", and can be found on many Linux FTP sites.

Also, keep in mind that because you'll be shrinking your original partitions, you may not have space to reinstall everything. In this case, you need to delete enough unwanted software to allow the rest to fit on the smaller partitions.

The program used to repartition is known as **fdisk**. Each operating system has its own analogue of this program; for example, under MS-DOS, it is invoked with the FDISK command. You should consult your documentation for whatever operating systems you are currently running for information on repartitioning. Here, we'll discuss how to resize partitions for MS-DOS using FDISK, but this information should be easily extrapolated to other operating systems.

Please consult the documentation for your current operating systems before repartitioning your drive. This section is meant to be a general overview of the process; there are many subtleties that we do not cover here. You can lose all of the software on your system if you do not repartition the drive correctly.

A warning: Do not modify or create partitions for any other operating systems (including Linux) using FDISK under MS-DOS. You should only modify partitions for a particular operating system with the version of **fdisk** included with that operating system; for example, you will create Linux partitions using a version of **fdisk** for Linux. Later, in Section 2.3.3, we describe how to create Linux partitions, but for now we are concerned with resizing your current ones.

Let's say that you have a single hard drive on your system, currently devoted entirely to MS-DOS. Hence, your drive consists of a single MS-DOS partition, commonly known as "**C:**". Because this repartitioning method will destroy the data on that partition, you need to create a bootable MS-DOS "system disk" which contains everything necessary to run FDISK and restore the software from backup after the repartitioning is complete.

In many cases, you can use the MS-DOS installation disks for this purpose. However, if you need to create your own system disk, format a floppy with the command

```
FORMAT /s A:
```

Copy onto this floppy all of the necessary MS-DOS utilities (usually most of the software in the directory \DOS on your drive), as well as the programs FORMAT.COM and FDISK.EXE. You should now be able to boot this floppy, and run the command

    FDISK C:

to start up FDISK.

Use of FDISK should be self-explanatory, but consult the MS-DOS documentation for details. When you start FDISK, use the menu option to display the partition table, and *write down* the information displayed there. It is important to keep a record of your original setup in case you want to back out of the Linux installation.

To delete an existing partition, choose the FDISK menu option "Delete an MS-DOS Partition or Logical DOS Drive". Specify the type of partition that you wish to delete (primary, extended, or logical) and the number of the partition. Verify all of the warnings. Poof!

To create a new (smaller) partition for MS-DOS, just choose the FDISK option "Create an MS-DOS Partition or Logical DOS Drive". Specify the type of partition (primary, extended, or logical), and the size of the partition to create (specified in megabytes). FDISK should create the partition and you're ready to roll.

After you're done using FDISK, you should exit the program and reformat any new partitions. For example, if you resized the first DOS partition on your drive (C:) you should run the command

    FORMAT /s C:

You may now reinstall your original software from backup.

2.3   Installing the Linux software

After you have resized your existing partitions to make space for Linux, you are ready to install the software. Here is a brief overview of the procedure:

- Boot the Linux installation media;

- Run fdisk under Linux to create Linux partitions;

- Run mke2fs and mkswap to create Linux filesystems and swap space;

- Install the Linux software;

- Finally, either install the LILO boot loader on your hard drive, or create a boot floppy in order to boot your new Linux system.

As we have said, one (or more) of these steps may be automated for you by the installation procedure, depending on the distribution of Linux which you are using. Please consult the documentation for your distribution for specific instructions.

2.3.1 Booting Linux

The first step is to boot the Linux installation media. In most cases, this is a "boot floppy" which contains a small Linux system. Upon booting the floppy, you will be presented with an installation menu of some kind which will lead you through the steps of installing the software. On other distributions, you will be presented with a login prompt when booting this floppy. Here, you usually login as **root** or **install** to begin the installation process.

The documentation which came with your particular distribution will explain what is necessary to boot Linux from the installation media.

If you are installing the Slackware distribution of Linux, all that is required is to boot the boot floppy which you created in the previous section.

Most distributions of Linux use a boot floppy which allows you to enter hardware parameters at a boot prompt, to force hardware detection of various devices. For example, if your SCSI controller is not detected when booting the floppy, you will need to reboot and specify the hardware parameters (such as I/O address and IRQ) at the boot prompt.

Likewise, IBM PS/1, ThinkPad, and ValuePoint machines do not store drive geometry in the CMOS, and you must specify it at boot time.

The boot prompt is often displayed automatically when booting the boot floppy. This is the case for the Slackware distribution. Other distributions require you to hold down `shift` or `ctrl` while booting the floppy. If successful, you should see the prompt

        boot:

and possibly other messages.

To try booting without any special parameters, just press **enter** at the boot prompt.

Watch the messages as the system boots. If you have a SCSI controller, you should see a listing of the SCSI hosts detected. If you see the message

        SCSI: 0 hosts

then your SCSI controller was not detected, and you will have to use the following procedure.

Also, the system will display information on the drive partitions and devices detected. If any of this information is incorrect or missing, you will have to force hardware detection.

On the other hand, if all goes well and you hardware seems to be detected, you can skip to the following section, Section 2.3.2.

To force hardware detection, you must enter the appropriate parameters at the boot prompt, using the following syntax:

> ramdisk ⟨*parameters...*⟩

There are a number of such parameters available; here are some of the most common.

hd=⟨*cylinders*⟩,⟨*heads*⟩,⟨*sectors*⟩
> Specify the harddrive geometry. Required for systems such as the IBM PS/1, ValuePoint, and ThinkPad. For example, if your drive has 683 cylinders, 16 heads, and 32 sectors per track, enter

> > ramdisk hd=683,16,32

tmc8xx=⟨*memaddr*⟩,⟨*irq*⟩
> Specify address and IRQ for BIOS-less Future Domain TMC-8xx SCSI controller. For example,

> > ramdisk tmc8xx=0xca000,5

> Note that the 0x prefix must be used for all values given in hexadecimal. This is true for all of the following options.

st0x=⟨*memaddr*⟩,⟨*irq*⟩
> Specify address and IRQ for BIOS-less Seagate ST02 controller.

t128=⟨*memaddr*⟩,⟨*irq*⟩
> Specify address and IRQ for BIOS-less Trantor T128B controller.

> ncr5380=⟨*port*⟩,⟨*irq*⟩,⟨*dma*⟩ Specify port, IRQ, and DMA channel for generic NCR5380 controller.

aha152x=⟨*port*⟩,⟨*irq*⟩,⟨*scsi_id*⟩,1
> Specify port, IRQ, and SCSI ID for BIOS-less AIC-6260 controllers. This includes Adaptec 1510, 152x, and Soundblaster-SCSI controllers.

For each of these, you must enter **ramdisk** followed by the parameter that you wish to use.

If you have questions about these boot-time options, please read the Linux *SCSI HOWTO*, which should be available on any Linux FTP archive site (or from wherever you obtained this book), as well as the Linux *CD-ROM HOWTO*. These documents describe hardware compatibility in much more detail.

2.3.2   Drives and partitions under Linux

Many distributions require you to create Linux partitions by hand using the **fdisk** program. Others may automatically create partitions for you. Either way, you should know the following information about Linux partitions and device names.

Drives and partitions under Linux are given different names than their counterparts under other operating systems. Under MS-DOS, floppy drives are referred to as **A:** and **B:**, while hard drive partitions are named **C:**, **D:**, and so on. Under Linux, the naming convention is quite different.

Device drivers, found in the directory **/dev**, are used to communicate with devices on your system (such as hard drives, mice, and so on). For example, if you have a mouse on your system, you access it through the driver **/dev/mouse**. Floppy drives, hard drives, and individual partitions are all given individual device drivers of their own. Don't worry about the device driver interface for now; it is important only to understand how the various devices are named in order to use them.

Table 2.1 lists the names of these various device drivers.

Device	Name
First floppy (**A:**)	/dev/fd0
Second floppy (**B:**)	/dev/fd1
First hard drive (entire drive)	/dev/hda
First hard drive, primary partition 1	/dev/hda1
First hard drive, primary partition 2	/dev/hda2
First hard drive, primary partition 3	/dev/hda3
First hard drive, primary partition 4	/dev/hda4
First hard drive, logical partition 1	/dev/hda5
First hard drive, logical partition 2	/dev/hda6
$\vdots$	
Second hard drive (entire drive)	/dev/hdb
Second hard drive, primary partition 1	/dev/hdb1
$\vdots$	
First SCSI hard drive (entire drive)	/dev/sda
First SCSI hard drive, primary partition 1	/dev/sda1
$\vdots$	
Second SCSI hard drive (entire drive)	/dev/sdb
Second SCSI hard drive, primary partition 1	/dev/sdb1
$\vdots$	

Table 2.1: Linux partition names

A few notes about this table. Note that **/dev/fd0** corresponds to the first floppy drive (**A:** under MS-DOS) and **/dev/fd1** corresponds to the second floppy (**B:**).

Also, SCSI hard drives are named differently than other drives. IDE, MFM, and RLL drives are accessed through the devices **/dev/hda**, **/dev/hdb**, and so on. The individual partitions on the drive **/dev/hda** are **/dev/hda1**, **/dev/hda2**, and so on. However, SCSI drives are named **/dev/sda**, **/dev/sdb**, etc., with partition names such as **/dev/sda1** and **/dev/sda2**.

Here's an example. Let's say that you have a single IDE hard drive, with 3 primary partitions. The first two are set aside for MS-DOS, and the third is an extended partition which contains two logical partitions, both for use by Linux. The devices referring to these partitions would be:

First MS-DOS partition (C:)	/dev/hda1
Second MS-DOS partition (D:)	/dev/hda2
Extended partition	/dev/hda3
First Linux logical partition	/dev/hda5
Second Linux logical partition	/dev/hda6

Note that **/dev/hda4** is skipped; it corresponds to the fourth primary partition, which we don't have in this example. Logical partitions are named consecutively starting with **/dev/hda5**.

2.3.3   Creating Linux partitions

Now you are ready to create Linux partitions with the **fdisk** command. As described in Section 2.2.3, in general you will need to create at least one partition for the Linux software itself, and another partition for swap space.

After booting the installation media, run **fdisk** by typing

    fdisk ⟨drive⟩

where ⟨drive⟩ is the Linux device name of the drive you plan to add partitions to (see Table 2.1). For instance, if you want to run **fdisk** on the first SCSI disk in your system, use the command **fdisk /dev/sda**. **/dev/hda** (the first IDE drive) is the default if you don't specify one.

If you are creating Linux partitions on more than one drive, run **fdisk** once for each drive.

    # fdisk /dev/hda
    Command (m for help):

Here **fdisk** is waiting for a command; you can type **m** to get a list of options.

```
Command (m for help):  m
Command action
a toggle a bootable flag
d delete a partition
l list known partition types
m print this menu
n add a new partition
p print the partition table
q quit without saving changes
t change a partition's system id
u change display/entry units
v verify the partition table
w write table to disk and exit
x extra functionality (experts only)

Command (m for help):
```

The **n** command is used to create a new partition. Most of the other options you won't need to worry about. To quit **fdisk** without saving any changes, use the **q** command. To quit **fdisk** and write the changes to the partition table to disk, use the **w** command.

The first thing you should do is display your current partition table and write the information down, for later reference. Use the **p** command.

```
Command (m for help):  p
Disk /dev/hda:  16 heads, 38 sectors, 683 cylinders
Units = cylinders of 608 * 512 bytes

   Device Boot  Begin   Start    End  Blocks   Id  System
/dev/hda1    *      1       1    203   61693    6  DOS 16-bit >=32M


Command (m for help):
```

In this example, we have a single MS-DOS partition on **/dev/hda1**, which is 61693 blocks (about 60 megs).[6] This partition starts at cylinder number 1, and ends on cylinder 203. We have a total of 683 cylinders in this disk; so there are 480 cylinders left to create Linux partitions on.

To create a new partition, use the **n** command. In this example, we'll create two primary partitions (**/dev/hda2** and **/dev/hda3**) for Linux.

```
Command (m for help):  n
Command action
e extended
p primary partition (1-4)
p
```

---

[6] A block, under Linux, is 1024 bytes.

Here, **fdisk** is asking the type of the partition to create: extended or primary. In our example, we're creating only primary partitions, so we choose **p**.

```
Partition number (1-4):
```

fdisk will then ask for the number of the partition to create; since partition 1 is already used, our first Linux partition will be number 2.

```
Partition number (1-4):  2
First cylinder (204-683):
```

Now enter the starting cylinder number of the partition. Since cylinders 204 through 683 are unused, we'll use the first available one (numbered 204). There's no reason to leave empty space between partitions.

```
First cylinder (204-683):  204
Last cylinder or +size or +sizeM or +sizeK (204-683):
```

fdisk is asking for the size of the partition to create. We can either specify an ending cylinder number, or a size in bytes, kilobytes, or megabytes. Since we want our partition to be 80 megs in size, we specify **+80M**. When specifying a partition size in this way, **fdisk** will round the actual partition size to the nearest number of cylinders.

```
Last cylinder or +size or +sizeM or +sizeK (204-683):  +80M
Warning:  Linux cannot currently use 33090 sectors of this partition
```

If you see a warning message such as this, it can be ignored. **fdisk** prints the warning because it's an older program, and dates before the time that Linux partitions were allowed to be larger than 64 megabytes.

Now we're ready to create our second Linux partition. For sake of demonstration, we'll create it with a size of 10 megabytes.

```
Command (m for help):  n
Command action
e extended
p primary partition (1-4)
p
Partition number (1-4):  3
First cylinder (474-683):  474
Last cylinder or +size or +sizeM or +sizeK (474-683):  +10M
```

At last, we'll display the partition table. Again, write down all of this information—especially the block sizes of your new partitions. You'll need to know the sizes of the partitions when creating filesystems, later. Also, verify that none of your partitions overlap.

```
Command (m for help):  p

Disk /dev/hda:  16 heads, 38 sectors, 683 cylinders
Units = cylinders of 608 * 512 bytes

    Device Boot  Begin   Start    End  Blocks  Id  System
    /dev/hda1    *     1       1    203   61693   6  DOS 16-bit >=32M
    /dev/hda2        204     204    473   82080  81  Linux/MINIX
    /dev/hda3        474     474    507   10336  81  Linux/MINIX
```

As you can see, **/dev/hda2** is now a partition of size 82080 blocks (which corresponds to about 80 megabytes), and **/dev/hda3** is 10336 blocks (about 10 megs).

Note that many distributions (such as Slackware) require you to use the **t** command in **fdisk** to change the type of the swap partition to "Linux swap", which is usually numbered 82. You can use the **L** command to print a list of known partition type codes, and then use **t** to set the type of the swap partition to that which corresponds to "Linux swap".

In this way, the installation software will be able to automatically find your swap partitions based on type. If the installation software doesn't seem to recognize your swap partition, you might want to re-run **fdisk** and use the **t** command on the partition in question.

In the example above, the remaining cylinders on the disk (numbered 508 to 683) are unused. You may wish to leave unused space on the disk, in case you wish to create additional partitions later.

Finally, we use the **w** command to write the changes to disk and exit **fdisk**.

```
Command (m for help):  w
#
```

Keep in mind that none of the changes you make while running **fdisk** will take effect until you give the **w** command, so you can toy with different configurations and save them when you're done. Also, if you want to quit **fdisk** at any time without saving the changes, use the **q** command. Remember that you shouldn't modify partitions for operating systems other than Linux with the Linux **fdisk** program.

Remember that you may not be able to boot Linux from a partition using cylinders numbered over 1023. Therefore, you should try to create your Linux root partition within the sub-1024 cylinder range. Again, if this is impossible, you can simply boot Linux from floppy.

Some Linux distributions require you to reboot the system after running **fdisk**. This is to allow the changes to the partition table to take effect before installing the software. Newer versions of **fdisk** automatically update the partition information in the kernel, so rebooting isn't necessary. To be on the safe side, after running **fdisk** you should reboot the installation media, as before, before proceeding.

2.3.4   Creating the swap space

If you are planning to use a swap partition for virtual RAM, you're ready to prepare it for use.[7] In Chapter 4 we will discuss the preparation of a swap file in case you don't want to use an individual partition.

Many distributions require you to create and activate swap space before installing the software. If you have a small amount of physical RAM, the installation procedure may not be successful unless you have some amount of swap space enabled.

The Slackware distribution requires you to create swap space, before installation, if you have 4 megabytes of RAM or less. If this is not the case, the Slackware installation procedure can be used to prepare swap space automatically. If in doubt, go ahead and follow the procedure described here; it can't hurt.

The command used to prepare a swap partition is **mkswap**, and it takes the form

> mkswap -c ⟨partition⟩ ⟨size⟩

where ⟨partition⟩ is the name of the swap partition, and ⟨size⟩ is the size of the partition, in blocks.[8] For example, if your swap partition is **/dev/hda3** and is 10336 blocks in size, use the command

> # *mkswap −c /dev/hda3 10336*

The **-c** option tells **mkswap** to check for bad blocks on the partition when creating the swap space.

If you are using multiple swap partitions, you will need to execute the appropriate **mkswap** command for each partition.

After formatting the swap space, you need to enable it for use by the system. Usually, the system automatically enables swap space at boot time. However, because you have not yet installed the Linux software, you need to enable it by hand.

The command to enable swap space is **swapon**, and it takes the form

> swapon ⟨partition⟩

In the example above, to enable the swap space on **/dev/hda3**, we use the command

> # *swapon /dev/hda3*

---

[7] Again, some distributions of Linux will prepare the swap space automatically for you, or via an installation menu option.

[8] This is the size as reported by **fdisk**, using the **p** menu option. A block under Linux is 1024 bytes.

2.3.5   Creating the filesystems

Before you can use your Linux partitions to store files, you must create **filesystems** on them. Creating a filesystem is analogous to formatting a partition under MS-DOS or other operating systems. We discussed filesystems briefly in Section 2.2.3.

There are several types of filesystems available for Linux. Each filesystem type has its own format and set of characteristics (such as filename length, maximum file size, and so on). Linux also supports several "third-party" filesystem types such as the MS-DOS filesystem.

The most commonly used filesystem type is the **Second Extended Filesystem**, or *ext2fs*. The *ext2fs* is one of the most efficient and flexible filesystems; it allows filenames up to 256 characters and filesystem sizes of up to 4 terabytes. In Chapter 4, we'll discuss the various filesystem types available for Linux. Initially, however, we suggest that you use the *ext2fs* filesystem.

If you are installing the Slackware distribution, filesystems are created automatically for you by the installation procedure described in the next section. If you wish to create your filesystems by hand, however, follow the procedure described here.

To create an *ext2fs* filesystem, use the command

```
mke2fs -c ⟨partition⟩ ⟨size⟩
```

where ⟨*partition*⟩ is the name of the partition, and ⟨*size*⟩ is the size of the partition in blocks. For example, to create a 82080-block filesystem on **/dev/hda2**, use the command

```
# mke2fs -c /dev/hda2 82080
```

If you're using multiple filesystems for Linux, you'll need to use the appropriate **mke2fs** command for each filesystem.

If you have encountered any problems at this point, see Section 2.5 at the end of this chapter.

2.3.6   Installing the software

Finally, you are ready to install the software on your system. Every distribution has a different mechanism for doing this. Many distributions have a self-contained program which will step you through the installation. On other distributions, you will have to **mount** your filesystems in a certain subdirectory (such as **/mnt**) and copy the software to them by hand. On CD-ROM distributions, you may be given the option to install a portion of the software on your hard drives, and leave most of the software on the CD-ROM.

Some distributions offer several different ways to install the software. For example, you may be able to install the software directly from an MS-DOS partition on your hard drive,

instead of from floppies. Or, you may be able to install over a TCP/IP network via FTP or
NFS. See your distribution's documentation for details.

For example, the Slackware distribution only requires you to create partitions with
fdisk, optionally create swap space with **mkswap** and **swapon** (if you have 4 megs or less of
RAM), and then run the **setup** program. **setup** leads you through a very self-explanatory
menu system to install the software. Use of **setup** is described in detail below.

The exact method used to install the Linux software differs greatly with each distribution.
We're hoping that installing the Linux software should be self-explanatory, as it is with most
distributions.

2.3.6.1 Installing Slackware with setup

If you are installing Slackware, after creating partitions (and possibly swap space), use the
command

> **#** *setup*

This will present you will a menu-based procedure to walk you through the remaining steps
of installation.

The procedure described here corresponds to that found on the **color144** and **colrlite**
root disks; the other root disks may have slightly different procedures.

The **setup** menu consists of the following items. Use the arrow keys to move over the
items, and press ⏎enter or ⏎spacebar to select an item.

Help	View the **setup** help file.
Keymap	This option allows you to specify the keyboard mapping for your system if you do not have a US keyboard. A list of keymaps will be presented; select the appropriate item from the list.
Quick	This allows you to select between "quick" and "verbose" installation modes. "Verbose" is the default, and is recommended for most installations (unless you've installed Slackware a dozen times, in which case you already know this).
Make tags	This allows Slackware installation experts to create customized "tag files" for preselecting packages. This is only necessary for customizing the installation procedure in some way; you shouldn't have to concern yourself with this.
Addswap	This will be the first item that most users will select to install Slackware. A list of available swap partitions will be displayed (those partitions with

type "Linux swap" as set in **fdisk**). You will be able to specify which partitions you wish to use for swap space. You will then be asked if you wish to run **mkswap** on these partitions.

If you have already executed **mkswap** and **swapon** (as described in Section 2.3.4) on your swap partitions, then you should *not* allow **setup** to execute **mkswap** on these partitions.

Even if you have already executed **mkswap** and **swapon**, it is necessary to use the **Addswap** menu item: This ensures that your swap partitions will be available once you have the system installed.

◇   Be warned! Creating swap space on a partition will destroy data on that partition. Be sure that you're not wiping out data that you want to keep.

If you select this menu item, you will be automatically prompted if you wish to proceed with the following items. In general, you should do this.

Target   This item allows you to specify the partitions upon which Linux is to be installed. A list of available partitions (those with type "Linux native", as specified by **fdisk**) will be displayed, and you will be asked to enter the name of your Linux root partition, such as **/dev/hda2**. You will then be prompted for the type of filesystem that you wish to create; we suggest using the **ext2fs** filesystem type as described in Section 2.3.5. This will create a filesystem on the named partition—somewhat analogous to "formatting" the partition under MS-DOS.

You will also be prompted for any other partitions that you might wish to use for Linux. For example, if you created a separate partition for **/usr** (see Section 2.2.3), you will be able to specify the name of the partition and the location where it should be mounted (as in **/usr** or **/usr/bin**).

◇   Be warned! Creating a filesystem on a partition will destroy all data on that partition. Be sure that you're not wiping out data that you want to keep.

Even if you already created your filesystems using **mke2fs** (see Section 2.3.5), you must use the **Target** menu item to specify the partitions where Linux will be installed.

Source   This menu item allows you to specify where you will be installing Slackware from, such as floppy, hard drive, or CD-ROM.

If you are installing from hard drive, you will be asked what partition the Slackware files are found on, as well as the type of partition. For example, if you have the Slackware files on an MS-DOS partition, enter the name of the partition (such as **/dev/hda1**) and select **MS-DOS FAT** as the type. You will then be asked what directory the files may be found under on this partition. For example, if you have the Slackware files stored under the directory **C:\SLACK** on your MS-DOS partition, enter

```
/slack
```

as the location. Note that you should use forward slashes, not backslashes, in the pathname.

If you are installing from CD-ROM, you will be asked the type of CD-ROM device that you are using, as well as what directory on the CD-ROM the files may be found in. Many CD-ROMs have the files contained within the directory **/slakware**, but this depends on the release.

If you are installing Slackware Professional,[9] two directories are used on the CD-ROM. **slakware** is used for the standard system which will install the files directly to your hard drive. **slackpro** is used for the CD-ROM-based system where many files are accessed directly from the CD-ROM. This can save diskspace, but accessing many files is also noticeably slower. Several other Slackware vendors provide the ability to run the software from the CD-ROM as well. However, if you have the diskspace to spare, we recommend not running Slackware from the CD-ROM itself. Performance is generally slower.

If you are attempting a hard drive or CD-ROM install, Slackware may report that there is a **mount** error at this point. This is usually an indication that there was a problem accessing the hard drive or CD-ROM. See Section 2.5.3 for more information if you see such an error message.

Disk sets   This menu option allows you to select the disk sets that you wish to install. You must install at least the **A** disk set. Simply use the arrow keys and spacebar to select which disk sets you wish to install.

Note that selecting a particular disk set does not mean that all packages on the disk set will be installed; you will be prompted before installing packages on the disk set marked as "optional" or "recommended."

Install   At long last, this menu item will install the software on your system. You will be prompted for the prompting method; most users should select "normal." For each disk set that you selected, the "required" packages will be installed, and you will be prompted when installing the "optional" and "recommended" packages. If you are installing from floppy you will be asked to insert each floppy in succession.

As each package is installed a short description will be printed. Unless you have background in UNIX or Linux, many of these descriptions will not mean much to you. Take note of which packages are being installed, so you know what's there, but don't worry about trying to jot down everything that's printed on the display.

---

[9] Slackware Professional is a version of Slackware available from Morse Telecommunications.

The most common error encountered here is that a file cannot be found on a floppy, or an I/O error when attempting to read the floppy. The former is an indication that the files on your floppy might be corrupted or incomplete; the latter that the floppy itself is bad. Any floppies which give these errors should be replaced, and you should re-install the disk set containing those floppies. See Section 2.5.3 for suggestions.

You may also have read errors when attempting to access a CD-ROM; be sure that the CD-ROM is clean, has no fingerprints, etc.

Configure This menu item performs some post-installation configuration of your system. This is covered in the following section.

2.3.7 Creating the boot floppy or installing LILO

Every distribution provides some means of booting your new Linux system after you have installed the software. In many cases, the installation procedure will create a "boot floppy" which contains a Linux kernel configured to use your newly-created root filesystem. In order to boot Linux, you would boot from this floppy, and control would be transferred to your hard drive after booting. On other distributions, this "boot floppy" is the installation floppy itself.

Many distributions give you the option of installing **LILO** on your hard drive. LILO is a program that is installed on your drive's master boot record. It is able to boot a number of operating systems, including MS-DOS and Linux, and allows you to select at startup time which to boot.

For the Slackware distribution, the **Configure** item in the **setup** menu will allow you to create a boot floppy as well as install LILO. These options should be fairly self-explanatory. The **Configure** menu item also allows you to specify your modem, mouse, and timezone information.

In order for LILO to be installed successfully, it needs to know a good deal of information about your drive configuration—for example, which partitions contain which operating systems, how to boot each operating system, and so on. Many distributions, when installing LILO, attempt to "guess" at the appropriate parameters for your configuration. Although it's not often, the automated LILO installation provided by some distributions can fail, and leave your master boot record in shambles (although it's very doubtful that any damage to the actual data on your hard drive will take place). In particular, if you use OS/2's Boot Manager, you should *not* install LILO using the automated procedure—there are special instructions for using LILO with the Boot Manager, which will be covered later.

In many cases, it is best to use a boot floppy, until you have a chance to configure LILO yourself, by hand. If you're feeling exceptionally trustworthy, though, you can go ahead with the automated LILO installation if it is provided with your distribution.

In Chapter 4, we'll cover in detail how to configure and install LILO for your particular setup.

If everything goes well, then congratulations! You have just installed Linux on your system. Go have a Diet Coke or something—you deserve it.

In case you did run into any trouble, the next section will describe the most common sticking points for Linux installations, and how to get around them.

2.3.8   Additional installation procedures

Some distributions of Linux provide a number of additional installation procedures, allowing you to configure various software packages such as TCP/IP networking, the X Window System, and so on. If you are provided with these configuration options during installation, you may wish to read ahead in this book for more information on how to configure this software. Otherwise, you should put off these installation procedures until you have a complete understanding of how to configure the software.

It's up to you; if all else fails, just go with the flow and see what happens. It's very doubtful that anything that you do incorrectly now cannot be undone in the future. (Knock on wood.)

2.4   Postinstallation procedures

After you have completed installing the Linux software, there should be very little left to do before you can begin to use the system. In most cases, you should be able to reboot the system, login as **root**, and begin exploring the system. (Each distribution has a slightly different method for doing this.)

At this point it's a good idea to explain how to reboot and shutdown the system as you're using it. You should never reboot or shutdown your Linux system by pressing the reset switch or with the old "Vulcan Nerve Pinch"—that is, by pressing ctrl-alt-del in unison.[10] You shouldn't simply switch off the power, either. As with most UNIX systems, Linux caches disk writes in memory. Therefore, if you suddenly reboot the system without shutting down "cleanly", you can corrupt the data on your drives, causing untold damage.

The easiest way to shut down the system is with the **shutdown** command. As an example, to shutdown and reboot the system immediately, use the following command as **root**:

    # shutdown -r now

---

[10] On most Linux systems, however, ctrl-alt-del will cause the system to shutdown gracefully, as if you had used the **shutdown** command.

This will cleanly reboot your system. The man page for **shutdown** describes the other command-line arguments that are available.[11]

Note, however, that many Linux distributions do not provide the **shutdown** command on the installation media. This means that the first time you reboot your system after installation, you may need to use the boxed(ctrl-alt-del) combination after all. Thereafter, you should always use the **shutdown** command.

After you have a chance to explore and use the system, there are several configuration chores that you should undertake. The first is to create a user account for yourself (and, optionally, for any other users that might have access to the system). Creating user accounts is described in Section 4.4. Usually, all that you have to do is login as **root**, and run the **adduser** (sometimes **useradd**) program. This will lead you through several prompts to create a new user account.

If you created more than one filesystem for Linux, or if you're using a swap partition, you may need to edit the file **/etc/fstab** in order for those filesystems to be available automatically after rebooting. (For example, if you're using a separate filesystem for **/usr**, and none of the files that should be in **/usr** appear to be present, you may simply need to mount that filesystem.) Section 4.8 describes this procedure. Note that the Slackware distribution of Linux automatically configures your filesystems and swap space at installation time, so this usually isn't necessary.

2.5   Running Into Trouble

Almost everyone runs into some kind of snag or hangup when attempting to install Linux the first time. Most of the time, the problem is caused by a simple misunderstanding. Sometimes, however, it can be something more serious, such as an oversight by one of the developers, or a bug.

This section will describe some of the most common installation problems, and how to solve them. If your installation appears to be successful, but you received unexpected error messages during the installation, these are described here as well.

2.5.1   Problems with booting the installation media

When attempting to boot the installation media for the first time, you may encounter a number of problems. These are listed below. Note that the following problems are *not* related to booting your newly-installed Linux system. See Section 2.5.4 for information on these kinds of pitfalls.

- **Floppy or media error when attempting to boot.**

---

[11]Use the command **man shutdown** to see the manual page for **shutdown**.

The most popular cause for this kind of problem is a corrupt boot floppy. Either the floppy is physically damaged, in which case you should re-create the disk with a *brand new* floppy, or the data on the floppy is bad, in which case you should verify that you downloaded and transferred the data to the floppy correctly. In many cases, simply re-creating the boot floppy will solve your problems. Retrace your steps and try again.

If you received your boot floppy from a mail order vendor or some other distributor, instead of downloading and creating it yourself, contact the distributor and ask for a new boot floppy—but only after verifying that this is indeed the problem.

- **System "hangs" during boot or after booting.**

  After the installation media boots, you will see a number of messages from the kernel itself, indicating which devices were detected and configured. After this, you will usually be presented with a login prompt, allowing you to proceed with installation (some distributions instead drop you right into an installation program of some kind). The system may appear to "hang" during several of these steps. During all of these steps, be patient; loading software from floppy is very slow. In many cases, the system has not hung at all, but is merely taking a long time. Verify that there is no drive or system activity for at least several minutes before assuming that the system is hung.

  1. After booting from the **LILO** prompt, the system must load the kernel image from floppy. This may take several seconds; you will know that things are going well if the floppy drive light is still on.

  2. While the kernel boots, SCSI devices must be probed for. If you do not have any SCSI devices installed, the system will "hang" for up to 15 seconds while the SCSI probe continues; this usually occurs after the line

     ```
     lp_init: lp1 exists (0), using polling driver
     ```

     appears on your screen.

  3. After the kernel is finished booting, control is transferred to the system bootup files on the floppy. Finally, you will be presented with a login prompt, or be dropped into an installation program. If you are presented with a login prompt such as

     ```
     Linux login:
     ```

     you should then login (usually as **root** or **install**—this varies with each distribution). After entering the username, the system may pause for 20 seconds or more while the installation program or shell is being loaded from floppy. Again, the floppy drive light should be on. Don't assume that the system is hung.

Any of the above items may be the source of your problem. However, it is possible that the system actually may "hang" while booting, which can be due to several causes. First of all, you may not have enough available RAM to boot the installation media. (See the following item for information on disabling the ramdisk to free up memory.)

The cause of many system hangs is hardware incompatibility. Section 1.8 in the last chapter presented an overview of supported hardware under Linux. Even if your hardware is supported, you may run into problems with incompatible hardware configurations which are causing the system to hang. See Section 2.5.2, below, for a discussion of hardware incompatibilities.

- **System reports out of memory errors while attempting to boot or install the software.**

  This item deals with the amount of RAM that you have available. On systems with 4 megabytes of RAM or less, you may run into trouble booting the installation media or installing the software itself. This is because many distributions use a "ramdisk", which is a filesystem loaded directly into RAM, for operations while using the installation media. The entire image of the installation boot floppy, for example, may be loaded into a ramdisk, which may require more than a megabyte of RAM.

  The solution to this problem is to disable the ramdisk option when booting the install media. Each release has a different procedure for doing this; on the SLS release, for example, you type "**floppy**" at the LILO prompt when booting the **a1** disk. See your distribution's documentation for details.

  You may not see an "out of memory" error when attempting to boot or install the software; instead, the system may unexpectedly hang, or fail to boot. If your system hangs, and none of the explanations in the previous section seem to be the cause, try disabling the ramdisk.

  Keep in mind that Linux itself requires at least 2 megabytes of RAM to run at all; some distributions of Linux require 4 megabytes or more.

- **The system reports an error such as "permission denied" or "file not found" while booting.**

  This is an indication that your installation bootup media is corrupt. If you attempt to boot from the installation media (and you're sure that you're doing everything correctly), you should not see any errors such as this. Contact the distributor of your Linux software and find out about the problem, and perhaps obtain another copy of the boot media if necessary. If you downloaded the bootup disk yourself, try re-creating the bootup disk, and see if this solves your problem.

- **The system reports the error "VFS: Unable to mount root" when booting.**

  This error message means that the root filesystem (found on the boot media itself), could not be found. This means that either your boot media is corrupt in some way, or that you are not booting the system correctly.

  For example, many CD-ROM distributions require that you have the CD-ROM in the drive when booting. Also be sure that the CD-ROM drive is on, and check for any activity. It's also possible that the system is not locating your CD-ROM drive at boot time; see Section 2.5.2 for more information.

  If you're sure that you are booting the system correctly, then your bootup media may indeed be corrupt. This is a very uncommon problem, so try other solutions before attempting to use another boot floppy or tape.

2.5.2   Hardware problems

The most common form of problem when attempting to install or use Linux is an incompatibility with hardware. Even if all of your hardware is supported by Linux, a misconfiguration or hardware conflict can sometimes cause strange results—your devices may not be detected at boot time, or the system may hang.

It is important to isolate these hardware problems if you suspect that they may be the source of your trouble. In the following sections we will describe some common hardware problems and how to resolve them.

2.5.2.1   Isolating hardware problems

If you experience a problem that you believe to be hardware-related, the first thing that you should to do is attempt to isolate the problem. This means eliminating all possible variables and (usually) taking the system apart, piece-by-piece, until the offending piece of hardware is isolated.

This is not as frightening as it may sound. Basically, you should remove all nonessential hardware from your system, and then determine which device is actually causing the trouble—possibly by reinserting each device, one at a time. This means that you should remove all hardware other than the floppy and video controllers, and of course the keyboard. Even innocent-looking devices such as mouse controllers can wreak unknown havoc on your peace of mind unless you consider them nonessential.

For example, let's say that the system hangs during the Ethernet board detection sequence at boot time. You might hypothesize that there is a conflict or problem with the Ethernet board in your machine. The quick and easy way to find out is to pull the Ethernet board, and try booting again. If everything goes well, then you know that either (a) the Ethernet board is not supported by Linux (see Section 1.8 for a list of compatible boards), or (b) there is an address or IRQ conflict with the board.

"Address or IRQ conflict?" What on earth does that mean? All devices in your machine use an *IRQ*, or *interrupt request line*, to tell the system that they need something done on their behalf. You can think of the IRQ as a cord that the device tugs when it needs the system to take care of some pending request. If more than one device is tugging on the same cord, the kernel won't be able to detemine which device it needs to service. Instant mayhem.

Therefore, be sure that all of your installed devices are using unique IRQ lines. In general the IRQ for a device can be set by jumpers on the card; see the documentation for the particular device for details. Some devices do not require the use of an IRQ at all, but it is suggested that you configure them to use one if possible (the Seagate ST01 and ST02 SCSI controllers being good examples).

In some cases, the kernel provided on your installation media is configured to use a certain IRQ for certain devices. For example, on some distributions of Linux, the kernel is preconfigured to use IRQ 5 for the TMC-950 SCSI controller, the Mitsumi CD-ROM controller, and the bus mouse driver. If you want to use two or more of these devices, you'll need to first install Linux with only one of these devices enabled, then recompile the kernel in order to change the default IRQ for one of them. (See Chapter 4 for information on recompiling the kernel.)

Another area where hardware conflicts can arise is with DMA (direct memory access) channels, I/O addresses, and shared memory addresses. All of these terms describe mechanisms through which the system interfaces with hardware devices. Some Ethernet boards, for example, use a shared memory address as well as an IRQ to interface with the system. If any of these are in conflict with other devices, then the system may behave unexpectedly. You should be able to change the DMA channel, I/O or shared memory addresses for your various devices with jumper settings. (Unfortunately, some devices don't allow you to change these settings.)

The documentation for your various hardware devices should specify the IRQ, DMA channel, I/O address, or shared memory address that the devices use, and how to configure them. Again, the simple way to get around these problems is just to temporarily disable the conflicting devices until you have time to determine the cause of the problem.

Table 2.2 is a list of IRQ and DMA channels used by various "standard" devices found on most systems. Almost all systems will have some of these devices, so you should avoid setting the IRQ or DMA of other devices in conflict with these values.

Device	I/O address	IRQ	DMA
ttyS0 (COM1)	3f8	4	n/a
ttyS1 (COM2)	2f8	3	n/a
ttyS2 (COM3)	3e8	4	n/a
ttyS3 (COM4)	2e8	3	n/a
lp0 (LPT1)	378 - 37f	7	n/a
lp1 (LPT2)	278 - 27f	5	n/a
fd0, fd1 (floppies 1 and 2)	3f0 - 3f7	6	2
fd2, fd3 (floppies 3 and 4)	370 - 377	10	3

Table 2.2: Common device settings

2.5.2.2 Problems recognizing hard drive or controller

When Linux boots, you should see a series of messages on your screen such as:

```
Console:  colour EGA+ 80x25, 8 virtual consoles
Serial driver version 3.96 with no serial options enabled
tty00 at 0x03f8 (irq = 4) is a 16450
```

```
tty03 at 0x02e8 (irq = 3) is a 16550A
lp_init:  lp1 exists (0), using polling driver
...
```

Here, the kernel is detecting the various hardware devices present on your system. At some point, you should see the line

```
Partition check:
```

followed by a list of recognized partitions, for example:

```
Partition check:
hda:   hda1 hda2
hdb:   hdb1 hdb2 hdb3
```

If, for some reason, your drives or partitions are not recognized, then you will not be able to access them in any way.

There are several things that can cause this to happen:

- **Hard drive or controller not supported.** If you are using a hard drive controller (IDE, SCSI, or otherwise) that is not supported by Linux, the kernel will not recognize your partitions at boot time.

- **Drive or controller improperly configured.** Even if your controller is supported by Linux, it may not be configured correctly. (This is particularly a problem for SCSI controllers; most non-SCSI controllers should work fine without any additional configuration).

  Refer to the documentation for your hard drive and/or controller for information on solving these kinds of problems. In particular, many hard drives will need to have a jumper set if they are to be used as a "slave" drive (for example, as the second hard drive). The acid test for this kind of condition is to boot up MS-DOS, or some other operating system, known to work with your drive and controller. If you can access the drive and controller from another operating system, then it is not a problem with your hardware configuration.

  See Section 2.5.2.1, above, for information on resolving possible device conflicts, and Section 2.5.2.3, below, for information on configuring SCSI devices.

- **Controller properly configured, but not detected.** Some BIOS-less SCSI controllers require the user to specify information about the controller at boot time. Section 2.5.2.3, below, describes how to force hardware detection for these controllers.

- **Hard drive geometry not recognized.** Some systems, such as the IBM PS/ValuePoint, do not store hard drive geometry information in the CMOS memory, where Linux expects to find it. Also, certain SCSI controllers need to be told where to find drive geometry in order for Linux to recognize the layout of your drive.

Most distributions provide a bootup option to specify the drive geometry. In general, when booting the installation media, you can specify the drive geometry at the LILO boot prompt with a command such as:

boot: *linux hd=⟨cylinders⟩,⟨heads⟩,⟨sectors⟩*

where ⟨*cylinders*⟩, ⟨*heads*⟩, and ⟨*sectors*⟩ correspond to the number of cylinders, heads, and sectors per track for your hard drive.

After installing the Linux software, you will be able to install LILO, allowing you to boot from the hard drive. At that time, you can specify the drive geometry to the LILO installation procedure, making it unnecessary to enter the drive geometry each time you boot. See Chapter 4 for more about LILO.

2.5.2.3 Problems with SCSI controllers and devices

Presented here are some of the most common problems with SCSI controllers and devices such as CD-ROMs, hard drives, and tape drives. If you are having problems getting Linux to recognize your drive or controller, read on.

The Linux SCSI HOWTO (see Appendix A) contains much useful information on SCSI devices in addition to that listed here. SCSI can be particularly tricky to configure at times.

- **A SCSI device is detected at all possible ID's.** This is caused by strapping the device to the same address as the controller. You need to change the jumper settings so that the drive uses a different address from the controller itself.

- **Linux reports sense errors, even if the devices are known to be error-free.** This can be caused by bad cables, or by bad termination. If your SCSI bus is not terminated at both ends, you may have errors accessing SCSI devices. When in doubt, always check your cables.

- **SCSI devices report timeout errors.** This is usually caused by a conflict with IRQ, DMA, or device addresses. Also check that interrupts are enabled correctly on your controller.

- **SCSI controllers using BIOS are not detected.** Detection of controllers using BIOS will fail if the BIOS is disabled, or if your controller's "signature" is not recognized by the kernel. See the Linux SCSI HOWTO for more information about this.

- **Controllers using memory mapped I/O do not work.** This is caused when the memory-mapped I/O ports are incorrectly cached. Either mark the board's address space as uncacheable in the XCMOS settings, or disable cache altogether.

- **When partitioning, you get a warning that "cylinders > 1024", or you are unable to boot from a partition using cylinders numbered above 1023.** BIOS limits the number of cylinders to 1024, and any partition using cylinders numbered above this won't be accessible from the BIOS. As far as Linux is concerned, this affects only booting; once the system has booted you should be able to access the partition. Your options are to either boot Linux from a boot floppy, or boot from a partition using cylinders numbered below 1024. See Section 2.3.7 for information on creating a boot diskette or installing LILO.

- **CD-ROM drive or other removeable media devices are not recognized at boot time.** Try booting with a CD-ROM (or disk) in the drive. This is necessary for some devices.

If your SCSI controller is not recognized, you may need to force hardware detection at boot time. This is particularly important for BIOS-less SCSI controllers. Most distributions allow you to specify the controller IRQ and shared memory address when booting the installation media. For example, if you are using a TMC-8xx controller, you may be able to enter

> boot: *linux tmx8xx=⟨interrupt⟩,⟨memory-address⟩*

at the LILO boot prompt, where ⟨*interrupt*⟩ is the IRQ of controller, and ⟨*memory-address*⟩ is the shared memory address. Whether or not you will be able to do this depends on the distribution of Linux you are using; consult your documentation for details.

2.5.3   Problems installing the software

Actually installing the Linux software should be quite trouble-free, if you're lucky. The only problems that you might experience would be related to corrupt installation media or lack of space on your Linux filesystems. Here is a list of these common problems.

- **System reports "Read error", "file not found", or other errors while attempting to install the software.** This is indicative of a problem with your installation media. If you are installing from floppy, keep in mind that floppies are quite succeptible to media errors of this type. Be sure to use brand-new, newly-formatted floppies. If you have an MS-DOS partition on your drive, many Linux distributions allow you to install the software from the hard drive. This may be faster and more reliable than using floppies.

  If you are using a CD-ROM, be sure to check the disc for scratches, dust, or other problems which might cause media errors.

  The cause of the problem may be that the media is in the incorrect format. For example, if using floppies, many Linux distributions require that the floppies be formatted in high-density MS-DOS format. (The boot floppy is the exception; it is not in MS-DOS format in most cases.) If all else fails, either obtain a new set of floppies, or recreate the floppies (using new diskettes) if you downloaded the software yourself.

- **System reports errors such as "`tar:  read error`" or "`gzip:  not in gzip format`".** This problem is usually caused by corrupt files on the installation media itself. In other words, your floppy may be error-free, but the data on the floppy is in some way corrupted. For example, if you downloaded the Linux software using text mode, rather than binary mode, then your files will be corrupt, and unreadable by the installation software.

- **System reports errors such as "`device full`" while installing.** This is a clear-cut sign that you have run out of space when installing the software. Not all Linux distributions will be able to cleanly pick up the mess; you shouldn't be able to abort the installation and expect the system to work.

  The solution is usually to re-create your filesystems (with the `mke2fs` command) which will delete the partially-installed software. You can then attempt to re-install the software, this time selecting a smaller amount of software to install. In other cases, you may need to start completely from scratch, and rethink your partition and filesystem sizes.

- **System reports errors such as "`read_intr:  0x10`" while accessing the hard drive.** This is usually an indication of bad blocks on your drive. However, if you receive these errors while using `mkswap` or `mke2fs`, the system may be having trouble accessing your drive. This can either be a hardware problem (see Section 2.5.2), or it might be a case of poorly specified geometry. If you used the

  hd=⟨cylinders⟩,⟨heads⟩,⟨sectors⟩

  option at boot time to force detection of your drive geometry, and incorrectly specified the geometry, you could be prone to this problem. This can also happen if your drive geometry is incorrectly specified in the system CMOS.

- **System reports errors such as "`file not found`" or "`permission denied`".** This problem can occur if not all of the necessary files are present on the installation media (see the next paragraph) or if there is a permissions problem with the installation software. For example, some distributions of Linux have been known to have bugs in the installation software itself. These are usually fixed very rapidly, and are quite infrequent. If you suspect that the distribution software contains bugs, and you're sure that you have not done anything wrong, contact the maintainer of the distribution to report the bug.

If you have other strange errors when installing Linux (especially if you downloaded the software yourself), be sure that you actually obtained all of the necessary files when downloading. For example, some people use the FTP command

```
mget *.*
```

when downloading the Linux software via FTP. This will download only those files that contain a ".." in their filenames; if there are any files without the ".", you will miss them. The correct command to use in this case is

```
mget *
```

The best advice is to retrace your steps when something goes wrong. You may think that you have done everything correctly, when in fact you forgot a small but important step somewhere along the way. In many cases, just attempting to re-download or re-install the Linux software can solve the problem. Don't beat your head against the wall any longer than you have to!

Also, if Linux unexpectedly hangs during installation, there may be a hardware problem of some kind. See Section 2.5.2 for hints.

2.5.4   Problems after installing Linux

You've spent an entire afternoon installing Linux. In order to make space for it, you wiped your MS-DOS and OS/2 partitions, and tearfully deleted your copies of SimCity and Wing Commander. You reboot the system, and nothing happens. Or, even worse, *something* happens, but it's not what should happen. What do you do?

In Section 2.5.1, we covered some of the most common problems that can occur when booting the Linux installation media—many of those problems may apply here. In addition, you may be victim to one of the following maladies.

2.5.4.1   Problems booting Linux from floppy

If you are using a floppy to boot Linux, you may need to specify the location of your Linux root partition at boot time. This is especially true if you are using the original installation floppy itself, and not a custom boot floppy created during installation.

While booting the floppy, hold down shift or ctrl. This should present you with a boot menu; press tab to see a list of available options. For example, many distributions allow you to type

```
boot:  linux hd=⟨partition⟩
```

at the boot menu, where ⟨partition⟩ is the name of the Linux root partition, such as /dev/hda2. Consult the documentation for your distribution for details.

2.5.4.2 Problems booting Linux from the hard drive

If you opted to install LILO, instead of creating a boot floppy, then you should be able to boot Linux from the hard drive. However, the automated LILO installation procedure used by many distributions is not always perfect. It may make incorrect assumptions about your partition layout, in which case you will need to re-install LILO to get everything right. Installing LILO is covered in Chapter 4.

- **System reports "Drive not bootable---Please insert system disk."** You will get this error message if the hard drive's master boot record is corrupt in some way. In most cases, it's harmless, and everything else on your drive is still intact. There are several ways around this:

  1. While partitioning your drive using **fdisk**, you may have deleted the partition that was marked as "active". MS-DOS and other operating systems attempt to boot the "active" partition at boot time (Linux pays no attention to whether the partition is "active" or not). You may be able to boot MS-DOS from floppy and run **FDISK** to set the active flag on your MS-DOS parition, and all will be well. Another command to try (with MS-DOS 5.0 and higher) is

     ```
     FDISK /MBR
     ```

     This command will attempt to rebuild the hard drive master boot record for booting MS-DOS, overwriting LILO. If you no longer have MS-DOS on your hard drive, you'll need to boot Linux from floppy and attempt to install LILO later.

  2. If you created an MS-DOS partition using Linux's version of **fdisk**, or vice versa, you may get this error. You should create MS-DOS partitions only using MS-DOS's version **FDISK**. (The same applies to operating systems other than MS-DOS.) The best solution here is either to start from scratch and repartition the drive correctly, or to merely delete and re-create the offending partitions using the correct version of **fdisk**.

  3. The LILO installation procedure may have failed. In this case, you should either boot from your Linux boot floppy (if you have one), or from the original installation media. Either of these should provide options for specifying the Linux root partition to use when booting. Hold down ⎡shift⎤ or ⎡ctrl⎤ at boot time, and press ⎡tab⎤ from the boot menu for a list of options.

- **When booting the system from the hard drive, MS-DOS (or another operating system) starts instead of Linux.** First of all, be sure that you actually installed LILO when installing the Linux software. If not, then the system will still boot MS-DOS (or whatever other operating system you may have) when you attempt to boot from the hard drive. In order to boot Linux from the hard drive, you will need to install LILO (see Chapter 4).

On the other hand, if you *did* install LILO, and another operating system boots instead of Linux, then you have LILO configured to boot that other operating system by default. While the system is booting, hold down $\boxed{\texttt{shift}}$ or $\boxed{\texttt{ctrl}}$, and press $\boxed{\texttt{tab}}$ at the boot prompt. This should present you with a list of possible operating systems to boot; select the appropriate option (usually just "`linux`") to boot Linux.

If you wish to select Linux as the default operating system to boot, you will need to re-install LILO. See Chapter 4.

It also may be possible that you attempted to install LILO, but the installation procedure failed in some way. See the previous item.

2.5.4.3   Problems logging in

After booting Linux, you should be presented with a login prompt, like so:

```
linux login:
```

At this point, either the distribution's documentation or the system itself will tell you what to do. For many distributions, you simply login as **root**, with no password. Other possible usernames to try are **guest** or **test**.

Most newly-installed Linux systems should not require a password for the initial login. However, if you are asked to enter a password, there may be a problem. First, try using a password equivalent to the username; that is, if you are logging in as **root**, use "**root**" as the password.

If you simply can't login, there may be a problem. First, consult your distribution's documentation; the username and password to use may be buried in there somewhere. The username and password may have been given to you during the installation procedure, or they may be printed on the login banner.

One cause of this may be a problem with installing the Linux login and initialization files. If this is the case, you may need to reinstall (at least parts of) the Linux software, or boot your installation media and attempt to fix the problem by hand—see Chapter 4 for hints.

2.5.4.4   Problems using the system

If login is successful, you should be presented with a shell prompt (such as "**#**" or "**$**") and can happily roam around your system. However, there are some initial problems with using the system that sometimes creep up.

The most common initial configuration problem is incorrect file or directory permissions. This can cause the error message

```
Shell-init:  permission denied
```

to be printed after logging in (in fact, any time you see the message "**permission denied**" you can be fairly certain that it is a problem with file permissions).

In many cases, it's a simple matter of using the **chmod** command to fix the permissions of the appropriate files or directories. For example, some distributions of Linux once used the (incorrect) file mode 0644 for the root directory (/). The fix was to issue the command

> **#** *chmod 755 /*

as **root**. However, in order to issue this command, you needed to boot from the installation media and mount your Linux root filesystem by hand—a hairy task for most newcomers.

As you use the system, you may run into places where file and directory permissions are incorrect, or software does not work as configured. Welcome to the world of Linux! While most distributions are quite trouble-free, very few of them are perfect. We don't want to cover all of those problems here. Instead, throughout the book we help you to solve many of these configuration problems by teaching you how to find them and fix them yourself. In Chapter 1 we discussed this philosophy in some detail. In Chapter 4, we give hints for fixing many of these common configuration problems.

Chapter 3

Linux Tutorial

3.1 Introduction

New users of UNIX and Linux may be a bit intimidated by the size and apparent complexity of the system before them. There are many good books on using UNIX out there, for all levels of expertise from novice to expert. However, none of these books covers, specifically, an introduction to using Linux. While 95% of using Linux is exactly like using other UNIX systems, the most straightforward way to get going on your new system is with a tutorial tailored for Linux. Herein is such a tutorial.

This chapter does not go into a large amount of detail or cover many advanced topics. Instead, it is intended to get the new Linux user running, on both feet, so that he or she may then read a more general book about UNIX and understand the basic differences between other UNIX systems and Linux.

Very little is assumed here, except perhaps some familiarity with personal computer systems, and MS-DOS. However, even if you're not an MS-DOS user, you should be able to understand everything here. At first glance, UNIX looks a lot like MS-DOS (after all, parts of MS-DOS were modeled on the CP/M operating system, which in turn was modeled on UNIX). However, only the very superficial features of UNIX resemble MS-DOS in any way. Even if you're completely new to the PC world, this tutorial should be of help.

And, before we begin: *Don't be afraid to experiment.* The system won't bite you. You can't destroy anything by working on the system. UNIX has some amount of security built in, to prevent "normal" users (the role which you will now assume) from damaging files which are essential to the system. Even so, the absolute worst thing that can happen is that you'll delete all of your files—and you'll have to go back and re-install the system. So, at this point, you have nothing to lose.

3.2   Basic UNIX Concepts

UNIX is a multitasking, multiuser operating system. This means that there can be many people using one computer at the same time, running many different applications. (This differs from MS-DOS, where only one person can use the system at any one time.) Under UNIX, for users to identify themselves to the system, they must **log in**, which entails two steps: Entering your **login name** (the name which the system identifies you as), and entering your **password**, which is your personal secret key to logging into your account. Because only you know your password, no one else can login to the system under your username.

On traditional UNIX systems, the system administrator will assign you a username and an initial password when you are given an account on the system. However, because you are the system administrator, you must set up your own account before you can login—see Section 3.2.1, below. For the following discussions, we'll use the imaginary username "`larry`".

In addition, each UNIX system has a **hostname** assigned to it. It is this hostname that gives your machine a name, gives it character and charm. The hostname is used to identify individual machines on a network, but even if your machine isn't networked, it should have a hostname. In Section 4.10.2 we'll cover setting your system's hostname. For our examples, below, the system's hostname is "`mousehouse`".

3.2.1   Creating an account

Before you can use the system, you must set up a user account for yourself. This is because it's usually not a good idea to use the **root** account for normal use. The **root** account should be reserved for running privileged commands and for maintaining the system, as discussed in Section 4.1.

In order to create an account for yourself, you need to login as **root** and use the **useradd** or **adduser** command. See Section 4.4 for information on this procedure.

3.2.2   Logging in

At login time, you'll see a prompt resembling the following on your screen:

```
mousehouse login:
```

Here, enter your username, and press the Return key. Our hero, **larry**, would type the following:

```
mousehouse login:  larry
Password:
```

Now, enter your password. It won't be echoed to the screen when you login, so type carefully. If you mistype your password, you'll see the message

```
Login incorrect
```

and you'll have to try again.

Once you have correctly entered the username and password, you are officially logged into the system, and are free to roam.

3.2.3 Virtual consoles

The system's **console** is the monitor and keyboard connected directly to the system. (Because UNIX is a multiuser operating system, you may have other terminals connected to serial ports on your system, but these would not be the console.) Linux, like some other versions of UNIX, provides access to **virtual consoles** (or VC's), which allow you to have more than one login session from your console at a time.

To demonstrate this, login to your system (as demonstrated above). Now, press $\boxed{\text{alt-F2}}$. You should see the **login:** prompt again. You're looking at the second virtual console—you logged into the first. To switch back to the first VC, press $\boxed{\text{alt-F1}}$. *Voila!* You're back to your first login session.

A newly-installed Linux system probably allows you to access the first four VC's, using $\boxed{\text{alt-F1}}$ through $\boxed{\text{alt-F4}}$. However, it is possible to enable up to 12 VC's—one for each function key on your keyboard. As you can see, use of VC's can be very powerful—you can be working on several different VC's at once.

While the use of VC's is somewhat limiting (after all, you can only be looking at one VC at a time), it should give you a feel for UNIX's multiuser capabilities. While you're working on VC #1, you can switch over to VC #2 and start working on something else.

3.2.4 Shells and commands

For most of your explorations in the world of UNIX, you'll be talking to the system through the use of a **shell**. A shell is just a program which takes user input (e.g., commands which you type) and translates them into instructions. This can be compared to the **COMMAND.COM** program under MS-DOS, which does essentially the same thing. The shell is just one interface to UNIX. There are many possible interfaces—such as the X Window System, which lets you run commands by using the mouse and keyboard in conjunction.

As soon as you login, the system starts the shell, and you can type commands to it. Here's a quick example. Here, Larry logs in, and is left sitting at the shell **prompt**.

```
mousehouse login: larry
Password: larry's password
```

```
Welcome to Mousehouse!

/home/larry#
```

"`/home/larry#`" is the shell's prompt, indicating that it's ready to take commands. (More on what the prompt itself means later.) Let's try telling the system to do something interesting:

```
/home/larry# make love
make:  *** No way to make target 'love'.  Stop.
/home/larry#
```

Well, as it turns out **make** was the name of an actual program on the system, and the shell executed this program when given the command. (Unfortunately, the system was being unfriendly.)

This brings us to one burning question: What are commands? What happens when you type "**make love**"? The first word on the command line, "**make**", is the name of the command to be executed. Everything else on the command line is taken as arguments to this command. Examples:

```
/home/larry# cp foo bar
```

Here, the name of the command is "**cp**", and the arguments are "**foo**" and "**bar**".

When you type a command, the shell does several things. First of all, it looks at the command name, and checks to see if it is a command which is internal to the shell. (That is, a command which the shell knows how to execute itself. There are a number of these commands, and we'll go into them later.) The shell also checks to see if the command is an alias, or substitute name, for another command. If neither of these conditions apply, the shell looks for a program, on the disk, with the command's name. If it finds such a program, the shell runs it, giving the program the arguments specified on the command line.

In our example, the shell looks for the program called **make**, and runs it with the argument **love**. **Make** is a program often used to compile large programs, and it takes as arguments the name of a "target" to compile. In the case of "**make love**", we instructed **make** to compile the target **love**. Because **make** can't find a target by this name, it fails with a humorous error message, and we are returned to the shell prompt.

What happens if we type a command to a shell, and the shell can't find a program with the command name to run? Well, we can try it:

```
/home/larry# eat dirt
eat:  command not found
/home/larry#
```

Quite simply, if the shell can't find a program with the name given on the command line (here, "eat"), it prints an error message which should be self-explanatory. You'll often see this error message if you mistype a command (for example, if you had typed "mkae love" instead of "make love").

3.2.5 Logging out

Before we delve much further, we should tell you how to log out of the system. At the shell prompt, use the command

   /home/larry# *exit*

to logout. There are other ways of logging out as well, but this is the most foolproof one.

3.2.6 Changing your password

You should also be aware of how to change your password. The command **passwd** will prompt you for your old password, and your new password. It will ask you to reenter the new password for validation. Be careful not to forget your password—if you do, you will have to ask the system administrator to reset it for you. (If you're the system administrator, see Section 4.4.)

3.2.7 Files and directories

Under most operating systems (UNIX included), there is the concept of a **file**, which is just a bundle of information which is given a name (called a **filename**). Examples of files would be your history term paper, an e-mail message, or an actual program which can be executed. Essentially, anything which is saved on disk is saved in an individual file.

Files are identified by their filenames. For example, the file containing your history paper might be saved with the filename **history-paper**. These names usually identify the file and its contents in some form which is meaningful to you. There is no standard format for filenames as there is under MS-DOS and other operating systems; in general, filenames may contain any character (except /—see the discussion of pathnames, below), and are limited to 256 characters in length.

With the concept of files comes the concept of directories. A **directory** is just a collection of files. It can be thought of as a "folder" which contains many different files. Directories themselves are given names, with which you can identify them. Furthermore, directories are maintained in a tree-like structure; that is, directories may contain other directories.

A file may be referred to by its **pathname**, which is made up of the filename, preceded by the name of the directory which contains the file. For example, let's say that Larry has a directory called **papers**, which contains three files: `history-final`, `english-lit`, and `masters-thesis`. (Each of these three files contains information for three of Larry's ongoing projects.) To refer to the file `english-lit`, Larry can specify the file's pathname:

> `papers/english-lit`

As you can see, the directory and file names are separated by a single slash (/). For this reason, filenames themselves cannot contain the / character. MS-DOS users will find this convention familiar, although in the MS-DOS world, the backslash (\) is used instead.

As mentioned, directories can be nested within each other as well. For example, let's say that Larry has another directory, within **papers**, called **notes**. This directory contains the files `math-notes` and `cheat-sheet`. The pathname of the file `cheat-sheet` would be

> `papers/notes/cheat-sheet`

Therefore, the pathname really is a "path" which you take to locate a certain file. The directory above a given subdirectory is known as the **parent directory**. Here, the directory **papers** is the parent of the **notes** directory.

3.2.8   The directory tree

Most UNIX systems have a standard layout for files, so that system resources and programs can be easily located. This layout forms a directory tree, which starts at the "/" directory, also known as "the root directory". Directly underneath / are some important subdirectories: `/bin`, `/etc`, `/dev`, and `/usr`, among others. These directories in turn contain other directories which contain system configuration files, programs, and so on.

In particular, each user has a **home directory**, which is the directory set aside for that user to store his or her files. In the examples above, all of Larry's files (such as `cheat-sheet` and `history-final`) were contained in Larry's home directory. Usually, user home directories are contained under `/home`, and are named for the user who owns that directory. Therefore, Larry's home directory is `/home/larry`.

In Figure 3.2.8 a sample directory tree is represented. It should give you some idea of how the directory tree on your system is organized.

3.2.9   The current working directory

At any given time, commands that you type to the shell are given in terms of your **current working directory**. You can think of your working directory as the directory in which you are currently "located". When you first login, your working directory is set to your home directory—`/home/larry` in our case. Whenever you reference a file, you may refer to it in relationship to your current working directory, instead of specifying the full pathname of the file.

Here's an example. Larry has the directory **papers**, and **papers** contains the file **history-final**. If Larry wants to look at this file, he can use the command

    /home/larry# *more /home/larry/papers/history-final*

The **more** command simply displays a file, one screen at a time. However, because Larry's current working directory is **/home/larry**, he can instead refer to the file *relative* to his current location. The command would be

    /home/larry# *more papers/history-final*

Therefore, if you begin a filename (such as **papers/final**) with a character other than "/", the system assumes that you're referring to the file in terms relative to your current working directory. This is known as a **relative pathname**.

On the other hand, if you begin a filename with a "/", the system interprets this as a full pathname—that is, a pathname including the entire path to the file, starting from the root directory, /. This is known as an **absolute pathname**.

3.2.10 Referring to home directories

Under both **tcsh** and **bash**,[1] your home directory can be referred to using the tilde character ("~"). For example, the command

    /home/larry# *more ~/papers/history-final*

is equivalent to

    /home/larry# *more /home/larry/papers/history-final*

The "~" character is simply replaced with the name of your home directory by the shell.

In addition, you can specify other user's home directories with the tilde as well. The pathname "~karl/letters" translates to "/home/karl/letters" by the shell (if **/home/karl** is karl's home directory). The use of the tilde is simply a shortcut; there is no directory named "~"—it's just syntactic sugar provided by the shell.

---

[1]**tcsh** and **bash** are two *shells* running under Linux. The shell is the program which reads user commands and executes them; most Linux systems enable either **tcsh** or **bash** for new user accounts.

3.3   First Steps into UNIX

Before we begin, it is important to note that all file and command names on a UNIX system are case-sensitive (unlike operating systems such as MS-DOS). For example, the command `make` is very different than `Make` or `MAKE`. The same hold for file and directory names.

3.3.1   Moving around

Now that we can login, and know how to refer to files using pathnames, how can we change our current working directory, to make life easier?

The command for moving around in the directory structure is `cd`, short for "change directory". You'll notice that many often-used Unix commands are two or three letters. The usage of the `cd` command is:

    cd ⟨directory⟩

where ⟨directory⟩ is the name of the directory which you wish to change to.

As we said, when you login, you begin in your home directory. If Larry wanted to move down into the **papers** subdirectory, he'd use the command

    /home/larry# cd papers
    /home/larry/papers#

As you can see, Larry's prompt changes to reflect his current working directory (so he knows where he is). Now that he's in the **papers** directory, he can look at his history final with the command

    /home/larry/papers# more history-final

Now, Larry is stuck in the **papers** subdirectory. To move back up to the parent directory, use the command

    /home/larry/papers# cd ..
    /home/larry#

(Note the space between the "cd" and the "..".) Every directory has an entry named ".." which refers to the parent directory. Similarly, every directory has an entry named "." which refers to itself. Therefore, the command

    /home/larry/papers# cd .

gets us nowhere.

You can also use absolute pathnames in the **cd** command. To **cd** into Karl's home directory, we can use the command

```
/home/larry/papers# cd /home/karl
/home/karl#
```

Also, using **cd** with no argument will return you to your own home directory.

```
/home/karl# cd
/home/larry#
```

3.3.2 Looking at the contents of directories

Now that you know how to move around directories you probably think, "So what?" The basic skill of moving around directories is fairly useless, so let's introduce a new command, **ls**. **ls** prints a listing of files and directories, by default from your current directory. For example:

```
/home/larry# ls
Mail
letters
papers
/home/larry#
```

Here we can see that Larry has three entries in his current directory: **Mail**, **letters**, and **papers**. This doesn't tell us much—are these directories or files? We can use the **-F** option on the **ls** command to tell us more.

```
/home/larry# ls -F
Mail/
letters/
papers/
/home/larry#
```

From the / appended to each filename, we know that these three entries are in fact subdirectories.

Using **ls -F** may also append "*" to the end of a filename. This indicates that the file is an **executable**, or a program which can be run. If nothing is appended to the filename using **ls -F**, the file is a "plain old file", that is, it's neither a directory, or an executable.

In general, each UNIX command may take a number of options in addition to other arguments. These options usually begin with a "–", as demonstrated above with `ls -F`. The `-F` option tells `ls` to give more information about the type of the files involved—in this case, printing a / after each directory name.

If you give `ls` a directory name, it will print the contents of that directory.

```
/home/larry# ls –F papers
english-lit
history-final
masters-thesis
notes/
/home/larry#
```

Or, for a more interesting listing, let's see what's in the system's **/etc** directory.

```
/home/larry# ls /etc
```

Images	ftpusers	lpc	rc.new	shells
adm	getty	magic	rc0.d	startcons
bcheckrc	gettydefs	motd	rc1.d	swapoff
brc	group	mount	rc2.d	swapon
brc~	inet	mtab	rc3.d	syslog.conf
csh.cshrc	init	mtools	rc4.d	syslog.pid
csh.login	init.d	pac	rc5.d	syslogd.reload
default	initrunlvl	passwd	rmt	termcap
disktab	inittab	printcap	rpc	umount
fdprm	inittab.old	profile	rpcinfo	update
fstab	issue	psdatabase	securetty	utmp
ftpaccess	lilo	rc	services	wtmp
/home/larry#				

(For those MS-DOS users out there, notice how the filenames can be longer than 8 characters, and can contain periods in any position. It is even possible to have more than one period in a filename.)

Let's **cd** up to the top of the directory tree, using "**cd ..**", and then down to another directory: **/usr/bin**.

```
/home/larry# cd ..
/home# cd ..
/# cd usr
/usr# cd bin
/usr/bin#
```

You can also move into directories in multiple steps, as in **cd /usr/bin**.

Try moving around various directories, using **ls** and **cd**. In some cases, you may run into a foreboding "**Permission denied**" error message. This is simply the concept of UNIX security kicking in: in order to **ls** or to **cd** into a directory, you must have permission to do so. We'll talk more about this in   Section 3.9.

3.3.3   Creating new directories

It's time to learn how to create directories. This involves the use of the **mkdir** command. Try the following:

```
/home/larry# mkdir foo
/home/larry# ls -F
Mail/
foo/
letters/
papers/
/home/larry# cd foo
/home/larry/foo# ls
/home/larry/foo#
```

Congrats! You've just made a new directory and moved into it. Since there aren't any files in this new directory, let's learn how to copy files from one place to another.

3.3.4   Copying files

Copying files is done with the command **cp**:

```
/home/larry/foo# cp /etc/termcap .
/home/larry/foo# cp /etc/shells .
/home/larry/foo# ls -F
shells      termcap
/home/larry/foo# cp shells bells
/home/larry/foo# ls -F
bells      shells      termcap
/home/larry/foo#
```

The **cp** command copies the files listed on the command line to the file or directory given as the last argument. Notice how we use the directory "**.**" to refer to the current directory.

3.3.5 Moving files

A new command named **mv** moves files, instead of copying them. The syntax is very straight-forward.

```
/home/larry/foo# mv termcap sells
/home/larry/foo# ls -F
bells        sells        shells
/home/larry/foo#
```

Notice how **termcap** no longer exists, but in its place is the file **sells**. This can be used to rename files, as we have just done, but also to move a file to a completely new directory.

◇   **Note:** mv and **cp** will overwrite the destination file (if it already exists) without asking you. Be careful when you move a file into another directory: there may already be a file with the same name in that directory, which you'll overwrite!

3.3.6 Deleting files and directories

You now have an ugly rhyme developing with the use of the **ls** command. To delete a file, use the **rm** command. ("**rm**" stands for "remove").

```
/home/larry/foo# rm bells sells
/home/larry/foo# ls -F
shells
/home/larry/foo#
```

We're left with nothing but shells, but we won't complain. Note that **rm** by default won't prompt you before deleting a file—so be careful.

A related command to **rm** is **rmdir**. This command deletes a directory, but only if the directory is empty. If the directory contains any files or subdirectories, **rmdir** will complain.

3.3.7 Looking at files

The commands **more** and **cat** are used for viewing the contents of files. **more** displays a file, one screenful at a time, while **cat** displays the whole file at once.

To look at the file **shells**, we can use the command

```
/home/larry/foo# more shells
```

In case you're interested what **shells** contains, it's a list of valid shell programs on your system. On most systems, this includes **/bin/sh**, **/bin/bash**, and **/bin/csh**. We'll talk about these different types of shells later.

While using **more**, press ⎡Space⎤ to display the next page of text, and ⎡b⎤ to display the previous page. There are other commands available in **more** as well, these are just the basics. Pressing ⎡q⎤ will quit **more**.

Quit **more** and try **cat /etc/termcap**. The text will probably fly by much too quickly for you to read it. The name "**cat**" actually stands for "concatenate", which is the real use of the program. The **cat** command can be used to concatenate the contents of several files and save the result to another file. This will be discussed later.

3.3.8   Getting online help

Almost every UNIX system, Linux included, provides a facility known as "manual pages", or "man pages" for short. These man pages contain online documentation for all of the various system commands, resources, configuration files, and so on.

The command used to access man pages is **man**. For example, if you're interested in finding out about the other options of the **ls** command, you can type

    /home/larry# *man ls*

and the man page for **ls** will be displayed.

Unfortunately, most of the man pages out there are written for those who already have some idea of what the command or resource does. For this reason, man pages usually only contain the hardcore technical details of the command, without a lot of tutorial. However, man pages can be an invaluable resource for jogging your memory if you forget the syntax of a command. Man pages will also tell you a lot about the commands which we won't tell you in this book.

I suggest that you try **man** for the commands we've already gone over, and whenever I introduce a new command. You'll notice some of these commands won't have man pages. This could be for several reasons. For one, the man pages haven't been written yet (the Linux Documentation Project is responsible for man pages under Linux as well. We are gradually accumulating most of the man pages available for the system). Secondly, the the command might be an internal shell command, or an alias (as discussed in Section 3.2.4), in which case it would not have a man page of its own. One example is **cd**, which is a shell internal command. The shell actually processes the **cd**—there is no separate program which contains this command.

3.4   Summary of Basic Commands

This section introduces some of the most useful basic commands on a UNIX system, including those covered in the last section.

Note that options usually begin with a "-", and in most cases multiple one-letter options may be combined using a single "-". For example, instead of using the command `ls -l -F`, it is adequate to use `ls -lF`.

Instead of listing all of the options available for each of these commands, we'll only talk about those which are useful or important at this time. In fact, most of these commands have a large number of options (most of which you'll never use). You can use `man` to see the manual pages for each command, which list all of the available options.

Also note that many of these commands take a list of files or directories as arguments, denoted by "⟨file1⟩ ... ⟨fileN⟩". For example, the `cp` command takes as arguments a list of files to copy, followed by the destination file or directory. When copying more than one file, the destination must be a directory.

`cd`	Change the current working directory. Syntax: `cd` ⟨directory⟩ ⟨directory⟩ is the directory to change to. ("." refers to the current directory, ".." the parent directory.) Example: `cd ../foo` sets the current directory to `../foo`.
`ls`	Displays information about the named files and directories. Syntax: `ls` ⟨file1⟩ ⟨file2⟩ ... ⟨fileN⟩ Where ⟨file1⟩ through ⟨fileN⟩ are the filenames or directories to list. Options: There are more options than you want to think about. The most commonly used are `-F` (used to display some information about the type of the file), and `-l` (gives a "long" listing including file size, owner, permissions, and so on. This will be covered in detail later.) Example: `ls -lF /home/larry` will display the contents of the directory `/home/larry`.
`cp`	Copies file(s) to another file or directory. Syntax: `cp` ⟨file1⟩ ⟨file2⟩ ... ⟨fileN⟩ ⟨destination⟩ Where ⟨file1⟩ through ⟨fileN⟩ are the files to copy, and ⟨destination⟩ is the destination file or directory. Example: `cp ../frog joe` copies the file `../frog` to the file or directory `joe`.
`mv`	Moves file(s) to another file or directory. This command does the equivalent of a copy followed by the deletion of the original. This can be used to rename files, as in the MS-DOS command `RENAME`. Syntax: `mv` ⟨file1⟩ ⟨file2⟩ ... ⟨fileN⟩ ⟨destination⟩

Where ⟨*file1*⟩ through ⟨*fileN*⟩ are the files to move, and ⟨*destination*⟩ is the destination file or directory.

Example: `mv ../frog joe` moves the file `../frog` to the file or directory `joe`.

`rm`   Deletes files. Note that when files are deleted under UNIX, they are unrecoverable (unlike MS-DOS, where you can usually "undelete" the file).

Syntax: `rm` ⟨*file1*⟩ ⟨*file2*⟩ ...⟨*fileN*⟩

Where ⟨*file1*⟩ through ⟨*fileN*⟩ are the filenames to delete.

Options: `-i` will prompt for confirmation before deleting the file.

Example: `rm -i /home/larry/joe /home/larry/frog` deletes the files `joe` and `frog` in `/home/larry`.

`mkdir`   Creates new directories.

Syntax: `mkdir` ⟨*dir1*⟩ ⟨*dir2*⟩ ...⟨*dirN*⟩

Where ⟨*dir1*⟩ through ⟨*dirN*⟩ are the directories to create.

Example: `mkdir /home/larry/test` creates the directory `test` under `/home/larry`.

`rmdir`   This command deletes empty directories. When using `rmdir`, your current working directory must not be within the directory to be deleted.

Syntax: `rmdir` ⟨*dir1*⟩ ⟨*dir2*⟩ ...⟨*dirN*⟩

Where ⟨*dir1*⟩ through ⟨*dirN*⟩ are the directories to delete.

Example: `rmdir`
`/home/larry/papers` deletes the directory `/home/larry/papers`, if it is empty.

`man`   Displays the manual page for the given command or resource (that is, any system utility which isn't a command, such as a library function.) Syntax: `man` ⟨*command*⟩

Where ⟨*command*⟩ is the name of the command or resource to get help on.

Example: `man ls` gives help on the `ls` command.

`more`   Displays the contents of the named files, one screenful at a time.

Syntax: `more` ⟨*file1*⟩ ⟨*file2*⟩ ...⟨*fileN*⟩

Where ⟨*file1*⟩ through ⟨*fileN*⟩ are the files to display.

Example: `more papers/history-final`   displays   the   file
`papers/history-final`.

`cat`   Officially used to concatenate files, `cat` is also used to display the entire contents of a file at once.

Syntax: `cat` ⟨*file1*⟩ ⟨*file2*⟩ ...⟨*fileN*⟩

Where ⟨*file1*⟩ through ⟨*fileN*⟩ are the files to display.

Example: `cat letters/from-mdw` displays the file `letters/from-mdw`.

echo
Simply echoes the given arguments.
Syntax: echo ⟨arg1⟩ ⟨arg2⟩ ... ⟨argN⟩
Where ⟨arg1⟩ through ⟨argN⟩ are the arguments to echo.
Example: echo "Hello world" displays the string "Hello world".

grep
Display all of the lines in the named file(s) matching the given pattern.
Syntax: grep ⟨pattern⟩ ⟨file1⟩ ⟨file2⟩ ... ⟨fileN⟩
Where ⟨pattern⟩ is a regular expression pattern, and ⟨file1⟩ through ⟨fileN⟩ are the files to search.
Example: grep loomer /etc/hosts will display all lines in the file /etc/hosts which contain the pattern "loomer".

3.5   Exploring the File System

The **file system** is the collection of files and the hierarchy of directories on your system. I promised before to escort you around the filesystem and the time has come.

You have the skills and the knowledge to make sense out of what I'm saying, and you have a roadmap. (Refer to Figure 3.2.8 on page 134).

First, change to the root directory (cd /), and do an ls -F. You'll probably see these directories[2]: bin, dev, etc, home, install, lib, mnt, proc, root, tmp, user, usr, and var.

Let's take a look at each of these directories.

/bin
/bin is short for "binaries", or executables. This is where many essential system programs reside. Use the command "ls -F /bin" to list the files here. If you look down the list you may see a few commands that you recognize, such as cp, ls, and mv. These are the actual programs for these commands. When you use the cp command, you're running the program /bin/cp.

Using ls -F, you'll see that most (if not all) of the files in /bin have an asterisk ("*") appended to their filenames. This indicates that the files are executables, as described in Section 3.3.2.

/dev
Next on our stop is /dev. Take a look, again with ls -F.

The "files" in /dev are known as **device drivers**—they are used to access system devices and resources, such as disk drives, modems, memory, and so on. For example, just as you can read data from a file, you can read input from the mouse by accessing /dev/mouse.

---

[2]You may see others, and you might not see all of them. Don't worry. Every release of Linux differs in some respects.

The filenames beginning with **fd** are floppy disk devices. **fd0** is the first floppy disk drive, **fd1** the second. Now, the astute among you will notice that there are more floppy disk devices then just the two I've listed above: they represent specific types of floppy disks. For example, **fd1H1440** will access high-density, 3.5" diskettes in drive 1.

Here is a list of some of the most commonly used device files. Note that even though you may not have some of the devices listed below, the chances are that you'll have entries in **/dev** for them anyway.

- **/dev/console** refers to the system's console—that is, the monitor connected directly to your system.

- The various **/dev/ttyS** and **/dev/cua** devices are used for accessing serial ports. For example, **/dev/ttyS0** refers to "**COM1**" under MS-DOS. The **/dev/cua** devices are "callout" devices, which are used in conjunction with a modem.

- The device names beginning with **hd** access hard drives. **/dev/hda** refers to the *whole* first hard disk, while **hda1** refers to the first *partition* on **/dev/hda**.

- The device names beginning with **sd** are SCSI drives. If you have a SCSI hard drive, instead of accessing it through **/dev/hda**, you would access **/dev/sda**. SCSI tapes are accessed via **st** devices, and SCSI CD-ROM via **sr** devices.

- The device names beginning with **lp** access parallel ports. **/dev/lp0** refers to "LPT1" in the MS-DOS world.

- **/dev/null** is used as a "black hole"—any data sent to this device is gone forever. Why is this useful? Well, if you wanted to suppress the output of a command appearing on your screen, you could send that output to **/dev/null**. We'll talk more about this later.

- The device names beginning with **/dev/tty** refer to the "virtual consoles" on your system (accessed via by pressing $\boxed{\texttt{alt-F1}}$, $\boxed{\texttt{alt-F2}}$, and so on). **/dev/tty1** refers to the first VC, **/dev/tty2** refers to the second, and so on.

- The device names beginning with **/dev/pty** are "pseudo-terminals". They are used to provide a "terminal" to remote login sessions. For example, if your machine is on a network, incoming **telnet** logins would use one of the **/dev/pty** devices.

/etc   **/etc** contains a number of miscellaneous system configuration files. These include **/etc/passwd** (the user database), **/etc/rc** (the system initialization script), and so on.

/sbin   sbin is used for storing essential system binaries, to be used by the system administrator.

/home   /home contains user's home directories. For example, /home/larry is the home directory for the user "larry". On a newly-installed system, there may not be any users in this directory.

/lib   /lib contains **shared library images**. These files contain code which many programs share in common. Instead of each program containing its own copy of these shared routines, they are all stored in one common place, in /lib. This makes executable files smaller, and saves space on your system.

/proc   /proc is a "virtual filesystem", the files in which are stored in memory, not on the drive. They refer to the various **processes** running on the system, and allow you to get information about what programs and processes are running at any given time. We'll go into more detail in Section 3.11.1.

/tmp   Many programs have a need to generate some information and store it in a temporary file. The canonical location for these files is in /tmp.

/usr   /usr is a very important directory. It contains a number of subdirectories which in turn contain some of the most important and useful programs and configuration files used on the system.

                 The various directories described above are essential for the system to operate, but most of the things found in /usr are optional for the system. However, it is those optional things which make the system useful and interesting. Without /usr, you'd more or less have a boring system, only with programs like cp and ls. /usr contains most of the larger software packages and the configuration files which accompany them.

/usr/X386   /usr/X386 contains The X Window System, if you installed it. The X Window System is a large, powerful graphical environment which provides a large number of graphical utilities and programs, displayed in "windows" on your screen. If you're at all familiar with the Microsoft Windows or Macintosh environments, X Windows will look very familiar. The /usr/X386 directory contains all of the X Windows executables, configuration files, and support files. This will be covered in more detail in Section 5.1.

/usr/bin   /usr/bin is the real warehouse for software on any UNIX system. It contains most of the executables for programs not found in other places, such as /bin.

/usr/etc   Just as /etc contained miscellaneous system programs and configuration files, /usr/etc contains even more of these utilities and files. In general, the files found in **/usr/etc** are not essential to the system, unlike those found in **/etc**, which are.

/usr/include   **/usr/include** contains **include files** for the C compiler. These files (most of which end in **.h**, for "header") declare data structure names, subroutines, and constants used when writing programs in C. Those files found in **/usr/include/sys** are generally used when programming on the UNIX system level. If you are familiar with the C programming language, here you'll find header files such as **stdio.h**, which declares functions such as **printf()**.

/usr/g++-include

/usr/g++-include contains include files for the C++ compiler (much like **/usr/include**).

/usr/lib   **/usr/lib** contains the "stub" and "static" library equivalents to the files found in **/lib**. When compiling a program, the program is "linked" with the libraries found in **/usr/lib**, which then directs the program to look in **/lib** when it needs the actual code in the library. In addition, various other programs store configuration files in **/usr/lib**.

/usr/local   **/usr/local** is a lot like **/usr**—it contains various programs and files not essential to the system, but which make the system fun and exciting. In general, those programs found in **/usr/local** are specialized for your system specifically—that is, **/usr/local** differs greatly between UNIX systems.

Here, you'll find large software packages such as TEX (a document formatting system) and Emacs (a large and powerful editor), if you installed them.

/usr/man   This directory contains the actual man pages. There are two subdirectories for every man page "section" (use the command **man man** for details). For example, **/usr/man/man1** contains the source (that is, the unformatted original) for man pages in section 1, and **/usr/man/cat1** contains the formatted man pages for section 1.

/usr/src   **/usr/src** contains the source code (the uncompiled program) for various programs on your system. The most important thing here is **/usr/src/linux**, which contains the source code for the Linux kernel.

/var   **/var** holds directories that often change in size or tend to grow. Many of those directories used to reside in **/usr**, but since we are trying to keep it relatively unchangeable, the directories that change often have been moved to **/var**. Some of those directories are:

/var/adm   **/var/adm** contains various files of interest to the system administrator, specifically system logs, which record any errors or problems with the system. Other files record logins to the system, as well as failed login attempts. This will be covered in Chapter 4.

/var/spool   **/var/spool** contains files which are to be "spooled" to another program. For example, if your machine is connected to a network, incoming mail will be stored in **/var/spool/mail**, until you read it or delete it. Outgoing or incoming news articles may be found in **/var/spool/news**, and so on.

3.6   Types of shells

As I have mentioned too many times before, UNIX is a multitasking, multiuser operating system. Multitasking is *very* useful, and once you get used to it, you'll use it all of the time. Before long, you'll be able to run programs in the "background", switch between multiple tasks, and "pipeline" programs together to achieve complicated results with a single command.

Many of the features we'll be covering in this section are features provided by the shell itself. Be careful not to confuse UNIX (the actual operating system) with the shell—the shell is just an interface to the underlying system. The shell provides a great deal of functionality on top of UNIX itself.

The shell is not only an interpreter for your interactive commands, which you type at the prompt. It is also a powerful programming language, which allows you to write **shell scripts**, to "batch" several shell commands together in a file. MS-DOS users will recognize the similarity to "batch files". Use of shell scripts is a very powerful tool, which will allow you to automate and expand your usage of UNIX. See Section 3.13.1 for more information.

There are several types of shells in the UNIX world. The two major types are the "Bourne shell" and the "C shell". The Bourne shell uses a command syntax like the original shell on early UNIX systems, such as System III. The name of the Bourne shell on most UNIX systems is **/bin/sh** (where **sh** stands for "shell"). The C shell (not to be confused with sea shell) uses a different syntax, somewhat like the programming language C, and on most UNIX systems is named **/bin/csh**.

Under Linux, there are several variations of these shells available. The two most commonly used are the Bourne Again Shell, or "Bash" (**/bin/bash**), and Tcsh (**/bin/tcsh**). Bash is a form of the Bourne shell with many of the advanced features found in the C shell. Because Bash supports a superset of the Bourne shell syntax, any shell scripts written in the standard Bourne shell should work with Bash. For those who prefer to use the C shell syntax, Linux supports Tcsh, which is an expanded version of the original C shell.

The type of shell that you decide to use is mostly a religious issue. Some folks prefer the Bourne shell syntax with the advanced features of Bash, and some prefer the more structured C shell syntax. As far as normal commands, such as **cp** and **ls**, are concerned, the type of shell you're using doesn't matter—the syntax is the same. Only when you start to write shell scripts or use some of the advanced features of the shell do the differences between shell types begin to matter.

As we're discussing some of the features of the shell, below, we'll note those differences between Bourne and C shells. However, for the purposes of this manual, most of those differences are minimal. (If you're really curious at this point, read the man pages for **bash** and **tcsh**).

3.7 Wildcards

A key feature of most Unix shells is the ability to reference more than one filename using special characters. These so-called **wildcards** allow you to refer to, say, all filenames which contain the character "n".

The wildcard "*" refers to any character or string of characters in a filename. For example, when you use the character "*" in a filename, the shell replaces it with all possible substitutions from filenames in the directory which you're referencing.

Here's a quick example. Let's suppose that Larry has the files **frog**, **joe**, and **stuff** in his current directory.

```
/home/larry# ls
frog      joe       stuff
/home/larry#
```

To access all files with the letter "o" in the filename, we can use the command

```
/home/larry# ls *o*
frog      joe
/home/larry#
```

As you can see, the use of the "*" wildcard was replaced with all substitutions which matched the wildcard from filenames in the current directory.

The use of "*" by itself simply matches all filenames, because all characters match the wildcard.

```
/home/larry# ls *
frog      joe       stuff
/home/larry#
```

Here are a few more examples.

```
/home/larry# ls f*
frog
/home/larry# ls *ff
stuff
/home/larry# ls *f*
frog      stuff
/home/larry# ls s*f
stuff
/home/larry#
```

The process of changing a "*" into filenames is called **wildcard expansion** and is done by the shell. This is important: the individual commands, such as ls, *never* see the "*" in their list of parameters. The shell expands the wildcard to include all of the filenames which match. So, the command

```
/home/larry# ls *o*
```

is expanded by the shell to actually be

```
/home/larry# ls frog joe
```

One important note about the "*" wildcard. Using this wildcard will *not* match filenames which begin with a single period ("."). These files are treated as "hidden" files—while they are not really hidden, they don't show up on normal ls listings, and aren't touched by the use of the "*" wildcard.

Here's an example. We already mentioned that each directory has two special entries in it: "." refers to the current directory, and ".." refers to the parent directory. However, when you use ls, these two entries don't show up.

```
/home/larry# ls
frog      joe      stuff
/home/larry#
```

If you use the -a switch with ls, however, you can display filenames which begin with ".". Observe:

```
/home/larry# ls -a
.      ..      .bash_profile    .bashrc    frog     joe     stuff
/home/larry#
```

Now we can see the two special entries, "." and "..", as well as two other "hidden" files— .bash_profile and .bashrc. These two files are startup files used by **bash** when larry logs in. More on them in Section 3.13.3.

Note that when we use the "*" wildcard, none of the filenames beginning with "." are displayed.

```
/home/larry# ls *
frog      joe       stuff
/home/larry#
```

This is a safety feature: if the "*" wildcard matched filenames beginning with ".", it would also match the directory names "." and "..". This can be dangerous when using certain commands.

Another wildcard is "?". The "?" wildcard will only expand a single character. Thus, "ls ?" will display all one character filenames, and "ls termca?" would display "termcap" but *not* "termcap.backup". Here's another example:

```
/home/larry# ls j?e
joe
/home/larry# ls f??g
frog
/home/larry# ls ????f
stuff
/home/larry#
```

As you can see, wildcards allow you to specify many files at one time. In the simple command summary, in Section 3.4, we said that the cp and mv commands actually can copy or move multiple files at one time. For example,

```
/home/larry# cp /etc/s* /home/larry
```

will copy all filenames in **/etc** beginning with "s" to the directory **/home/larry**. Therefore, the format of the cp command is really

cp ⟨file1⟩ ⟨file2⟩ ⟨file3⟩ ... ⟨fileN⟩ ⟨destination⟩

where ⟨file1⟩ through ⟨fileN⟩ is a list of filenames to copy, and ⟨destination⟩ is the destination file or directory to copy them to. mv has an identical syntax.

Note that if you are copying or moving more than one file, the ⟨destination⟩ must be a directory. You can only copy or move a *single* file to another file.

3.8   UNIX Plumbing

3.8.1   Standard input and output

Many UNIX commands get input from what is known as **standard input** and send their output to **standard output** (often abbreviated as "stdin" and "stdout"). Your shell sets things up so that standard input is your keyboard, and standard output is the screen.

Here's an example using the command **cat**. Normally, **cat** reads data from all of the filenames given on the command line and sends this data directly to stdout. Therefore, using the command

>   /home/larry/papers# *cat history-final masters-thesis*

will display the contents of the file **history-final** followed by **masters-thesis**.

However, if no filenames are given to **cat** as parameters, it instead reads data from stdin, and sends it back to stdout. Here's an example.

>   /home/larry/papers# *cat*
>   *Hello there.*
>   Hello there.
>   *Bye.*
>   Bye.
>   ctrl-D
>   /home/larry/papers#

As you can see, each line that the user types (displayed in italics) is immediately echoed back by the **cat** command. When reading from standard input, commands know that the input is "finished" when they receive an EOT (end-of-text) signal. In general, this is generated by pressing ctrl-D.

Here's another example. The command **sort** reads in lines of text (again, from stdin, unless files are given on the command line), and sends the sorted output to stdout. Try the following.

>   /home/larry/papers# *sort*
>   *bananas*
>   *carrots*
>   *apples*
>   ctrl-D
>   apples
>   bananas
>   carrots
>   /home/larry/papers#

Now we can alphabetize our shopping list... isn't UNIX useful?

3.8.2 Redirecting input and output

Now, let's say that we wanted to send the output of **sort** to a file, to save our shopping list elsewhere. The shell allows us to **redirect** standard output to a filename, using the ">" symbol. Here's how it works.

```
/home/larry/papers# sort > shopping-list
bananas
carrots
apples
ctrl-D
/home/larry/papers#
```

As you can see, the result of the **sort** command isn't displayed, instead it's saved to the file **shopping-list**. Let's look at this file.

```
/home/larry/papers# cat shopping-list
apples
bananas
carrots
/home/larry/papers#
```

Now we can sort our shopping list, and save it, too! But let's suppose that we were storing our unsorted, original shopping list in the file **items**. One way of sorting the information and saving it to a file would be to give **sort** the name of the file to read, in lieu of standard input, and redirect standard output as we did above. As so:

```
/home/larry/papers# sort items > shopping-list
/home/larry/papers# cat shopping-list
apples
bananas
carrots
/home/larry/papers#
```

However, there's another way of doing this. Not only can we redirect standard output, but we can redirect standard *input* as well, using the "<" symbol.

```
/home/larry/papers# sort < items
apples
bananas
carrots
/home/larry/papers#
```

Technically, **sort < items** is equivalent to **sort items**, but the former allows us to demonstrate the point: **sort < items** behaves as if the data in the file **items** was typed to standard input. The shell handles the redirection. **sort** wasn't given the name of the file (**items**) to read; as far as **sort** is concerned, it was still reading from standard input as if you had typed the data from your keyboard.

This introduces the concept of a **filter**. A filter is a program which reads data from standard input, processes it in some way, and sends the processed data to standard output. Using redirection, standard input and/or standard output can be referenced from files. **sort** is a simple filter: it sorts the incoming data and sends the result to standard output. **cat** is even simpler: it doesn't do anything with the incoming data, it simply outputs whatever was given to it.

3.8.3 Using pipes

We've already demonstrated how to use **sort** as a filter. However, these examples assumed that you had data in a file somewhere, or were willing to type the data to standard input yourself. What if the data you wanted to sort came from the output of another command, such as **ls**? For example, using the **-r** option with **sort** sorts the data in reverse-alphabetical order. If you wanted to list the files in your current directory in reverse order, one way to do it would be:

```
/home/larry/papers# ls
english-list
history-final
masters-thesis
notes
/home/larry/papers# ls > file-list
/home/larry/papers# sort -r file-list
notes
masters-thesis
history-final
english-list
/home/larry/papers#
```

Here, we saved the output of **ls** in a file, and then ran **sort -r** on that file. But this is unwieldy and causes us to use a temporary file to save the data from **ls**.

The solution is to use **pipelining**. Pipelining is another feature of the shell which allows you to connect a string of commands in a "pipe", where the stdout of the first command is sent directly to the stdin of the second command, and so on. Here, we wish to send the stdout of **ls** to the stdin of **sort**. The "|" symbol is used to create a pipe:

```
/home/larry/papers# ls | sort -r
notes
```

```
masters-thesis
history-final
english-list
/home/larry/papers#
```

This command is much shorter, and obviously easier to type.

Another useful example—using the command

/home/larry/papers# *ls /usr/bin*

is going to display a long list a files, most of which will fly past the screen too quickly for you to read them. Instead, let's use **more** to display the list of files in **/usr/bin**.

/home/larry/papers# *ls /usr/bin | more*

Now you can page down the list of files at your own leisure.

But the fun doesn't stop here! We can pipe more than two commands together. The command **head** is a filter which displays the first lines from an input stream (here, input from a pipe). If we wanted to display the last filename in alphabetical order in the current directory, we can use:

```
/home/larry/papers# ls | sort -r | head -1
notes
/home/larry/papers#
```

where **head** **-1** simply displays the first line of input that it receives (in this case, the stream of reverse-sorted data from **ls**).

3.8.4 Non-destructive redirection

Using ">" to redirect output to a file is destructive: in other words, the command

/home/larry/papers# *ls > file-list*

overwrites the contents of the file **file-list**. If, instead, you redirect with the symbol ">>", the output will be appended to the named file, instead of overwriting it.

/home/larry/papers# *ls >> file-list*

will append the output of the **ls** command to **file-list**.

Just keep in mind that redirection and using pipes are features provided by the shell— the shell provides this handy syntax using ">" and ">>" and "|". It has nothing to do with the commands themselves, but the shell.

3.9 File Permissions

3.9.1 Concepts of file permissions

Because there are multiple users on a UNIX system, in order to protect individual user's files from tampering by other users, UNIX provides a mechanism known as **file permissions**. This mechanism allows files and directories to be "owned" by a particular user. As an example, because Larry created the files in his home directory, Larry owns those files, and has access to them.

UNIX also allows files to be shared between users and groups of users. If Larry so desired, he could cut off access to his files, such that no other user could access them. However, on most systems the default is to allow other users to read your files, but not modify or delete them in any way.

As explained above, every file is owned by a particular user. However, files are also owned by a particular **group**, which is a system-defined group of users. Every user is placed into at least one group when that user is created. However, the system administrator may also grant the user access to more than one group.

Groups are usually defined by the type of users which access the machine. For example, on a university UNIX system, users may be placed into the groups **student**, **staff**, **faculty** or **guest**. There are also a few system-defined groups (such as **bin** and **admin**) which are used by the system itself to control access to resources—very rarely do actual users belong to these system groups.

Permissions fall into three main divisions: read, write, and execute. These permissions may be granted to three classes of users: the owner of the file, the group to which the file belongs, and to all users, regardless of group.

Read permission allows a user to read the contents of the file, or in the case of directories, to list the contents of the directory (using **ls**). Write permission allows the user to write to and modify the file. For directories, write permission allows the user to create new files or delete files within that directory. Finally, execute permission allows the user to run the file as a program or shell script (if the file happens to be a program or shell script, that is). For directories, having execute permission allows the user to **cd** into the directory in question.

3.9.2 Interpreting file permissions

Let's look at an example to demonstrate file permissions. Using the **ls** command with the **-l** option will display a "long" listing of the file, including file permissions.

```
/home/larry/foo# ls -l stuff

-rw-r--r--   1 larry     users        505 Mar 13 19:05 stuff
```

`/home/larry/foo#`

The first field printed in the listing represents the file permissions. The third field is the owner of the file (`larry`), and the fourth field is the group to which the file belongs (`users`). Obviously, the last field is the name of the file (`stuff`), and we'll cover the other fields later.

This file is owned by `larry`, and belongs to the group `users`. Let's look at the file permissions. The string `-rw-r--r--` lists, in order, the permissions granted to the file's owner, the file's group, and everybody else.

The first character of the permissions string ("`-`") represents the type of file. A "`-`" just means that this is a regular file (as opposed to a directory or device driver). The next three letters ("`rw-`") represent the permissions granted to the file's owner, `larry`. The "`r`" stands for "read" and the "`w`" stands for "write". Thus, `larry` has read and write permission to the file `stuff`.

As we mentioned, besides read and write permission, there is also "execute" permission—represented by an "`x`". However, there is a "`-`" here in place of the "`x`", so Larry doesn't have execute permission on this file. This is fine, the file `stuff` isn't a program of any kind. Of course, because Larry owns the file, he may grant himself execute permission for the file if he so desires. This will be covered shortly.

The next three characters, `r--`, represent the group's permissions on the file. The group which owns this file is `users`. Because only an "`r`" appears here, any user which belongs to the group `users` may read this file.

The last three characters, also `r--`, represent the permissions granted to every other user on the system (other than the owner of the file and those in the group `users`). Again, because only an "`r`" is present, other users may read the file, but not write to it or execute it.

Here are some other examples of group permissions.

`-rwxr-xr-x`   The owner of the file may read, write, and execute the file. Users in the file's group, and all other users, may read and execute the file.

`-rw-------`   The owner of the file may read and write the file. No other user can access the file.

`-rwxrwxrwx`   All users may read, write, and execute the file.

3.9.3 Dependencies

It is important to note that the permissions granted to a file also depend on the permissions of the directory in which the file is located. For example, even if a file is set to `-rwxrwxrwx`, other users cannot access the file unless they have read and execute access to the directory in which the file is located. For example, if Larry wanted to restrict access to all of his files, he could simply set the permissions on his home directory /home/larry to -rwx------. In this way, no other user has access to his directory, and all files and directories within it. Larry doesn't need to worry about the individual permissions on each of his files.

In other words, to access a file at all, you must have execute access to all directories along the file's pathname, and read (or execute) access to the file itself.

Usually, users on a UNIX system are very open with their files. The usual set of permissions given to files is -rw-r--r--, which will allow other users to read the file, but not change it in any way. The usual set of permissions given to directories is -rwxr-xr-x, which will allow other users to look through your directories, but not create or delete files within them.

However, many users wish to keep other users out of their files. Setting the permissions of a file to -rw------- will not allow any other user to access the file. Likewise, setting the permissions of a directory to -rwx------ will keep other users out of the directory in question.

3.9.4   Changing permissions

The command chmod is used to set the permissions on a file. Only the owner of a file may change the permissions on that file. The syntax of chmod is:

> chmod {a,u,g,o}{+,-}{r,w,x} ⟨filenames⟩

Briefly, you supply one or more of **all**, **user**, **group**, or **other**. Then you specify whether you are adding rights (**+**) or taking them away (**-**). Finally, you specify one or more of **read**, **write**, and **execute**. Some examples of legal commands are:

chmod a+r stuff
> Gives all users read access to the file.

chmod +r stuff
> Same as above—if none of **a**, **u**, **g**, or **o** is specified, **a** is assumed.

chmod og-x stuff
> Remove execute permission from users other than the owner.

chmod u+rwx stuff
> Allow the owner of the file to read, write, and execute the file.

chmod o-rwx stuff
> Remove read, write, and execute permission from users other than the owner and users in the file's group.

3.10 Managing file links

Links allow you to give a single file multiple names. Files are actually identified to the system by their **inode number**, which is just the unique filesystem identifier for the file[3]. A directory is actually a listing of inode numbers with their corresponding filenames. Each filename in a directory is a **link** to a particular inode.

3.10.1 Hard links

The `ln` command is used to create multiple links for one file. For example, let's say that you have the file `foo` in a directory. Using `ls -i`, we can look at the inode number for this file.

```
# ls -i foo
22192 foo
#
```

Here, the file `foo` has an inode number of 22192 in the filesystem. We can create another link to `foo`, named `bar`:

```
# ln foo bar
```

With `ls -i`, we see that the two files have the same inode.

```
# ls -i foo bar
22192 bar    22192 foo
#
```

Now, accessing either `foo` or `bar` will access the same file. If you make changes to `foo`, those changes will be made to `bar` as well. For all purposes, `foo` and `bar` are the same file.

These links are known as *hard links* because they directly create a link to an inode. Note that you can only hard-link files on the same filesystem; symbolic links (see below) don't have this restriction.

When you delete a file with **rm**, you are actually only deleting one link to a file. If you use the command

```
# rm foo
```

then only the link named `foo` is deleted; `bar` will still exist. A file is only actually deleted on the system when it has no links to it. Usually, files have only one link, so using the **rm**

---

[3] The command `ls -i` will display file inode numbers.

command deletes the file. However, if a file has multiple links to it, using **rm** will only delete a single link; in order to delete the file, you must delete all links to the file.

The command **ls -l** will display the number of links to a file (among other information).

```
# ls -l foo bar
-rw-r--r--   2 root      root            12 Aug  5 16:51 bar
-rw-r--r--   2 root      root            12 Aug  5 16:50 foo
#
```

The second column in the listing, "**2**", specifies the number of links to the file.

As it turns out, a directory is actually just a file containing information about link-to-inode translations. Also, every directory has at least two hard links in it: "**.**" (a link pointing to itself), and "**..**" (a link pointing to the parent directory). The root directory (**/**) "**..**" link just points back to **/**.

3.10.2 Symbolic links

Symbolic links are another type of link, which are somewhat different than hard links. A symbolic link allows you to give a file another name, but it doesn't link the file by inode.

The command **ln -s** will create a symbolic link to a file. For example, if we use the command

```
# ln -s foo bar
```

we will create the symbolic link **bar** pointing to the file **foo**. If we use **ls -i**, we will see that the two files have different inodes, indeed.

```
# ls -i foo bar
22195 bar    22192 foo
#
```

However, using **ls -l**, we see that the file **bar** is a symlink pointing to **foo**.

```
# ls -l foo bar
lrwxrwxrwx   1 root      root             3 Aug  5 16:51 bar -> foo
-rw-r--r--   1 root      root            12 Aug  5 16:50 foo
#
```

The permission bits on a symbolic link are not used (they always appear as **rwxrwxrwx**). Instead, the permissions on the symbolic link are determined by the permissions on the target of the symbolic link (in our example, the file **foo**).

Functionally, hard links and symbolic links are similar, but there are some differences. For one thing, you can create a symbolic link to a file which doesn't exist; the same is not true for hard links. Symbolic links are processed by the kernel differently than hard links are, which is just a technical difference but sometimes an important one. Symbolic links are helpful because they identify what file they point to; with hard links, there is no easy way to determine which files are linked to the same inode.

Links are used in many places on the Linux system. Symbolic links are especially important to the shared library images in **/lib**. See Section 4.7.2 for more information.

3.11 Job Control

3.11.1 Jobs and processes

Job control is a feature provided by many shells (Bash and Tcsh included) which allows you to control multiple running commands, or **jobs**, at once. Before we can delve much further, we need to talk about **processes**.

Every time you run a program, you start what is known as a *process*—which is just a fancy name for a running program. The command **ps** displays a list of currently running processes. Here's an example:

```
/home/larry# ps

    PID TT STAT   TIME COMMAND
     24  3 S      0:03 (bash)
    161  3 R      0:00 ps

/home/larry#
```

The **PID** listed in the first column is the **process ID**, a unique number given to every running process. The last column, **COMMAND**, is the name of the running command. Here, we're only looking at the processes which Larry is currently running[4]. These are **bash** (Larry's shell), and the **ps** command itself. As you can see, **bash** is running concurrently with the **ps** command. **bash** executed **ps** when Larry typed the command. After **ps** is finished running (after the table of processes is displayed), control is returned to the **bash** process, which displays the prompt, ready for another command.

A running process is known as a *job* to the shell. The terms *process* and *job* are interchangeable. However, a process is usually referred to as a "job" when used in conjunction with **job control**—a feature of the shell which allows you to switch between several independent jobs.

---

[4]There are many other processes running on the system as well—"ps -aux" lists them all.

In most cases users are only running a single job at a time—that being whatever command they last typed to the shell. However, using job control, you can run several jobs at once, switching between them as needed. How might this be useful? Let's say that you're editing a text file and need to suddenly interrupt your editing and do something else. With job control, you can temporarily suspend the editor, and back at the shell prompt start to work on something else. When you're done, you can start the editor back up, and be back where you started, as if you never left the editor. This is just one example. There are many practical uses for job control.

3.11.2 Foreground and background

Jobs can either be in the **foreground** or in the **background**. There can only be one job in the foreground at any one time. The foreground job is the job which you interact with—it receives input from the keyboard and sends output to your screen. (Unless, of course, you have redirected input or output, as described in Section 3.8). On the other hand, jobs in the background do not receive input from the terminal—in general, they run along quietly without need for interaction.

Some jobs take a long time to finish, and don't do anything interesting while they are running. Compiling programs is one such job, as is compressing a large file. There's no reason why you should sit around being bored while these jobs complete their tasks; you can just run them in the background. While the jobs are running in the background, you are free to run other programs.

Jobs may also be **suspended**. A suspended job is a job that is not currently running, but is temporarily stopped. After you suspend a job, you can tell the job to continue, in the foreground or the background as needed. Resuming a suspended job will not change the state of the job in any way—the job will continue to run where it left off.

Note that suspending a job is not equal to *interrupting* a job. When you interrupt a running process (by hitting your interrupt key, which is usually $\boxed{\text{ctrl-C}}$)[5], it kills the process, for good. Once the job is killed, there's no hope of resuming it; you'll have to re-run the command. Also note that some programs trap the interrupt, so that hitting $\boxed{\text{ctrl-C}}$ won't immediately kill the job. This is to allow the program to perform any necessary cleanup operations before exiting. In fact, some programs simply don't allow you to kill them with an interrupt at all.

3.11.3 Backgrounding and killing jobs

Let's begin with a simple example. The command **yes** is a seemingly useless command which sends an endless stream of **y**'s to standard output. (This is actually useful. If you

---

[5]The interrupt key can be set using the **stty** command. The default on most systems is $\boxed{\text{ctrl-C}}$, but we can't guarantee the same for your system.

piped the output of **yes** to another command which asked a series of yes and no questions, the stream of **y**'s would confirm all of the questions.)

Try it out.

```
/home/larry# yes
y
y
y
y
y
```

The **y**'s will continue *ad infinitum*. You can kill the process by hitting your interrupt key, which is usually `ctrl-C`. So that we don't have to put up with the annoying stream of **y**'s, let's redirect the standard output of **yes** to **/dev/null**. As you may remember, **/dev/null** acts as a "black hole" for data. Any data sent to it will disappear. This is a very effective method of quieting an otherwise verbose program.

```
/home/larry# yes > /dev/null
```

Ah, much better. Nothing is printed, but the shell prompt doesn't come back. This is because **yes** is still running, and is sending those inane **y**'s to **/dev/null**. Again, to kill the job, hit the interrupt key.

Let's suppose that we wanted the **yes** command to continue to run, but wanted to get our shell prompt back to work on other things. We can put **yes** into the background, which will allow it to run, but without need for interaction.

One way to put a process in the background is to append an "**&**" character to the end of the command.

```
/home/larry# yes > /dev/null &
[1] 164
/home/larry#
```

As you can see, we have our shell prompt back. But what is this "[1] 164"? And is the **yes** command really running?

The "[1]" represents the **job number** for the **yes** process. The shell assigns a job number to every running job. Because **yes** is the one and only job that we're currently running, it is assigned job number 1. The "164" is the process ID, or PID, number given by the system to the job. Either number may be used to refer to the job, as we'll see later.

You now have the **yes** process running in the background, continuously sending a stream of **y**'s to **/dev/null**. To check on the status of this process, use the shell internal command **jobs**.

```
/home/larry# jobs
[1]+  Running                     yes >/dev/null  &
/home/larry#
```

Sure enough, there it is. You could also use the **ps** command as demonstrated above to check on the status of the job.

To terminate the job, use the command **kill**. This command takes either a job number or a process ID number as an argument. This was job number 1, so using the command

```
/home/larry# kill %1
```

will kill the job. When identifying the job with the job number, you must prefix the number with a percent ("%") character.

Now that we've killed the job, we can use **jobs** again to check on it:

```
/home/larry# jobs

[1]+  Terminated                  yes >/dev/null

/home/larry#
```

The job is in fact dead, and if we use the **jobs** command again nothing should be printed.

You can also kill the job using the process ID (PID) number, which is printed along with the job ID when you start the job. In our example, the process ID is 164, so the command

```
/home/larry# kill 164
```

is equivalent to

```
/home/larry# kill %1
```

You don't need to use the "%" when referring to a job by its process ID.

3.11.4 Stopping and restarting jobs

There is another way to put a job into the background. You can start the job normally (in the foreground), **stop** the job, and then restart it in the background.

First, start the **yes** process in the foreground, as you normally would:

```
/home/larry# yes > /dev/null
```

Again, because **yes** is running in the foreground, you shouldn't get your shell prompt back.

Now, instead of interrupting the job with $\boxed{\texttt{ctrl-C}}$, we'll *suspend* the job. Suspending a job doesn't kill it: it only temporarily stops the job until you restart it. To do this, you hit the suspend key, which is usually $\boxed{\texttt{ctrl-Z}}$.

```
/home/larry# yes > /dev/null
ctrl-Z
[1]+  Stopped                  yes >/dev/null
/home/larry#
```

While the job is suspended, it's simply not running. No CPU time is used for the job. However, you can restart the job, which will cause the job to run again as if nothing ever happened. It will continue to run where it left off.

To restart the job in the foreground, use the command **fg** (for "foreground").

```
/home/larry# fg
yes >/dev/null
```

The shell prints the name of the command again so you're aware of which job you just put into the foreground. Stop the job again, with $\boxed{\texttt{ctrl-Z}}$. This time, use the command **bg** to put the job into the background. This will cause the command to run just as if you started the command with "**&**" as in the last section.

```
/home/larry# bg
[1]+ yes >/dev/null &
/home/larry#
```

And we have our prompt back. **jobs** should report that **yes** is indeed running, and we can kill the job with **kill** as we did before.

How can we stop the job again? Using $\boxed{\texttt{ctrl-Z}}$ won't work, because the job is in the background. The answer is to put the job in the foreground, with **fg**, and then stop it. As it turns out you can use **fg** on either stopped jobs or jobs in the background.

There is a big difference between a job in the background and a job which is stopped. A stopped job is not running—it's not using any CPU time, and it's not doing any work (the job still occupies system memory, although it may be swapped out to disk). A job in the background is running, and using memory, as well as completing some task while you do other work. However, a job in the background may try to display text on to your terminal, which can be annoying if you're trying to work on something else. For example, if you used the command

```
/home/larry# yes &
```

without redirecting stdout to **/dev/null**, a stream of **y**'s would be printed to your screen, without any way of interrupting it (you can't use ⎥ctrl-C⎥ to interrupt jobs in the background). In order to stop the endless **y**'s, you'd have to use the **fg** command, to bring the job to the foreground, and then use ⎥ctrl-C⎥ to kill it.

Another note. The **fg** and **bg** commands normally foreground or background the job which was last stopped (indicated by a "+" next to the job number when you use the command **jobs**). If you are running multiple jobs at once, you can foreground or background a specific job by giving the job ID as an argument to **fg** or **bg**, as in

/home/larry# *fg %2*

(to foreground job number 2), or

/home/larry# *bg %3*

(to background job number 3). You can't use process ID numbers with **fg** or **bg**.

Furthermore, using the job number alone, as in

/home/larry# *%2*

is equivalent to

/home/larry# *fg %2*

Just remember that using job control is a feature of the shell. The commands **fg**, **bg** and **jobs** are internal to the shell. If for some reason you use a shell which does not support job control, don't expect to find these commands available.

In addition, there are some aspects of job control which differ between Bash and Tcsh. In fact, some shells don't provide job control at all—however, most shells available for Linux support job control.

3.12   Using the vi Editor

A **text editor** is simply a program used to edit files which contain text, such as a letter, C program, or a system configuration file. While there are many such editors available for Linux, the only editor which you are guaranteed to find on any UNIX system is **vi**— the "visual editor". **vi** is not the easiest editor to use, nor is it very self-explanatory. However, because it is so common in the UNIX world, and at times you may be required to use it, it deserves some documentation here.

Your choice of an editor is mostly a question of personal taste and style. Many users prefer the baroque, self-explanatory and powerful **Emacs**—an editor with more features than any other single program in the UNIX world. For example, Emacs has its own built-in dialect of the LISP programming language, and has many extensions (one of which is an "Eliza"-like AI program). However, because Emacs and all of its support files are relatively large, you may not have access to it on many systems. vi, on the other hand, is small and powerful, but more difficult to use. However, once you know your way around vi, it's actually very easy. It's just the learning curve which is sometimes difficult to cross.

This section is a coherent introduction to vi—we won't discuss all of its features, just the ones you need to know to get you started. You can refer to the man page for vi if you're interested in learning about more of this editor's features. Or, you can read the book *Learning the vi Editor* from O'Reilly and Associates. See Appendix A for information.

3.12.1 Concepts

While using vi, at any one time you are in one of three modes of operation. These modes are known as *command mode, insert mode,* and *last line mode.*

When you start up vi, you are in *command mode.* This mode allows you to use certain commands to edit files or to change to other modes. For example, typing "x" while in command mode deletes the character underneath the cursor. The arrow keys move the cursor around the file which you're editing. Generally, the commands used in command mode are one or two characters long.

You actually insert or edit text within *insert mode.* When using vi, you'll probably spend most of your time within this mode. You start insert mode by using a command such as "i" (for "insert") from command mode. While in insert mode, you are inserting text into the document from your current cursor location. To end insert mode and return to command mode, press ⌈esc⌋.

Last line mode is a special mode used to give certain extended commands to vi. While typing these commands, they appear on the last line of the screen (hence the name). For example, when you type ":" from command mode, you jump into last line mode, and can use commands such as "wq" (to write the file and quit vi), or "q!" (to quit vi without saving changes). Last line mode is generally used for vi commands which are longer than one character. In last line mode, you enter a single-line command and press ⌈enter⌋ to execute it.

3.12.2 Starting vi

The best way to understand these concepts is to actually fire up vi and edit a file. In the example "screens" below, we're only going to show a few lines of text, as if the screen was only six lines high (instead of twenty-four).

The syntax for vi is

        `vi` ⟨*filename*⟩

where ⟨*filename*⟩ is the name of the file that you wish to edit.

    Start up **vi** by typing

        `/home/larry#` *vi test*

which will edit the file **test**. You should see something like

```
~
~
~
~
~
~
"test" [New file]
```

The column of "~" characters indicates that you are the end of the file.

3.12.3 Inserting text

You are now in command mode; in order to insert text into the file, press $\boxed{\texttt{i}}$ (which will place you into insert mode), and begin typing.

```
Now is the time for all good men to come to the aid of the party.
~
~
~
~
```

    While inserting text, you may type as many lines as you wish (pressing $\boxed{\texttt{return}}$ after each, of course), and you may correct mistakes using the backspace key.

    To end insert mode, and return to command mode, press $\boxed{\texttt{esc}}$.

    While in command mode, you can use the arrow keys to move around the file. Here, because we only have one line of text, trying to use the up- or down-arrow keys will probably cause **vi** to beep at you.

    There are several ways to insert text, other than using the i command. For example, the **a** command inserts text beginning *after* the current cursor position, instead of on the current cursor position. For example, use the left arrow key to move the cursor between the words "good" and "men".

```
Now is the time for all good_men to come to the aid of the party.
~
~
~
~
~
```

Press a , to start insert mode, type "**wo**", and then hit esc to return to command mode.

```
Now is the time for all good women to come to the aid of the party.
~
~
~
~
~
```

To begin inserting text at the line below the current one, use the o command. For example, press o and type another line or two:

```
Now is the time for all good women to come to the aid of the party.
Afterwards, we'll go out for pizza and beer.
~
~
~
~
```

Just remember that at any time you're either in command mode (where commands such as i, a, or o are valid), or in insert mode (where you're inserting text, followed by esc to return to command mode), or last line mode (where you're entering extended commands, as discussed below).

3.12.4 Deleting text

From command mode, the x command deletes the character under the cursor. If you press x five times, you'll end up with:

```
Now is the time for all good women to come to the aid of the party.
Afterwards, we'll go out for pizza and_
~
~
~
~
```

Now press a , insert some text, followed by esc :

```
Now is the time for all good women to come to the aid of the party.
Afterwards, we'll go out for pizza and Diet Coke_.
~
~
~
~
```

You can delete entire lines using the command **dd** (that is, press d twice in a row). If your cursor is on the second line, and you type **dd**,

```
Now is the time for all good women to come to the aid of the party.
~
~
~
~
~
```

To delete the word which the cursor is on, use the **dw** command. Place the cursor on the word "good", and type **dw**.

```
Now is the time for all women to come to the aid of the party.
~
~
~
~
~
```

3.12.5   Changing text

You can replace sections of text using the **R** command. Place the cursor on the first letter in "party", press R, and type the word "hungry".

```
Now is the time for all women to come to the aid of the hungry_.
~
~
~
~
~
```

Using **R** to edit text is much like the **i** and **a** commands, but **R** overwrites text, instead of inserting it.

The **r** command replaces the single character under the cursor. For example, move the cursor to the beginning of the word "Now", and type **r** followed by **C**, you'll have:

```
Cow is the time for all women to come to the aid of the hungry.
~
~
~
~
```

The "~" command changes the case of the letter under the cursor from upper- to lower-case, and vise versa, For example, if you place the cursor on the "o" in "Cow", above, and repeatedly press ⌐~⌐, you'll end up with:

```
COW IS THE TIME FOR ALL WOMEN TO COME TO THE AID OF THE HUNGRY.
~
~
~
~
~
```

3.12.6 Moving commands

You already know how to use the arrow keys to move around the document. In addition, you can use the h, j, k, and l commands to move the cursor left, down, up, and right, respectively. This comes in handy when (for some reason) your arrow keys aren't working correctly.

The w command moves the cursor to the beginning of the next word; the b moves it to the beginning of the previous word.

The 0 (that's a zero) command moves the cursor to the beginning of the current line, and the $ command moves it to the end of the line.

When editing large files, you'll want to move forwards or backwards through the file a screenful at a time. Pressing ctrl-F moves the cursor one screenful forward, and ctrl-B moves it a screenful back.

In order to move the cursor to the end of the file, type G. You can also move to an arbitrary line; for example, typing the command 10G would move the cursor to line 10 in the file. To move to the beginning of the file, use 1G.

You can couple moving commands with other commands, such as deletion. For example, the command d$ will delete everything from the cursor to the end of the line; dG will delete everything from the cursor to the end of the file, and so on.

3.12.7   Saving files and quitting `vi`

To quit `vi` without making changes to the file, use the command `:q!`. When you type the
":", the cursor will move to the last line on the screen; you'll be in last line mode.

```
COW IS THE TIME FOR ALL WOMEN TO COME TO THE AID OF THE HUNGRY.
~
~
~
~
~
:_
```

In last line mode, certain extended commands are available. One of them is `q!`, which quits
`vi` without saving. The command `:wq` saves the file and then exits `vi`. The command `ZZ`
(from command mode, without the ":") is equivalent to `:wq`. Remember that you must
press enter after a command entered in last line mode.

   To save the file without quitting vi, just use `:w`.

3.12.8   Editing another file

To edit another file, use the `:e` command. For example, to stop editing **test**, and edit the
file **foo** instead, use the command

```
COW IS THE TIME FOR ALL WOMEN TO COME TO THE AID OF THE HUNGRY.
~
~
~
~
~
:e foo_
```

If you use `:e` without saving the file first, you'll get the error message

```
No write since last change (":edit!" overrides)
```

which simply means that `vi` doesn't want to edit another file until you save the first one.
At this point, you can use `:w` to save the original file, and then use `:e`, or you can use the
command

```
┌─────────────────────────────────────────────────────────────────────┐
│ COW IS THE TIME FOR ALL WOMEN TO COME TO THE AID OF THE HUNGRY.       │
│ ~                                                                     │
│ ~                                                                     │
│ ~                                                                     │
│ ~                                                                     │
│ ~                                                                     │
│ :e!  foo_                                                             │
└─────────────────────────────────────────────────────────────────────┘
```

The "!" tells **vi** that you really mean it—edit the new file without saving changes to the first.

3.12.9 Including other files

If you use the `:r` command, you can include the contents of another file in the current file. For example, the command

```
:r foo.txt
```

would insert the contents of the file **foo.txt** in the text at the current cursor location.

3.12.10 Running shell commands

You can also run shell commands from within **vi**. The `:r!` command works like `:r`, but instead of reading a file, it inserts the output of the given command into the buffer at the current cursor location. For example, if you use the command

```
:r! ls -F
```

you'll end up with

```
┌─────────────────────────────────────────────────────────────────────┐
│ COW IS THE TIME FOR ALL WOMEN TO COME TO THE AID OF THE HUNGRY.       │
│ letters/                                                              │
│ misc/                                                                 │
│ papers/                                                               │
│ ~                                                                     │
│ ~                                                                     │
└─────────────────────────────────────────────────────────────────────┘
```

You can also "shell out" of **vi**, in other words, run a command from within **vi**, and return to the editor when you're done. For example, if you use the command

```
:! ls -F
```

the **ls -F** command will be executed, and the results displayed on the screen, but not inserted into the file which you're editing. If you use the command

```
:shell
```

vi will start an instance of the shell, allowing you to temporarily put vi "on hold" while you execute other commands. Just logout of the shell (using the **exit** command) to return to vi.

3.12.11 Getting help

vi doesn't provide much in the way of interactive help (most UNIX programs don't), but you can always read the man page for vi. vi is a visual front-end to the **ex** editor; it is **ex** which handles many of the last-line mode commands in vi. So, in addition to reading the man page for vi, see **ex** as well.

3.13 Customizing your Environment

The shell provides many mechanisms to customize your work environment. As we've mentioned before, the shell is more than a command interpreter—it is also a powerful programming language. While writing shell scripts is an extensive subject, we'd like to introduce you to some of the ways that you can simplify your work on a UNIX system by using these advanced features of the shell.

As we have mentioned before, different shells use different syntaxes when executing shell scripts. For example, Tcsh uses a C-like syntax, while Bourne shells use another type of syntax. In this section, we won't be running into many of the differences between the two, but we will assume that shell scripts are executed using the Bourne shell syntax.

3.13.1 Shell scripts

Let's say that you use a series of commands often, and would like to shorten the amount of required typing by grouping all of them together into a single "command". For example, the commands

```
/home/larry# cat chapter1 chapter2 chapter3 > book
/home/larry# wc -l book
/home/larry# lp book
```

would concatenate the files **chapter1**, **chapter2**, and **chapter3** and place the result in the file **book**. Then, a count of the number of lines in **book** would be displayed, and finally **book** would be printed with the **lp** command.

Instead of typing all of these commands, you could group them into a **shell script**. We described shell scripts briefly in Section 3.13.1. The shell script used to run all of these commands would look like

```
#!/bin/sh
# A shell script to create and print the book

cat chapter1 chapter2 chapter3 > book
wc -l book
lp book
```

If this script was saved in the file **makebook**, you could simply use the command

/home/larry# *makebook*

to run all of the commands in the script. Shell scripts are just plain text files; you can create them with an editor such as **emacs** or **vi** [6].

Let's look at this shell script. The first line, "`#!/bin/sh`", identifies the file as a shell script, and tells the shell how to execute the script. It instructs the shell to pass the script to **/bin/sh** for execution, where **/bin/sh** is the shell program itself. Why is this important? On most UNIX systems, **/bin/sh** is a Bourne-type shell, such as Bash. By forcing the shell script to run using **/bin/sh**, we are ensuring that the script will run under a Bourne-syntax shell (instead of, say, a C shell). This will cause your script to run using the Bourne syntax even if you use Tcsh (or another C shell) as your login shell.

The second line is a *comment*. Comments begin with the character "#" and continue to the end of the line. Comments are ignored by the shell—they are commonly used to identify the shell script to the programmer.

The rest of the lines in the script are just commands, as you would type them to the shell directly. In effect, the shell reads each line of the script and runs that line as if you had typed it at the shell prompt.

Permissions are important for shell scripts. If you create a shell script, you must make sure that you have execute permission on the script in order to run it[7]. The command

/home/larry# *chmod u+x makebook*

can be used to give yourself execute permission on the shell script **makebook**.

3.13.2 Shell variables and the environment

The shell allows you to define **variables**, as most programming languages do. A variable is just a piece of data which is given the name.

◇   Note that Tcsh, as well as other C-type shells, use a different mechanism for setting variables than is described here. This discussion assumes the use of a Bourne shell, such as Bash (which you're probably using). See the Tcsh man page for details.

---

[6] **vi** is covered in Section 3.12.
[7] When you create text files, the default permissions usually don't include execute permission.

When you assign a value to a variable (using the "=" operator), you can access the variable by prepending a "**$**" to the variable name, as demonstrated below.

```
/home/larry# foo="hello there"
```

The variable **foo** is given the value "**hello there**". You can now refer to this value by the variable name, prefixed with a "**$**" character. The command

```
/home/larry# echo $foo
hello there
/home/larry#
```

produces the same results as

```
/home/larry# echo "hello there"
hello there
/home/larry#
```

These variables are internal to the shell. This means that only the shell can access these variables. This can be useful in shell scripts; if you need to keep track of a filename, for example, you can store it in a variable, as above. Using the command **set** will display a list of all defined shell variables.

However, the shell allows you to **export** variables to the **environment**. The environment is the set of variables which all commands that you execute have access to. Once you define a variable inside the shell, exporting it makes that variable part of the environment as well. The **export** command is used to export a variable to the environment.

◇   Again, here we differ between Bash and Tcsh. If you're using Tcsh, another syntax is used for setting environment variables (the **setenv** command is used). See the Tcsh man page for more information.

The environment is very important to the UNIX system. It allows you to configure certain commands just by setting variables which the commands know about.

Here's a quick example. The environment variable **PAGER** is used by the **man** command. It specifies the command to use to display man pages one screenful at a time. If you set **PAGER** to be the name of a command, it will use that command to display the man pages, instead of **more** (which is the default).

Set **PAGER** to "cat". This will cause output from **man** to be displayed to the screen all at once, without breaking it up into pages.

```
/home/larry# PAGER="cat"
```

Now, export **PAGER** to the environment.

/home/larry# *export PAGER*

Try the command **man ls**. The man page should fly past your screen without pausing for you.

Now, if we set **PAGER** to "**more**", the **more** command will be used to display the man page.

/home/larry# *PAGER="more"*

Note that we don't have to use the **export** command after we change the value of **PAGER**. We only need to export a variable once; any changes made to it thereafter will automatically be propagated to the environment.

The man pages for a particular command will tell you if the command uses any environment variables; for example, the **man** man page explains that **PAGER** is used to specify the pager command. Some commands share environment variables; for example, many commands use the **EDITOR** environment variable to specify the default editor to use when one is needed.

The environment is also used to keep track of important information about your login session. An example is the **HOME** environment variable, which contains the name of your home directory.

/home/larry/papers# *echo $HOME*
/home/larry

Another interesting environment variable is **PS1**, which defines the main shell prompt. For example,

/home/larry# *PS1="Your command, please: "*
Your command, please:

To set the prompt back to our usual (which contains the current working directory followed by a "#" symbol),

Your command, please: *PS1="\w# "*
/home/larry#

The **bash** man page describes the syntax used for setting the prompt.

3.13.2.1   The PATH environment variable

When you use the **ls** command, how does the shell find the **ls** executable itself? In fact, **ls** is found in /bin/ls on most systems. The shell uses the environment variable **PATH** to locate executable files for commands which you type.

For example, your **PATH** variable may be set to:

```
/bin:/usr/bin:/usr/local/bin:.
```

This is a list of directories for the shell to search, each directory separated by a ":". When you use the command **ls**, the shell first looks for **/bin/ls**, then **/usr/bin/ls**, and so on.

Note that the **PATH** has nothing to do with finding regular files. For example, if you use the command

```
/home/larry#  cp foo bar
```

The shell does not use **PATH** to locate the files **foo** and **bar**—those filenames are assumed to be complete. The shell only uses **PATH** to locate the **cp** executable.

This saves you a lot of time; it means that you don't have to remember where all of the command executables are stored. On many systems, executables are scattered about in many places, such as **/usr/bin**, **/bin**, or **/usr/local/bin**. Instead of giving the command's full pathname (such as **/usr/bin/cp**), you can simply set **PATH** to the list of directories that you want the shell to automatically search.

Notice that **PATH** contains ".", which is the current working directory. This allows you to create a shell script or program and run it as a command from your current directory, without having to specify it directly (as in **./makebook**). If a directory isn't on your **PATH**, then the shell will not search it for commands to run—this includes the current directory.

3.13.3   Shell initialization scripts

In addition to shell scripts that you create, there are a number of scripts that the shell itself uses for certain purposes. The most important of these are your **initialization scripts**, scripts automatically executed by the shell when you login.

The initialization scripts themselves are simply shell scripts, as described above. However, they are very useful in setting up your environment by executing commands automatically when you login. For example, if you always use the **mail** command to check your mail when you login, you place the command in your initialization script so it will be executed automatically.

Both Bash and Tcsh distinguish between a **login shell** and other invocations of the shell. A login shell is a shell invoked at login time; usually, it's the only shell which you'll use. However, if you "shell out" of another program, such as **vi**, you start another instance of the shell, which isn't your login shell. In addition, whenever you run a shell script, you automatically start another instance of the shell to execute the script.

The initialization files used by Bash are: **/etc/profile** (set up by the system administrator, executed by all Bash users at login time), **$HOME/.bash_profile** (executed by a login Bash session), and `$HOME/.bashrc` (executed by all non-login instances of Bash). If `.bash_profile` is not present, `.profile` is used instead.

Tcsh uses the following initialization scripts: `/etc/csh.login` (executed by all Tcsh users at login time), `$HOME/.tcshrc` (executed a login time and by all new instances of Tcsh), and `$HOME/.login` (executed at login time, following `.tcshrc`). If `.tcshrc` is not present, `.cshrc` is used instead.

To fully understand the function of these files, you'll need to learn more about the shell itself. Shell programming is a complicated subject, far beyond the scope of this book. See the man pages for `bash` and/or `tcsh` to learn more about customizing your shell environment.

3.14 So You Want to Strike Out on Your Own?

Hopefully we have provided enough information to give you a basic idea of how to use the system. Keep in mind that most of the interesting and important aspects of Linux aren't covered here—these are the very basics. With this foundation, before long you'll be up and running complicated applications and fulfilling the potential of your system. If things don't seem exciting at first, don't despair—there is much to be learned.

One indispensable tool for learning about the system is to read the man pages. While many of the man pages may appear confusing at first, if you dig beneath the surface there is a wealth of information contained therein.

We also suggest reading a complete book on using a UNIX system. There is much more to UNIX than meets the eye—unfortunately, most of it is beyond the scope of this book. Some good UNIX books to look at are listed in Appendix A.

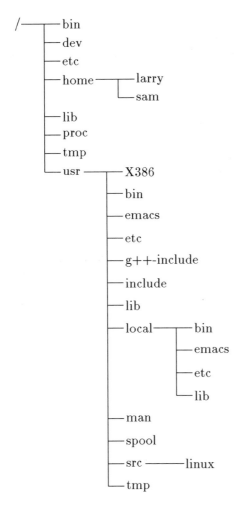

Figure 3.1: A typical (abridged) Unix directory tree.

Chapter 4

System Administration

This chapter is an overview to Linux system administration, including a number of advanced features which aren't necessarily for system administrators only. Just as every dog has its day, every system has its administrator, and running the system is a very important and sometimes time-consuming job, even if you're the only user on your system.

We have tried to cover here the most important things about system administration you need to know when you use Linux, in sufficient detail to get you comfortably started. In order to keep it short and sweet, we have only covered the very basics, and have skipped many an important detail. You should read the *Linux System Administrator's Guide* if you are serious about running Linux. It will help you understand better how things work, and how they hang together. At least skim through it so that you know what it contains and know what kind of help you can expect from it.

4.1 About Root, Hats, and the Feeling of Power

As you know, UNIX differentiates between different users, so that what they do to each other and to the system can be regulated (one wouldn't want anybody to be able to read one's love letters, for instance). Each user is given an **account**, which includes a username, home directory, and so on. In addition to accounts given to real people, there are special system-defined accounts which have special privileges. The most important of these is the **root account**, for the username **root**.

4.1.1 The root account

Ordinary users are generally restricted so that they can't do harm to anybody else on the system, just to themselves. File permissions on the system are arranged such that normal

135

users aren't allowed to delete or modify files in directories shared by all users (such as /bin and /usr/bin. Most users also protect their own files with the appropriate file permissions so that other users can't access or modify those files.

There are no such restrictions on root. The user root can read, modify, or delete any file on the system, change permissions and ownerships on any file, and run special programs, such as those which partition the drive or create filesystems. The basic idea is that the person or persons who run and take care of the system logs in as root whenever it is necessary to perform tasks that cannot be executed as a normal user. Because root can do anything, it is easy to make mistakes that have catastrophic consequences when logged in using this account.

For example, as a normal user, if you inadvertently attempt to delete all of the files in /etc, the system will not permit you to do so. However, when logged in as root, the system won't complain at all. It is very easy to trash your system when using root. The best way to prevent accidents is to:

- Sit on your hands before you press ⌸return⌸ on a command which may cause damage. For example, if you're about to clean out a directory, before hitting ⌸return⌸, re-read the entire command and make sure that it is correct.

- Don't get accustomed to using root. The more comfortable you are in the role of the root user, the more likely you are to confuse your privileges with those of a normal user. For example, you might *think* that you're logged in as larry, when you're really logged in as root.

- Use a different prompt for the root account. You should change root's .bashrc or .login file to set the shell prompt to something other than your regular user prompt. For example, many people use the character "$" in prompts for regular users, and reserve the character "#" for the root user prompt.

- Only login as root when absolutely necessary. And, as soon as you're finished with your work as root, log out. The less you use the root account, the less likely you'll be to do damage on your system.

Of course, there is a breed of UNIX hackers out there who use root for virtually everything. But every one of them has, at some point, made a silly mistake as root and trashed the system. The general rule is, until you're familiar with the lack of restrictions on root, and are comfortable using the system without such restrictions, login as root sparingly.

Of course, everyone makes mistakes. Linus Torvalds himself once accidentally deleted the entire kernel directory tree on his system. Hours of work were lost forever. Fortunately, however, because of his knowledge of the filesystem code, he was able to reboot the system and reconstruct the directory tree by hand on disk.

Put another way, if you picture using the root account as wearing a special magic hat that gives you lots of power, so that you can, by waving your hand, destroy entire cities, it is a good idea to be a bit careful about what you do with your hands. Since it is easy to move your hand in a destructive way by accident, it is not a good idea to wear the magic hat when it is not needed, despite the wonderful feeling.

4.1.2   Abusing the system

Along with the feeling of power comes the tendency to do harm. This is one of the grey areas of UNIX system administration, but everyone goes through it at some point in time. Most users of UNIX systems never have the ability to wield this power—on university and business UNIX systems, only the highly-paid and highly-qualified system administrators ever login as root. In fact, at many such institutions, the root password is a highly guarded secret: it is treated as the Holy Grail of the institution. A large amount of hubbub is made about logging in as root; it is portrayed as a wise and fearsome power, given only to an exclusive cabal.

This kind of attitude towards the root account is, quite simply, the kind of thing which breeds malice and contempt. Because root is so fluffed-up, when some users have their first opportunity to login as root (either on a Linux system or elsewhere), the tendency is to use root's privileges in a harmful manner. I have known so-called "system administrators" who read other user's mail, delete user's files without warning, and generally behave like children when given such a powerful "toy".

Because root has such privilege on the system, it takes a certain amount of maturity and self-control to use the account as it was intended—to run the system. There is an unspoken code of honor which exists between the system administrator and the users on the system. How would you feel if your system administrator was reading your e-mail or looking over your files? There is still no strong legal precedent for electronic privacy on time-sharing computer systems. On UNIX systems, the root user has the ability to forego all security and privacy mechanisms on the system. It is important that the system administrator develop a trusting relationship with the users on the system. I can't stress that enough.

4.1.3   Dealing with users

UNIX security is rather lax by design. Security on the system was an afterthought—the system was originally developed in an environment where users intruding upon other users was simply unheard of. Because of this, even with security measures, there is still the ability for normal users to do harm.

System administrators can take two stances when dealing with abusive users: they can be either paranoid or trusting. The paranoid system administrator usually causes more harm than he or she prevents. One of my favorite sayings is, "Never attribute to malice anything which can be attributed to stupidity." Put another way, most users don't have the ability or knowledge to do real harm on the system. 90% of the time, when a user is causing trouble on the system (by, for instance, filling up the user partition with large files, or running multiple instances of a large program), the user is simply unaware that what he or she is doing is a problem. I have come down on users who were causing a great deal of trouble, but they were simply acting out of ignorance—not malice.

When you deal with users who are causing potential trouble, don't be accusative. The old rule of "innocent until proven guilty" still holds. It is best to simply talk to the user, and question about the trouble, instead of causing a confrontation. The last thing you want to do is be on the user's bad side. This will raise a lot of suspicion about you—the system administrator—running the system correctly. If a user believes that you distrust or dislike them, they might accuse you of deleting files or breaching privacy on the system. This is certainly not the kind of position that you want to be in.

If you do find that a user has been attempting to "crack" the system, or was intentionally doing harm to the system, don't return the malicious behavior with malice of your own. Instead, simply provide a warning—but be flexible. In many cases, you may catch a user "in the act" of doing harm to the system—give them a warning. Tell them not to let it happen again. However, if you *do* catch them causing harm again, be absolutely sure that it is intentional. I can't even begin to describe the number of cases where it appeared as though a user was causing trouble, when in fact it was either an accident or a fault of my own.

4.1.4 Setting the rules

The best way to run a system is not with an iron fist. That may be how you run the military, but UNIX was not designed for such discipline. It makes sense to lay down a simple and flexible set of guidelines for users—but remember, the fewer rules you have, the less chance there is of breaking them. Even if your rules for using the system are perfectly reasonable and clear, users will always at times break these rules without intending to. This is especially true in the case of new UNIX users, who are just learning the ropes of the system. It's not patently obvious, for example, that you shouldn't download a gigabyte of files and mail them to everyone on the system. Users need help understanding the rules, and why they are there.

If you do specify usage guidelines for your system, make sure that the reason behind a particular guideline is made clear. If you don't, then users will find all sorts of creative ways to get around the rule, and not know that they are in fact breaking it.

4.1.5 What it all means

We can't tell you how to run your system to the last detail. Most of the philosophy depends on how you're using the system. If you have many users, things are much different than if you only have a few users, or if you're the only user on the system. However, it's always a good idea—in any situation—to understand what being the system administrator really means.

Being the system administrator doesn't make you a UNIX wizard. There are many system admins out there who know very little about UNIX. Likewise, there are many "normal" users out there who know more about UNIX than any system administrator could. Also, being the system administrator does not allow you to use malice against your users. Just because the system gives you the privilege to mess with user files does not mean that you have any right to do so.

Lastly, being the system administrator is really not a big deal. It doesn't matter if your system is a little 386 or a Cray supercomputer. Running the system is the same, regardless. Knowing the **root** password isn't going to earn you money or fame. It will allow you to maintain the system, and keep it running. That's it.

4.2   Booting the System

There are several ways to boot the system, either from floppy or from the hard drive.

4.2.1   Using a boot floppy

Many people boot Linux using a "boot floppy" which contains a copy of the Linux kernel. This kernel has the Linux root partition coded into it, so it will know where to look on the hard drive for the root filesystem. (The **rdev** command can be used to set the root partition in the kernel image; see below.) This is the type of floppy created by Slackware during installation, for example.

To create your own boot floppy, first locate the kernel image on your hard disk. It should be in the file **/Image** or **/etc/Image**. Some installations use the file **/vmlinux** for the kernel.

You may instead have a compressed kernel. A compressed kernel uncompresses itself into memory at boot time, and takes up much less space on the hard drive. If you have a compressed kernel, it may be found in the file **/zImage** or **/etc/zImage**.

Once you know where the kernel is, set the root device in the kernel image to the name of your Linux root partition with the **rdev** command. The format of the command is

> rdev ⟨*kernel-name*⟩ ⟨*root-device*⟩

where ⟨*kernel-name*⟩ is the name of the kernel image, and ⟨*root-device*⟩ is the name of the Linux root partition. For example, to set the root device in the kernel **/etc/Image** to **/dev/hda2**, use the command

> **#** *rdev /etc/Image /dev/hda2*

rdev can set other options in the kernel as well, such as the default SVGA mode to use at boot time. Just use "**rdev -h**" to get a help message.

After setting the root device, you can simply copy the kernel image to the floppy. Whenever copying data to a floppy, it's a good idea to MS-DOS format the floppy first. This lays down the sector and track information on the floppy, so it can be detected as either high or low density.

For example, to copy the kernel in the file **/etc/Image** to the floppy in **/etc/fd0**, use the command

> # *cp /etc/Image /dev/fd0*

This floppy should now boot Linux.

4.2.2   Using LILO

Another method of booting is to use LILO, a program which resides in the boot sector of your hard disk. This program is executed when the system is booted from the hard disk, and can automatically boot up Linux from a kernel image stored on the hard drive itself.

LILO can also be used as a first-stage boot loader for several operating systems, allowing you to select at boot time which operating system (such as Linux or MS-DOS) to boot. When you boot using LILO, the default operating system is booted unless you press ctrl , alt , or shift during the bootup sequence. If you press any of these keys, you will be provided with a boot prompt, at which you type the name of the operating system to boot (such as "**linux**" or "**msdos**"). If you press tab at the boot prompt, a listing of available operating systems will be provided.

The easy way to install LILO is to edit the configuration file, **/etc/lilo.conf**, and then run the command

> # */sbin/lilo*

The LILO configuration file contains a "stanza" for each operating system that you want to boot. The best way to demonstrate this is with an example LILO config file. The below setup is for a system which has a Linux root partition on **/dev/hda1**, and an MS-DOS partition on **/dev/hda2**.

```
# Tell LILO to modify the boot record on /dev/hda (the first
# non-SCSI hard drive). If you boot from a drive other than /dev/hda,
# change the following line.
boot = /dev/hda

# Name of the boot loader. No reason to modify this unless you're doing
# some serious hacking on LILO.
install = /boot/boot.b
```

```
# Have LILO perform some optimization.
compact

# Stanza for Linux root partition on /dev/hda1.
image = /etc/Image    # Location of kernel
   label = linux      # Name of OS (for the LILO boot menu)
   root = /dev/hda1   # Location of root partition
   vga = ask          # Tell kernel to ask for SVGA modes at boot time

# Stanza for MSDOS partition on /dev/hda2.
other = /dev/hda2     # Location of partition
   table = /dev/hda   # Location of partition table for /dev/hda2
   label = msdos      # Name of OS (for boot menu)
```

The first operating system stanza in the config file will be the default OS for LILO to boot. You can select another OS to boot at the LILO boot prompt, as discussed above.

Remember that every time you update the kernel image on disk, you should rerun /sbin/lilo in order for the changes to be reflected on the boot sector of your drive.

Also note that if you use the "root =" line, above, there's no reason to use **rdev** to set the root partition in the kernel image. LILO sets it for you at boot time.

The Linux FAQ (see Appendix A) provides more information on LILO, including how to use LILO to boot with OS/2's Boot Manager.

4.3 Shutting Down

Shutting down a Linux system is a bit tricky. Remember that you should never just turn off the power or hit the reset switch while the system is running. The kernel keeps track of disk I/O in memory buffers. If you reboot the system without giving the kernel the chance to write its buffers to disk, you can corrupt your filesystems.

Other precautions are taken at shutdown time as well. All processes are sent a signal, which allows them to die gracefully (writing and closing all files, and so on). Filesystems are unmounted for safety. If you wish, the system can also alert users that the system is going down and give them a change to log off.

The easiest way to shutdown is with the **shutdown** command. The format of the command is

shutdown ⟨time⟩ ⟨warning-message⟩

The ⟨time⟩ argument is the time to shutdown the system (in the format *hh:mm:ss*), and ⟨warning-message⟩ is a message displayed on all user's terminals before shutdown. Alternately, you can specify the ⟨time⟩ as "now", to shutdown immediately. The **-r** option may be given to **shutdown** to reboot the system after shutting down.

For example, to shutdown the system at 8:00pm, use the command

    # *shutdown -r 20:00*

The command **halt** may be used to force an immediate shutdown, without any warning messages or grace period. **halt** is useful if you're the only one using the system, and want to shut down the system and turn it off.

◇   Don't turn off the power or reboot the system until you see the message:

    `The system is halted`

It is very important that you shutdown the system "cleanly" using the **shutdown** or **halt** commands. On some systems, pressing `ctrl-alt-del` will be trapped and cause a **shutdown**; on other systems, however, using the "Vulcan nerve pinch" will reboot the system immediately and may cause disaster.

4.4   Managing Users

Whether or not you have many users on your system, it's important to understand the aspects of user management under Linux. Even if you're the only user, you should presumably have a separate account for yourself (an account other than **root** to do most of your work).

Each person using the system should have his or her own account. It is seldom a good idea to have several people share the same account. Not only is security an issue, but accounts are used to uniquely identify users to the system. You need to be able to keep track of who is doing what.

4.4.1   User management concepts

The system keeps track of a number of pieces of information about each user. They are summarized below.

username   The username is the unique identifier given to every user on the system. Examples of usernames are **larry**, **karl**, and **mdw**. Letters and digits may be used, as well as the characters "_" (underscore) and "." (period). Usernames are usually limited to 8 characters in length.

user ID   The user ID, or UID, is a unique number given to every user on the system. The system usually keeps track of information by UID, not username.

group ID   The group ID, or GID, is the ID of the user's default group. In Section 3.9 we discussed group permissions; each user belongs to one or more groups defined by the system administrator. More about this below.

password   The system also stores the user's encrypted password. The **passwd** command is used to set and change user passwords.

full name   The user's "real name" or "full name" is stored along with the username. For example, the user **schmoj** may have the name "Joe Schmo" in real life.

home directory

The home directory is the directory in which the user is initially placed at login time. Every user should have his or her own home directory, usually found under **/home**.

login shell   The user's login shell is the shell which is started for the user at login time. Examples are **/bin/bash** and **/bin/tcsh**.

The file **/etc/passwd** contains this information about users. Each line in the file contains information about a single user; the format of each line is

```
username:encrypted password:UID:GID:full name:home directory:login shell
```

An example might be:

```
kiwi:Xv8Q981g71oKK:102:100:Laura Poole:/home/kiwi:/bin/bash
```

As we can see, the first field, "**kiwi**", is the username.

The next field, "**Xv8Q981g71oKK**", is the encrypted password. Passwords are not stored on the system in any human-readable format. The password is encrypted using itself as the secret key. In other words, you need to know the password to decrypt it. This form of encryption is fairly secure.

Some systems use "shadow password" in which password information is relegated to the file **/etc/shadow**. Because **/etc/passwd** is world-readable, **/etc/shadow** provides some degree of extra security because it is not. Shadow password provides some other features such as password expiration and so on; we will not go into these features here.

The third field, "**102**", is the UID. This must be unique for each user. The fourth field, "**100**", is the GID. This user belongs to the group numbered 100. Group information, like user information, is stored in the file **/etc/group**. See Section 4.4.5 for more information.

The fifth field is the user's full name, "**Laura Poole**". The last two fields are the user's home directory (**/home/kiwi**) and login shell (**/bin/bash**), respectively. It is not required that the user's home directory be given the same name as the username. It does help identify the directory, however.

4.4.2   Adding users

When adding a user, there are several steps to be taken. First, the user must be given an entry in /etc/passwd, with a unique username and UID. The GID, fullname, and other information must be specified. The user's home directory must be created, and the permissions on the directory set so that the user owns the directory. Shell initialization files must be provided in the new home directory and other system-wide configuration must be done (for example, setting up a spool for incoming e-mail for the new user).

While it is not difficult to add users by hand (I do), when you are running a system with many users it is easy to forget something. The easiest way to add users is to use an interactive program which asks you for the required information and updates all of the system files automatically. The name of this program is **useradd** or **adduser**, depending on what software was installed. The man pages for these commands should be fairly self-explanatory.

4.4.3   Deleting users

Similarly, deleting users can be accomplished with the commands **userdel** or **deluser** depending on what software was installed on the system.

If you'd like to temporarily "disable" a user from logging into the system (without deleting the user's account), you can simply prepend an asterisk ("*") to the password field in /etc/passwd. For example, changing **kiwi**'s /etc/passwd entry to

```
kiwi:*Xv8Q981g71oKK:102:100:Laura Poole:/home/kiwi:/bin/bash
```

will restrict **kiwi** from logging in.

4.4.4   Setting user attributes

After you have created a user, you may need to change attributes for that user, such as home directory or password. The easiest way to do this is to change the values directly in /etc/passwd. To set a user's password, use the **passwd** command. For example,

```
# passwd larry
```

will change **larry**'s password. Only **root** may change other user's password in this manner. Users can change their own passwords with **passwd** as well.

On some systems, the commands **chfn** and **chsh** will be available to allow users to set their own fullname and login shell attributes. If not, they will have to ask the system administrator to change these attributes for them.

4.4.5 Groups

As we have mentioned, each user belongs to one or more groups. The only real importance of group relationships pertains to file permissions, as you'll recall from Section 3.9, each file has a "group ownership" and a set of group permissions which defines how users in that group may access the file.

There are several system-defined groups such as **bin**, **mail**, and **sys**. Users should not belong to any of these groups; they are used for system file permissions. Instead, users should belong to an individual group such as **users**. If you want to be cute, you can maintain several groups of users such as **student**, **staff**, and **faculty**.

The file **/etc/group** contains information about groups. The format of each line is

```
group name:password:GID:other members
```

Some example groups might be:

```
root:*:0:
users:*:100:mdw,larry
guest:*:200:
other:*:250:kiwi
```

The first group, **root**, is a special system group reserved for the **root** account. The next group, **users**, is for regular users. It has a GID of 100. The users **mdw** and **larry** are given access to this group. Remember that in **/etc/passwd** each user was given a default GID. However, users may belong to more than one group, by adding their usernames to other group lines in **/etc/group**. The **groups** command lists what groups you are given access to.

The third group, **guest**, is for guest users, and **other** is for "other" users. The user **kiwi** is given access to this group as well.

As you can see, the "password" field of **/etc/group** is rarely used. It is sometimes used to set a password on group access. This is seldom necessary. To protect users from changing into priveleged groups (with the **newgroup** command), set the password field to "*****".

The commands **addgroup** or **groupadd** may be used to add groups to your system. Usually, it's easier just to add entries in **/etc/group** yourself, as no other configuration needs to be done to add a group. To delete a group, simply delete its entry in **/etc/group**.

4.5 Archiving and Compressing Files

Before we can talk about backups, we need to introduce the tools used to archive files and software on UNIX systems.

4.5.1   Using tar

The **tar** command is most often used to archive files.

The format of the **tar** command is

> tar ⟨options⟩ ⟨file1⟩ ⟨file2⟩ ...⟨fileN⟩

where ⟨options⟩ is the list of commands and options for **tar**, and ⟨file1⟩ through ⟨fileN⟩ is
the list of files to add or extract from the archive.

For example, the command

> # tar cvf backup.tar /etc

would pack all of the files in **/etc** into the tar archive **backup.tar**. The first argument
to **tar**—"**cvf**"—is the **tar** "command". "**c**" tells **tar** to create a new archive file. The
"**v**" option forces **tar** into verbose mode—printing each filename as it is archived. The "**f**"
option tells **tar** that the next argument—**backup.tar**—is the name of the archive to create.
The rest of the arguments to **tar** are the file and directory names to add to the archive.

The command

> # tar xvf backup.tar

will extract the tar file **backup.tar** in the current directory.   This can sometimes be
dangerous—when extracting files from a tar file, old files are overwritten.

Furthermore, before extracting tar files it is important to know where the files should be
unpacked. For example, let's say you archived the following files: **/etc/hosts**, **/etc/group**,
and **/etc/passwd**. If you use the command

> # tar cvf backup.tar /etc/hosts /etc/group /etc/passwd

the directory name **/etc/** is added to the beginning of each filename. In order to extract
the files to the correct location, you would need to use the following commands:

> # cd /
> # tar xvf backup.tar

because files are extracted with the pathname saved in the archive file.

If, however, you archived the files with the command

> # cd /etc
> # tar cvf hosts group passwd

the directory name is not saved in the archive file. Therefore, you would need to "**cd /etc**" before extracting the files. As you can see, how the tar file is created makes a large difference in where you extract it. The command

> # *tar tvf backup.tar*

may be used to display an "index" of the tar file before unpacking it. In this way you can see what directory the filenames in the archive are stored relative to, and can extract the archive from the correct location.

4.5.2 gzip and compress

Unlike archiving programs for MS-DOS, **tar** does not automatically compress files as it archives them. Therefore, if you are archiving two 1-megabyte files, the resulting tar file will be two megabytes in size. The **gzip** command may be used to compress a file (the file to compress need not be a tar file). The command

> # *gzip -9 backup.tar*

will compress **backup.tar** and leave you with **backup.tar.gz**, the compressed version of the file. The **-9** switch tells **gzip** to use the highest compression factor.

The **gunzip** command may be used to uncompress a gzipped file. Equivalently, you may use "**gzip -d**".

gzip is a relatively new tool in the UNIX community. For many years, the **compress** command was used instead. However, because of several factors[1], **compress** is being phased out.

compressed files end in the extension **.Z**. For example, **backup.tar.Z** is the compressed version of **backup.tar**, while **backup.tar.gz** is the gzipped version[2]. The **uncompress** command is used to expand a **compress**ed file; **gunzip** knows how to handle **compress**ed files as well.

4.5.3 Putting them together

Therefore, to archive a group of files and compress the result, you can use the commands:

> # *tar cvf backup.tar /etc*
> # *gzip -9 backup.tar*

---

[1] These factors include a software patent dispute against the **compress** algorithm and the fact that **gzip** is much more efficient than **compress**.

[2] To add further confusion, for some time the extension **.z** (lowercase "z") was used for gzipped files. The official **gzip** extension is now **.gz**.

The result will be **backup.tar.gz**. To unpack this file, use the reverse set of commands:

> # *gunzip backup.tar.gz*
> # *tar xvf backup.tar*

Of course always make sure that you are in the correct directory before unpacking a tar file.

You can use some UNIX cleverness to do all of this on one command line, as in the following:

> # *tar cvf - /etc | gzip -9c > backup.tar.gz*

Here, we are sending the tar file to "–", which stands for **tar**'s standard output. This is piped to **gzip**, which compresses the incoming tar file, and the result is saved in **backup.tar.gz**. The **-c** option to **gzip** tells **gzip** to send its output to stdout, which is redirected to **backup.tar.gz**.

A single command used to unpack this archive would be:

> # *gunzip -c backup.tar.gz | tar xvf -*

Again, **gunzip** uncompresses the contents of **backup.tar.gz** and sends the resulting tar file to stdout. This is piped to **tar**, which reads "–", this time referring to **tar**'s standard input.

Happily, the **tar** command also includes the **z** option to automatically compress/uncompress files on the fly, using the **gzip** compression algorithm.

For example, the command

> # *tar cvfz backup.tar.gz /etc*

is equivalent to

> # *tar cvf backup.tar /etc*
> # *gzip backup.tar*

Just as the command

> # *tar xvfz backup.tar.Z*

may be used instead of

> # *uncompress backup.tar.Z*
> # *tar xvf backup.tar*

Refer to the man pages for **tar** and **gzip** for more information.

4.6 Using Floppies and Making Backups

Floppies are usually used as backup media. If you don't have a tape drive connected to your system, floppy disks can be used (although they are slower and somewhat less reliable).

You may also use floppies to hold individual filesystems—in this way, you can **mount** the floppy to access the data on it.

4.6.1 Using floppies for backups

The easiest way to make a backup using floppies is with **tar**. The command

> # *tar cvfzM /dev/fd0 /*

will make a complete backup of your system using the floppy drive **/dev/fd0**. The "M" option to **tar** allows the backup to be a multivolume backup; that is, when one floppy is full, **tar** will prompt for the next. The command

> # *tar xvfzM /dev/fd0*

can be used to restore the complete backup. This method can also be used if you have a tape drive (**/dev/rmt0**) connected to your system.

Several other programs exist for making multiple-volume backups; the **backflops** program found on **tsx-11.mit.edu** may come in handy.

Making a complete backup of the system can be time- and resource-consuming. Most system administrators use a incremental backup policy, in which every month a complete backup is taken, and every week only those files which have been modified in the last week are backed up. In this case, if you trash your system in the middle of the month, you can simply restore the last full monthly backup, and then restore the last weekly backups as needed.

The **find** command can be useful in locating files which have changed since a certain date. Several scripts for managing incremental backups can be found on **sunsite.unc.edu**.

4.6.2 Using floppies as filesystems

You can create a filesystem on a floppy just as you would on a hard drive partition. For example,

> # *mke2fs /dev/fd0 1440*

creates a filesystem on the floppy in **/dev/fd0**. The size of the filesystem must correspond to the size of the floppy. High-density 3.5" disks are 1.44 megabytes, or 1440 blocks, in size. High-density 5.25" disks are 1200 blocks.

In order to access the floppy, you must **mount** the filesystem contained on it. The command

> # *mount -t ext2 /dev/fd0 /mnt*

will mount the floppy in **/dev/fd0** on the directory **/mnt**. Now, all of the files on the floppy will appear under **/mnt** on your drive. The "**-t ext2**" specifies an ext2fs filesystem type. If you created another type of filesystem on the floppy, you'll need to specify its type to the **mount** command.

The "mount point" (the directory where you're mounting the filesystem) needs to exist when you use the **mount** command. If it doesn't exist, simply create it with **mkdir**.

See Section 4.8 for more information on filesystems, mounting, and mount points.

◇   Note that any I/O to the floppy is buffered just as hard disk I/O is. If you change data on the floppy, you may not see the drive light come on until the kernel flushes its I/O buffers. It's important that you not remove a floppy before you unmount it; this can be done with the command

> # *umount /dev/fd0*

Do not simply switch floppies as you would on an MS-DOS system; whenever you change floppies, **umount** the first one and **mount** the next.

4.7   Upgrading and Installing New Software

Another duty of the system administrator is upgrading and installing new software.

The Linux community is very dynamic. New kernel releases come out every few weeks, and other software is updated almost as often. Because of this, new Linux users often feel the need to upgrade their systems constantly to keep up the the rapidly changing pace. Not only is this unnecessary, it's a waste of time: to keep up with all of the changes in the Linux world, you would be spending all of your time upgrading and none of your time using the system.

So, when should you upgrade? Some people feel that you should upgrade when a new distribution release is made—for example, when Slackware comes out with a new version. Many Linux users completely reinstall their system with the newest Slackware release every time. This, also, is a waste of time. In general, changes to Slackware releases are small. Downloading and reinstalling 30 disks when only 10% of the software has been actually modified is, of course, pointless.

The best way to upgrade your system is to do it by hand: only upgrade those software packages which you know that you should upgrade. This scares a lot of people: they want to know what to upgrade, and how, and what will break if they don't upgrade. In order to be successful with Linux, it's important to overcome your fears of "doing it yourself"— which is what Linux is all about. In fact, once you have your system working and all software correctly configured, reinstalling with the newest release will no doubt wipe all of your configuration and things will be broken again, just as they were when you first installed your system. Setting yourself back in this manner is unnecessary—all that is needed is some know-how about upgrading your system, and how to do it right.

You'll find that when you upgrade one component of your system, other things should not break. For example, most of the software on my system is left over from an ancient 0.96 MCC Interim installation. Yet, I run the newest version of the kernel and libraries with this software with no problem. For the most part, senselessly upgrading to "keep up with the trend" is not important at all. This isn't MS-DOS or Microsoft Windows. There is no important reason to run the newest version of all of the software. If you find that you would like or need features in a new version, then upgrade. If not, then don't. In other words, only upgrade what you have to, and when you have to. Don't just upgrade for the sake of upgrading. That will waste a lot of time and effort trying to keep up.

The most important software to upgrade on your system is the kernel, the libraries, and the **gcc** compiler. These are the three essential parts of your system, and in some cases they all depend on each other for everything to work successfully. Most of the other software on your system does not need to be upgraded periodically.

4.7.1 Upgrading the kernel

Upgrading the kernel is simply a matter of getting the sources and compiling them yourself. You must compile the kernel yourself in order to enable or disable certain features, as well as to ensure that the kernel will be optimized to run on your machine. The process is quite painless.

The kernel sources may be retrieved from any of the Linux FTP sites (see Section C for a list). On **sunsite.unc.edu**, for instance, the kernel sources are found in **/pub/Linux/kernel**. Kernel versions are numbered using a version number and a patchlevel. For example, kernel version 0.99 patchlevel 11 is usually written as **0.99.pl11**, or just **0.99.11**.

The kernel sources are released as a gzipped tar file[3]. For example, the file containing the 0.99.pl11 kernel sources is **linux-0.99.11.tar.gz**.

Unpack this tar file from the directory **/usr/src**; it creates the directory **/usr/src/linux** which contains the kernel sources. You should delete or rename your

---

[3]Often, a patch file is also released for the current kernel version which allows you to patch your current kernel sources from the last patchlevel to the current one (using the program **patch**). In most cases, however, it's usually easier to install the entire new version of the kernel sources.

existing **/usr/src/linux** before unpacking the new version.

Once the sources are unpacked, you need to make sure that two symbolic links in **/usr/include** are correct. To create these links, use the commands

> **#** *ln -sf /usr/src/linux/include/linux /usr/include/linux*
> **#** *ln -sf /usr/src/linux/include/asm /usr/include/asm*

Once you have created these links once, there is no reason to create them again when you install the next version of the kernel sources. (See Section 3.10 for more about symbolic links.)

Note that in order to compile the kernel, you must have the **gcc** and **g++** C and C++ compilers installed on your system. You may need to have the most recent versions of these compilers: see Section 4.7.3, below, for more information.

To compile the kernel, first **cd** to **/usr/src/linux**. Run the command **make config**. This command will prompt you for a number of configuration options, such as what filesystem types you wish to include in the new kernel.

Next, edit **/usr/src/linux/Makefile**. Be sure that the definition for **ROOT_DEV** is correct—it defines the device used as the root filesystem at boot time. The usual definition is

>   ROOT_DEV = CURRENT

Unless you are changing your root filesystem device, there is no reason to change this.

Next, run the command **make dep** to fix all of the source dependencies. This is a very important step.

Finally, you're ready to compile the kernel. The command **make Image** will compile the kernel and leave the new kernel image in the file **/usr/src/linux/Image**. Alternately, the command **make zImage** will compile a compressed kernel image, which uncompresses itself at boot time and uses less drive space.

Once you have the kernel compiled, you need to either copy it to a boot floppy (with a command such as "**cp Image /dev/fd0**") or install it using LILO to boot from your hard drive. See Section 4.2.2 for more information.

4.7.2   Upgrading the libraries

As mentioned before, most of the software on the system is compiled to use shared libraries, which contain common subroutines shared among different programs.

If you see the message

>   Incompatible library version

when attempting to run a program, then you need to upgrade to the version of the libraries which the program requires. Libraries are back-compatible; that is, a program compiled to use an older version of the libraries should work with the new version of the libraries installed. However, the reverse is not true.

The newest version of the libraries can be found on the Linux FTP sites. On `sunsite.unc.edu`, they are located in `/pub/Linux/GCC`. The "release" files there should explain what files you need to download and how to install them. Briefly, you should get the files `image-`*version*`.tar.gz` and `inc-`*version*`.tar.gz` where *version* is the version of the libraries to install, such as `4.4.1`. These are gzipped tar files; the `image` file contains the library images to install in `/lib` and `/usr/lib`. The `inc` file contains include files to install in `/usr/include`

The `release-`*version*`.tar.gz` should explain the installation procedure in detail (the exact instructions vary for each release). In general you need to install the library `.a` and `.sa` files in `/usr/lib`. These are the libraries used at compilation time.

In addition, the shared library image files, `libc.so.`*version* are installed in `/lib`. These are the shared library images loaded at runtime by programs using the libraries. Each library has a symbolic link using the major version number of the library in `/lib`.

For example, the `libc` library version 4.4.1 has a major version number of **4**. The file containing the library is `libc.so.4.4.1`. A symbolic link of the name `libc.so.4` is also in `/lib` pointing to this file. You need to change this symbolic link when upgrading the libraries. For example, when upgrading from `libc.so.4.4` to `libc.so.4.4.1`, you need to change the symbolic link to point to the new version.

◇   It is very important that you change the symbolic link in one step, as given below. If you somehow delete the symbolic link `libc.so.4`, then programs which depend on the link (including basic utilities like `ls` and `cat`) will stop working. Use the following command to update the symbolic link `libc.so.4` to point to the file `libc.so.4.4.1`:

> `# ln -sf /lib/libc.so.4.4.1 /lib/libc.so.4`

You also need to change the symbolic link `libm.so.`*version* in the same manner. If you are upgrading to a different version of the libraries substitute to appropriate filenames above. The library release notice should explain the details. (See Section 3.10 for more information about symbolic links.)

4.7.3 Upgrading gcc

The **gcc** C and C++ compiler is used to compile software on your system, most importantly the kernel. The newest version of **gcc** is found on the Linux FTP sites. On `sunsite.unc.edu`, it is found in the directory `/pub/Linux/GCC` (along with the libraries). There should be a **release** file for the **gcc** distribution detailing what files you need to download and how to install them.

4.7.4   Upgrading other software

Upgrading other software is usually just a matter of downloading the appropriate files and installing them. Most software for Linux is distributed at gzipped tar files, including either sources or binaries or both. If binaries are not included in the release, you may need to compile them yourself; usually, this means typing **make** in the directory where the sources are held.

Reading the USENET newsgroup `comp.os.linux.announce` for announcements of new software releases is the easiest way to find out about new software. Whenever you are looking for software on an FTP site, downloading the `ls-lR` index file from the FTP site and using **grep** to find the files in question is the easiest way to locate software. If you have **archie** available to you, it can be of assistance as well[4]. See Appendix A for more details.

One handy source of Linux software is the Slackware distribution disk images. Each disk contains a number of `.tgz` files which are simply gzipped tar files. Instead of downloading the disks, you can download the desired `.tgz` files from the Slackware directories on the FTP site and install them directly. If you run the Slackware distribution, the **setup** command can be used to automatically load and install a complete series of disks.

Again, it's usually not a good idea to upgrade by reinstalling with the newest version of Slackware, or another distribution. If you reinstall in this way, you will no doubt wreck your current installation, including user directories and all of your customized configuration. The best way to upgrade software is piecewise; that is, if there is a program that you use often that has a new version, upgrade it. Otherwise, don't bother. Rule of thumb: If it ain't broke, don't fix it. If your current software works, there's no reason to upgrade.

4.8   Managing Filesystems

Another task of the system administrator is taking care of filesystems. Most of this job entails periodically checking the filesystems for damage or corrupted files; many systems automatically check the filesystems at boot time.

4.8.1   Mounting filesystems

First, a few concepts about filesystems. Before a filesystem is accessible to the system, it must be **mounted** on some directory. For example, if you have a filesystem on a floppy, you must mount it under some directory, say `/mnt`, in order to access the files on it (see Section 4.6.2). After mounting the filesystem, all of the files in the filesystem appear in that directory. After unmounting the filesystem, the directory (in this case, `/mnt`) will be empty.

---

[4] If you don't have **archie**, you can telnet to an **archie** server such as `archie.rutgers.edu`, login as "archie" and use the command "help"

The same is true of filesystems on the hard drive. The system automatically mounts filesystems on your hard drive for you at bootup time. The so-called "root filesystem" is mounted on the directory /. If you have a separate filesystem for **/usr**, for example, it is mounted on **/usr**. If you only have a root filesystem, all files (including those in **/usr**) exist on that filesystem.

The command **mount** is used to mount a filesystem. The command

```
mount -av
```

is executed from the file **/etc/rc** (which is the system initialization file executed at boot time; see Section 4.10.1). The **mount -av** command obtains information on filesystems and mount points from the file **/etc/fstab**. An example **fstab** file appears below.

```
# device       directory      type      options
/dev/hda2       /             ext2      defaults
/dev/hda3       /usr          ext2      defaults
/dev/hda4       none          swap      sw
/proc           /proc         proc      none
```

The first field is the device—the name of the partition to mount. The second field is the mount point. The third field is the filesystem type—such as **ext2** (for ext2fs) or **minix** (for Minix filesystems). Table 4.1 lists the various filesystem types available for Linux.[5] Not all of these filesystem types may be available on your system; your kernel must have support for them compiled in. See Section 4.7 for information on building the kernel.

Filesystem	Type name	Comment
Second Extended Filesystem	ext2	Most common Linux filesystem.
Extended Filesystem	ext	Superseded by ext2.
Minix Filesystem	minix	Original Minix filesystem; rarely used.
Xia Filesystem	xia	Like ext2, but rarely used.
UMSDOS Filesystem	umsdos	Used to install Linux on an MS-DOS partition.
MS-DOS Filesystem	msdos	Used to access MS-DOS files.
/proc Filesystem	proc	Provides process information for ps, etc.
ISO 9660 Filesystem	iso9660	Format used by most CD-ROMs.
Xenix Filesystem	xenix	Used to access files from Xenix.
System V Filesystem	sysv	Used to access files from System V variants for the x86.
Coherent Filesystem	coherent	Used to access files from Coherent.
HPFS Filesystem	hpfs	Read-only access for HPFS partitions (DoubleSpace).

Table 4.1: Linux Filesystem Types

The last field of the **fstab** file contains **mount** options—usually, this is set to "**defaults**".

---

[5]This table is current as of kernel version 1.1.37.

As you can see, swap partitions are included in /etc/fstab as well. They have a mount directory of **none**, and type **swap**. The **swapon -a** command, executed from /etc/rc as well, is used to enable swapping on all swap devices listed in /etc/fstab.

The **fstab** file contains one special entry—for the /proc filesystem. As mentioned in Section 3.11.1, the /proc filesystem is used to store information about system processes, available memory, and so on. If /proc is not mounted, commands such as **ps** will not work.

◇   The **mount** command may only be used by root. This is to ensure security on the system; you wouldn't want regular users mounting and unmounting filesystems on a whim. There are several software packages available which allow regular users to mount and unmount filesystems (floppies in particular) without compromising system security.

The **mount -av** command actually mounts all filesystems other than the root filesystem (in the table above, /dev/hda2). The root filesystem is automatically mounted at boot time by the kernel.

Instead of using **mount -av**, you can mount a filesystem by hand. The command

    # mount -t ext2 /dev/hda3 /usr

is equivalent to mounting the filesystem with the entry /dev/hda3 in the **fstab** example file above.

In general, you should never have to mount or unmount filesystems by hand. The **mount -av** command in /etc/rc takes care of mounting the filesystems at boot time. Filesystems are automatically unmounted by the **shutdown** or **halt** commands before bringing the system down.

4.8.2   Checking filesystems

It is usually a good idea to check your filesystems for damage or corrupt files every now and then. Some systems automatically check their filesystems at boot time (with the appropriate commands in /etc/rc).

The command used to check a filesystem depends on the type of the filesystem in question. For ext2fs filesystems (the most commonly used type), this command is **e2fsck**. For example, the command

    # e2fsck -av /dev/hda2

will check the ext2fs filesystem on /dev/hda2 and automatically correct any errors.

It is usually a good idea to unmount a filesystem before checking it. For example, the command

    # umount /dev/hda2

will unmount the filesystem on **/dev/hda2**, after which you can check it. The one exception is that you cannot unmount the root filesystem. In order to check the root filesystem when it's unmounted, you should use a maintenance boot/root diskette (see Section 4.11.1). You also cannot unmount a filesystem if any of the files in it are "busy"—that is, being used by a running process. For example, you cannot unmount a filesystem if any user's current working directory is on that filesystem. You will receive a "**Device busy**" error if you attempt to unmount a filesystem which is in use.

Other filesystem types use different forms of the **e2fsck** command, such as **efsck** and **xfsck**. On some systems, you can simply use the command **fsck**, which will determine the filesystem type and execute the appropriate command.

◇   It is important that you reboot your system immediately after checking a mounted filesystem if any corrections were made to that filesystem. (However, in general, you shouldn't check filesystems while they are mounted.) For example, if **e2fsck** reports that it corrected any errors with the filesystem, you should immediately **shutdown -r** in order to reboot the system. This is to allow the system to re-sync its information about the filesystem when **e2fsck** modifies it.

The **/proc** filesystem never needs to be checked in this manner. **/proc** is a memory filesystem, managed directly by the kernel.

4.9 Using a swap file

Instead of reserving an individual partition for swap space, you can use a file. However, to do so you'll need install the Linux software and get everything going *before* you create the swap file.

If you have a Linux system installed, you can use the following commands to create a swap file. Below, we're going to create a swap file of size 8208 blocks (about 8 megs).

   # *dd if=/dev/zero of=/swap bs=1024 count=8208*

This command creates the swap file itself. Replace the "**count=**" with the size of the swap file in blocks.

   # *mkswap /swap 8208*

This command will initialize the swapfile; again, replace the name and size of the swapfile with the appropriate values.

   # */etc/sync*
   # *swapon /swap*

Now we are swapping on the file **/swap** which we have created, after syncing, which ensures that the file has been written to disk.

The one major drawback to using a swapfile in this manner is that all access to the swap file is done through the filesystem. This means that the blocks which make up the swap file may not be contiguous. Therefore, performance may not be as great as using a swap partition, for which blocks are always contiguous and I/O requests are done directly to the device.

Another drawback in using a swapfile is the chance to corrupt your filesystem data—when using large swap files, there is the chance that you can corrupt your filesystem if something goes wrong. Keeping your filesystems and swap partitions separate will prevent this from happening.

Using a swap file can be very useful if you have a temporary need for more swap space. For example, if you're compiling a large program and would like to speed things up somewhat, you can temporarily create a swap file and use it in addition to your regular swap space.

To get rid of a swap file, first use **swapoff**, as in

> # *swapoff /swap*

And you can safely delete the file.

> # *rm /swap*

Remember that each swap file (or partition) may be as large as 16 megabytes, but you may use up to 8 swap files or partitions on your system.

4.10   Miscellaneous Tasks

Believe it or not, there are a number of housekeeping tasks for the system administrator which don't fall into any major category.

4.10.1   System startup files

When the system boots, a number of scripts are executed automatically by the system before any user logs in. Here is a description of what happens.

At bootup time, the kernel spawns the process **/etc/init**. **init** is a program which reads its configuration file, **/etc/inittab**, and spawns other processes based on the contents of this file. One of the important processes started from **inittab** is the **/etc/getty** process started on each virtual console. The **getty** process grabs the VC for use, and starts a **login** process on the VC. This allows you to login on each VC; if /etc/inittab does not contain a **getty** process for a certain VC, you will not be able to login on that VC.

Another process executed from /etc/inittab is /etc/rc, the main system initialization file. This file is a simple shell script which executes any initialization commands needed at boot time, such as mounting the filesystems (see Section 4.8) and initializing swap space.

Your system may execute other initialization scripts as well, such as /etc/rc.local. /etc/rc.local usually contains initialization commands specific to your own system, such as setting the hostname (see the next section). rc.local may be started from /etc/rc or from /etc/inittab directly.

4.10.2 Setting the hostname

In a networked environment, the hostname is used to uniquely identify a particular machine, while in a standalone environment the hostname just gives the system personality and charm. It's like naming a pet: you can always address to your dog as "The dog," but it's much more interesting to assign the dog a name such as Spot or Woofie.

Setting the system's hostname is a simple matter of using the **hostname** command. If you are on a network, your hostname should be the full hostname of your machine, such as **goober.norelco.com**. If you are not on a network of any kind, you can choose an arbitrary host and domainname, such as **loomer.vpizza.com**, **shoop.nowhere.edu**, or **floof.org**.

When setting the hostname, the hostname must appear in the file /etc/hosts, which assigns an IP address to each host. Even if your machine is not on a network, you should include your own hostname in /etc/hosts.

For example, if you are not on a TCP/IP network, and your hostname is **floof.org**, simply include the following line in /etc/hosts:

```
127.0.0.1       floof.org localhost
```

This assigns your hostname, **floof.org**, to the loopback address 127.0.0.1 (used if you're not on a network). The **localhost** alias is also assigned to this address.

If you are on a TCP/IP network, however, your real IP address and hostname should appear in /etc/hosts. For example, if your hostname is **goober.norelco.com**, and your IP address is 128.253.154.32, add the following line to /etc/hosts:

```
128.253.154.32       goober.norelco.com
```

If your hostname does not appear in /etc/hosts, you will not be able to set it.

To set your hostname, simply use the **hostname** command. For example, the command

 # hostname -S goober.norelco.com

sets the hostname to goober.norelco.com. In most cases, the hostname command is executed from one of the system startup files, such as /etc/rc or /etc/rc.local. Edit these two files and change the hostname command found there to set your own hostname; upon rebooting the system the hostname will be set to the new value.

4.11   What To Do In An Emergency

On some occasions, the system administrator will be faced with the problem of recovering from a complete disaster, such as forgetting the root password or trashing filesystems. The best advice is, *don't panic.* Everyone makes stupid mistakes—that's the best way to learn about system administration: the hard way.

Linux is not an unstable version of UNIX. In fact, I have had fewer problems with system hangs than with commercial versions of UNIX on many platforms. Linux also benefits from a strong complement of wizards who can help you get out of a bind.

The first step in investigating any problem is to attempt to fix it yourself. Poke around, see how things work. Too much of the time, a system administrator will post a desperate plea for help before looking into the problem at all. Most of the time, you'll find that fixing problems yourself is actually very easy. It is the path to guruhood.

There are very few cases where reinstalling the system from scratch is necessary. Many new users accidentally delete some essential system file, and immediately reach for the installation disks. This is not a good idea. Before taking such drastic measures, investigate the problem and ask others to help fix things up. In almost all cases, you can recover your system from a maintenance diskette.

4.11.1   Recovering using a maintenance diskette

One indispensable tool for the system administrator is the so called "boot/root disk"—a floppy which can be booted for a complete Linux system, independent of your hard drive. Boot/root disks are actually very simple—you create a root filesystem on the floppy, place all of the necessary utilities on it, and install LILO and a bootable kernel on the floppy. Another technique is to use one floppy for the kernel and another for the root filesystem. In any case, the result is the same: you are running a Linux system completely from floppy.

The canonical example of a boot/root disk is the Slackware boot disks[6]. These diskettes contain a bootable kernel and a root filesystem, all on floppy. They are intended to be used to install the Slackware distribution, but come in very handy when doing system maintenance.

The H.J Lu boot/root disk, available from /pub/Linux/GCC/rootdisk on sunsite.unc.edu, is another example of such a maintenance disk. Or, if you're ambi-

---

[6] See Section 2.1.1 for information on downloading these from the Internet. For this procedure, you don't need to download the entire Slackware release—only the boot and root diskettes.

tious, you can create your own. In most cases, however, using a pre-made boot/root disk is much easier and will probably be more complete.

Using a boot/root disk is very simple. Just boot the disk on your system, and login as **root** (usually no password). In order to access the files on your hard drive, you will need to mount your filesystems by hand. For example, the command

> **#** *mount -t ext2 /dev/hda2 /mnt*

will mount an ext2fs filesystem on **/dev/hda2** under **/mnt**. Remember that **/** is now on the boot/root disk itself; you need to mount your hard drive filesystems under some directory in order to access the files. Therefore, **/etc/passwd** on your hard drive is now **/mnt/etc/passwd** if you mount your root filesystem on **/mnt**.

4.11.2 Fixing the root password

If you forget your root password, no problem. Just boot the boot/root disk, mount your root filesystem on **/mnt**, and blank out the password field for **root** in **/mnt/etc/passwd**, as so:

> root::0:0:root:/:/bin/sh

Now **root** has no password; when you reboot from the hard drive you should be able to login as **root** and reset the password using **passwd**.

Aren't you glad you learned how to use **vi**? On your boot/root disk, other editors such as Emacs probably aren't available, but **vi** should be.

4.11.3 Fixing trashed filesystems

If you somehow trash your filesystems, you can run **e2fsck** (if you use the ext2fs filesystem type, that is) to correct any damaged data on the filesystems from floppy. Other filesystem types use different forms of the **fsck** command; see Section 4.8 for details.

When checking your filesystems from floppy, it's best for the filesystems to not be mounted.

One common cause of filesystem damage is superblock corruption. The *superblock* is the "header" of the filesystem that contains information on the filesystem status, size, free blocks, and so forth. If you corrupt your superblock (for example, by accidentally writing data directly to the filesystem's partition), the system may not recognize the filesystem at all. Any attempt to mount the filesystem could fail, and **e2fsck** won't be able to fix the problem.

Happily, the *ext2fs* filesystem type saves copies of the superblock at "block group" boundaries on the drive—usually, every 8K blocks. In order to tell **e2fsck** to use a copy of the superblock, you can use a command such as

> # *e2fsck -b 8193 ⟨partition⟩*

where ⟨*partition*⟩ is the partition on which the filesystem resides. The **−b 8193** option tells **e2fsck** to use the copy of the superblock stored at block 8193 in the filesystem.

4.11.4   Recovering lost files

If you accidentally deleted important files on your system, there's no way to "undelete" them. However, you can copy the relevant files from the floppy to your hard drive. For example, if you deleted **/bin/login** on your system (which allows you to login), simply boot the boot/root floppy, mount the root filesystem on **/mnt**, and use the command

> # *cp -a /bin/login /mnt/bin/login*

The **−a** option tells **cp** to preserve the permissions on the file(s) being copied.

Of course, if the files you deleted weren't essential system files which have counterparts on the boot/root floppy, you're out of luck. If you made backups, you can always restore from them.

4.11.5   Fixing trashed libraries

If you accidentally trashed your libraries or symbolic links in **/lib**, more than likely commands which depended on those libraries will no longer run (see Section 4.7.2). The easiest solution is to boot your boot/root floppy, mount your root filesystem, and fix the libraries in **/mnt/lib**.

Chapter 5

Advanced Features

This chapter will introduce you to some of the more interesting features of Linux. This assumes that you have at least basic UNIX experience, and understand the information contained in the previous chapters.

The most important aspect of Linux that distinguishes it from other implementations of UNIX is its open design and philosophy. Linux was not developed by a small team of programmers headed by a marketing committee with a single goal in mind. It was developed by an ever-increasing group of hackers, putting what they wanted into a homebrew UNIX system. The types of software and diversity of design in the Linux world is large. Some people dislike this lack of uniformity and conformity—however, some call it one of the strongest qualities of Linux.

5.1   The X Window System

The X Window System is a large and powerful (and somewhat complex) graphics environment for UNIX systems. The original X Window System code was developed at MIT; commercial vendors have since made X the industry standard for UNIX platforms. Virtually every UNIX workstation in the world runs some variant of the X Window system.

A free port of the MIT X Window System version 11, release 6 (X11R6) for 80386/80486/Pentium UNIX systems has been developed by a team of programmers headed by David Wexelblat[1]. The release, known as XFree86[2], is available for System V/386, 386BSD, and other x86 UNIX implementations, including Linux. It includes all of the required binaries, support files, libraries, and tools.

---

[1] David may be reached on the Internet at dwex@mtgzfs3.att.com.
[2] XFree86 is a trademark of The XFree86 Project, Inc.

Configuring and using the X Window System is far beyond the scope of this book. You are encouraged to read *The X Window System: A User's Guide*—see Appendix A for information on this book. In this section, we'll give a step-by-step description of how to install and configure XFree86 for Linux, but you will have to fill in some of the details yourself by reading the documentation released with XFree86 itself. (This documentation is discussed below.) The Linux *XFree86 HOWTO* is another good source of information.

5.1.1 Hardware requirements

As of XFree86 version 3.1, released in September 1994, the following video chipsets are supported. The documentation included with your video adaptor should specify the chipset used. If you are in the market for a new video card, or are buying a new machine that comes with a video card, have the vendor find out exactly what the make, model, and chipset of the video card is. This may require the vendor to call technical support on your behalf; in general vendors will be happy to do this. Many PC hardware vendors will state that the video card is a "standard SVGA card" which "should work" on your system. Explain that your software (mention Linux and XFree86!) does not support all video chipsets and that you must have detailed information.

You can also determine your videocard chipset by running the `SuperProbe` program included with the XFree86 distribution. This is covered in more detail below.

The following standard SVGA chipsets are supported:

- Tseng ET3000, ET4000AX, ET4000/W32

- Western Digital/Paradise PVGA1

- Western Digital WD90C00, WD90C10, WD90C11, WD90C24, WD90C30, WD90C31, WD90C33

- Genoa GVGA

- Trident TVGA8800CS, TVGA8900B, TVGA8900C, TVGA8900CL, TVGA9000, TVGA9000i, TVGA9100B, TVGA9200CX, TVGA9320, TVGA9400CX, TVGA9420

- ATI 18800, 18800-1, 28800-2, 28800-4, 28800-5, 28800-6, 68800-3, 68800-6, 68800AX, 68800LX, 88800

- NCR 77C22, 77C22E, 77C22E+

- Cirrus Logic CLGD5420, CLGD5422, CLGD5424, CLGD5426, CLGD5428, CLGD5429, CLGD5430, CLGD5434, CLGD6205, CLGD6215, CLGD6225, CLGD6235, CLGD6420

- Compaq AVGA

- OAK OTI067, OTI077

- Advance Logic AL2101

- MX MX68000, MX680010

- Video 7/Headland Technologies HT216-32

The following SVGA chipsets with accelerated features are also supported:

- 8514/A (and true clones)

- ATI Mach8, Mach32

- Cirrus CLGD5420, CLGD5422, CLGD5424, CLGD5426, CLGD5428, CLGD5429, CLGD5430, CLGD5434, CLGD6205, CLGD6215, CLGD6225, CLGD6235

- S3 86C911, 86C924, 86C801, 86C805, 86C805i, 86C928, 86C864, 86C964

- Western Digital WD90C31, WD90C33

- Weitek P9000

- IIT AGX-014, AGX-015, AGX-016

- Tseng ET4000/W32, ET4000/W32i, ET4000/W32p

Video cards using these chipsets are supported on all bus types, including VLB and PCI.

All of the above are supported in both 256 color and monochrome modes, with the exception of the Advance Logic, MX and Video 7 chipsets, which are only supported in 256 color mode. If your video card has enough DRAM installed, many of the above chipsets are supported in 16 and 32 bits-per-pixel mode (specifically, some Mach32, P9000, S3 and Cirrus boards). The usual configuration is 8 bits per pixel (that is, 256 colors).

The monochrome server also supports generic VGA cards, the Hercules monochrome card, the Hyundai HGC1280, Sigma LaserView, and Apollo monochrome cards. On the Compaq AVGA, only 64k of video memory is supported for the monochrome server, and the GVGA has not been tested with more than 64k.

This list will undoubtedly expand as time passes. The release notes for the current version of XFree86 should contain the complete list of supported video chipsets.

One problem faced by the XFree86 developers is that some video card manufacturers use non-standard mechanisms for determining clock frequencies used to drive the card. Some of these manufacturers either don't release specifications describing how to program the card, or they require developers to sign a non-disclosure statement to obtain the information. This would obviously restrict the free distribution of the XFree86 software, something that the XFree86 development team is not willing to do. Specifically, the Diamond Speedstar 24/Speedstar+, and Diamond's S3-based cards, are not supported for this reason.

The suggested setup for XFree86 under Linux is a 486 machine with at least 8 megabytes of RAM, and a video card with a chipset listed above. For optimal performance, we suggest using an accelerated card, such as an S3-chipset card. You should check the documentation for XFree86 and verify that your particular card is supported before taking the plunge and purchasing expensive hardware. Benchmark ratings comparisons for various video cards under XFree86 are posted routinely to the USENET newsgroups `comp.windows.x.i386unix` and `comp.os.linux.misc`.

As a side note, my personal Linux system is a 486DX2-66, 20 megabytes of RAM, and is equipped with a VLB S3-864 chipset card with 2 megabytes of DRAM. I have run X benchmarks on this machine as well as on Sun Sparc IPX workstations. The Linux system is roughly 7 times faster than the Sparc IPX (for the curious, XFree86-3.1 under Linux, with this video card, runs at around 171,000 xstones; the Sparc IPX at around 24,000). In general, XFree86 on a Linux system with an accelerated SVGA card will give you much greater performance than that found on commercial UNIX workstations (which usually employ simple framebuffers for graphics).

Your machine will need at least 4 megabytes of physical RAM, and 16 megabytes of virtual RAM (for example, 8 megs physical and 8 megs swap). Remember that the more physical RAM that you have, the less that the system will swap to and from disk when memory is low. Because swapping is inherently slow (disks are very slow compared to memory), having 8 megabytes of RAM or more is necessary to run XFree86 comfortably. A system with 4 megabytes of physical RAM could run *much* (up to 10 times) more slowly than one with 8 megs or more.

5.1.2   Installing XFree86

The Linux binary distribution of XFree86 can be found on a number of FTP sites. On `sunsite.unc.edu`, it is found in the directory `/pub/Linux/X11`. (As of the time of this writing, the current version is 3.1; newer versions are released periodically).

It's quite likely that you obtained XFree86 as part of a Linux distribution, in which case downloading the software separately is not necessary.

If you are downloading XFree86 directly, This table lists the files in the XFree86-3.1 distribution.

One of the following servers is required:

File	Description
XF86-3.1-8514.tar.gz	Server for 8514-based boards.
XF86-3.1-AGX.tar.gz	Server for AGX-based boards.
XF86-3.1-Mach32.tar.gz	Server for Mach32-based boards.
XF86-3.1-Mach8.tar.gz	Server for Mach8-based boards.
XF86-3.1-Mono.tar.gz	Server for monochrome video modes.
XF86-3.1-P9000.tar.gz	Server for P9000-based boards.
XF86-3.1-S3.tar.gz	Server for S3-based boards.
XF86-3.1-SVGA.tar.gz	Server for Super VGA-based boards.
XF86-3.1-VGA16.tar.gz	Server for VGA/EGA-based boards.
XF86-3.1-W32.tar.gz	Server for ET4000/W32-based boards.

All of the following files are required:

File	Description
XF86-3.1-bin.tar.gz	The rest of the X11R6 binaries.
XF86-3.1-cfg.tar.gz	Config files for xdm, xinit and fs.
XF86-3.1-doc.tar.gz	Documentation and manpages.
XF86-3.1-inc.tar.gz	Include files.
XF86-3.1-lib.tar.gz	Shared X libraries and support files.
XF86-3.1-fnt.tar.gz	Basic fonts.

The following files are optional:

File	Description
XF86-3.1-ctrb.tar.gz	Selected contrib programs.
XF86-3.1-extra.tar.gz	Extra XFree86 servers and binaries.
XF86-3.1-lkit.tar.gz	Server linkkit for customization.
XF86-3.1-fnt75.tar.gz	75-dpi screen fonts.
XF86-3.1-fnt100.tar.gz	100-dpi screen fonts.
XF86-3.1-fntbig.tar.gz	Large Kanji and other fonts.
XF86-3.1-fntscl.tar.gz	Scaled fonts (Speedo, Type1).
XF86-3.1-man.tar.gz	Manual pages.
XF86-3.1-pex.tar.gz	PEX binaries, includes and libraries.
XF86-3.1-slib.tar.gz	Static X libraries and support files.
XF86-3.1-usrbin.tar.gz	Daemons which reside in /usr/bin.
XF86-3.1-xdmshdw.tar.gz	Shadow password version of xdm.

The XFree86 directory should contain README files and installation notes for the current version.

All that is required to install XFree86 is to obtain the above files, create the directory /usr/X11R6 (as root), and unpack the files from /usr/X11R6 with a command such as:

```
# gzip –dc XF86-3.1-bin.tar.gz | tar xfBp –
```

Remember that these tar files are packed relative to /usr/X11R6, so it's important to unpack the files there.

After unpacking the files, you first need to link the file /usr/X11R6/bin/X to the server that you're using. For example, if you wish to use the SVGA color server, /usr/bin/X11/X should be linked to {\tt /usr/X11R6/bin/XF86_SVGA}. If you wish to use the monochrome server instead, relink this file to XF86_MONO with the command

> # *ln −sf /usr/X11R6/bin/XF86_MONO /usr/X11R6/bin/X*

The same holds true if you are using one of the other servers.

If you aren't sure which server to use, or don't know your video card chipset, you can run the SuperProbe program found in /usr/X11R6/bin (included in the XF86-3.1-bin listed above). This program will attempt to determine your video chipset type and other information; write down its output for later reference.

You need to make sure that /usr/X11R6/bin is on your path. This can be done by editing your system default /etc/profile or /etc/csh.login (based on the shell that you, or other users on your system, use). Or you can simply add the directory to your personal path by modifying /etc/.bashrc or /etc/.cshrc, based on your shell.

You also need to make sure that /usr/X11R6/lib can be located by ld.so, the runtime linker. To do this, add the line

> /usr/X11R6/lib

to the file /etc/ld.so.conf, and run /sbin/ldconfig, as root.

5.1.3   Configuring XFree86

Setting up XFree86 is not difficult in most cases. However, if you happen to be using hardware for which drivers ar under development, or wish to obtain the best performance or resolution from an accelerated graphics card, configuring XFree86 can be somewhat time-consuming.

In this section we will describe how to create and edit the XF86Config file, which configures the XFree86 server. In many cases it is best to start out with a "basic" XFree86 configuration, one which uses a low resolution, such as 640x480, which should be supported on all video cards and monitor types. Once you have XFree86 working at a lower, standard resolution, you can tweak the configuration to exploit the capabilities of your video hardware. The idea is that you want to know that XFree86 works at all on your system, and that something isn't wrong with your installation, before attempting the sometimes difficult task of setting up XFree86 for real use.

In addition to the information listed here, you should read the following documentation:

- The XFree86 documentation in **/usr/X11R6/lib/X11/doc** (contained within the **XFree86-3.1-doc** package). You should especially see the file **README.Config**, which is an XFree86 configuration tutorial.

- Several video chipsets have separate **README** files in the above directory (such as **README.Cirrus** and **README.S3**). Read one of these if applicable.

- The man page for **XFree86**.

- The man page for **XF86Config**.

- The man page for the particular server that you are using (such as **XF86_SVGA** or **XF86_S3**).

The main XFree86 configuration file is **/usr/X11R6/lib/X11/XF86Config**. This file contains information on your mouse, video card parameters, and so on. The file **XF86Config.eg** is provided with the XFree86 distribution as an example. Copy this file to **XF86Config** and edit it as a starting point.

The **XF86Config** man page explains the format of this file in detail. Read this man page now, if you have not done so already.

We are going to present a sample **XF86Config** file, piece by piece. This file may not look exactly like the sample file included in the XFree86 distribution, but the structure is the same.

◇ Note that the **XF86Config** file format may change with each version of XFree86; this information is only valid for XFree86 version 3.1.

◇ Also, you should not simply copy the configuration file listed here to your own system and attempt to use it. Attempting to use a configuration file which doesn't correspond to your hardware could drive the monitor at a frequency which is too high for it; there have been reports of monitors (especially fixed-frequency monitors) being damaged or destroyed by using an incorrectly configured **XF86Config** file. The bottom line is this: Make absolutely sure that your **XF86Config** file corresponds to your hardware before you attempt to use it.

Each section of the **XF86Config** file is surrounded by the pair of lines **Section "**⟨section-name⟩**"**...**EndSection**. The first part of the **XF86Config** file is **Files**, which looks like this:

```
Section "Files"
    RgbPath     "/usr/X11R6/lib/X11/rgb"
    FontPath    "/usr/X11R6/lib/X11/fonts/misc/"
    FontPath    "/usr/X11R6/lib/X11/fonts/75dpi/"
EndSection
```

The **RgbPath** line sets the path to the X11R6 RGB color database, and each **FontPath** line sets the path to a directory containing X11 fonts. In general you shouldn't have to modify these lines; just be sure that there is a FontPath entry for each font type that you have installed (that is, for each directory in /usr/X11R6/lib/X11/fonts).

The next section is ServerFlags, which specifies several global flags for the server. In general this section is empty.

```
Section "ServerFlags"
# Uncomment this to cause a core dump at the spot where a signal is
# received.  This may leave the console in an unusable state, but may
# provide a better stack trace in the core dump to aid in debugging
#    NoTrapSignals

# Uncomment this to disable the <Crtl><Alt><BS> server abort sequence
#    DontZap
EndSection
```

Here, we have all lines within the section commented out.

The next section is Keyboard. This should be fairly intuitive.

```
Section "Keyboard"
    Protocol    "Standard"
    AutoRepeat  500 5
    ServerNumLock
EndSection
```

Other options are available as well—see the XF86Config file if you wish to modify the keyboard configuration. The above should work for most systems.

The next section is Pointer which specifies parameters for the mouse device.

```
Section "Pointer"

    Protocol    "MouseSystems"
    Device      "/dev/mouse"

# Baudrate and SampleRate are only for some Logitech mice
#    BaudRate    9600
#    SampleRate 150

# Emulate3Buttons is an option for 2-button Microsoft mice
#    Emulate3Buttons

# ChordMiddle is an option for some 3-button Logitech mice
#    ChordMiddle

EndSection
```

The only options that you should concern yourself with now are `Protocol` and `Device`. `Protocol` specifies the mouse *protocol* that your mouse uses (not the make or brand of mouse). Valid types for `Protocol` (under Linux—there are other options available for other operating systems) are:

- BusMouse

- Logitech

- Microsoft

- MMSeries

- Mouseman

- MouseSystems

- PS/2

- MMHitTab

BusMouse should be used for the Logitech busmouse. Note that older Logitech mice should use `Logitech`, but newer Logitech mice use either `Microsoft` or `MouseSystems` protocols. This is a case in which the protocol doesn't necessarily have anything to do with the make of the mouse.

`Device` specifies the device file where the mouse can be accessed. On most Linux systems, this is `/dev/mouse`. `/dev/mouse` is usually a link to the appropriate serial port (such as `/dev/cua0`) for serial mice, or to the appropriate busmouse device for busmice. At any rate, be sure that the device file listed in `Device` exists.

The next section is `Monitor`, which specifies the characteristics of your monitor. As with other sections in the `XF86Config` file, there may be more than one `Monitor` section. This is useful if you have multiple monitors connected to a system, or use the same `XF86Config` file under multiple hardware configurations. In general, though, you will need a single `Monitor` section.

```
Section "Monitor"

    Identifier  "CTX 5468 NI"

    # These values are for a CTX 5468NI only! Don't attempt to use
    # them with your monitor (unless you have this model)

    Bandwidth    60
    HorizSync    30-38,47-50
    VertRefresh  50-90
```

```
# Modes: Name        dotclock  horiz                 vert

ModeLine "640x480"   25        640 664 760 800       480 491 493 525
ModeLine "800x600"   36        800 824 896 1024      600 601 603 625
ModeLine "1024x768"  65        1024 1088 1200 1328   768 783 789 818
```

EndSection

The `Identifier` line is used to give an arbitrary name to the `Monitor` entry. This can be any string; you will use it to refer to the `Monitor` entry later in the `XF86Config` file.

`Bandwidth` is the maximum video bandwidth of the monitor, specified in MHz. Essentially, this is the maximum rate at which pixels may be sent to the monitor by the video card. Your monitor manual should list this value in the technical specifications section. If you do not have this information available, you should either contact the manufacturer or vendor of your monitor to obtain it. There are other sources of information, as well; they are listed below.

`HorizSync` specifies the valid horizontal sync frequencies for your monitor, in kHz. If you have a multisync monitor, this can be a range of values (or several comma-separated ranges), as seen above. If you have a fixed-frequency monitor, this will be a list of discrete values, such as:

```
HorizSync    31.5, 35.2, 37.9, 35.5, 48.95
```

Again, your monitor manual should list these values.

`VertRefresh` specifies the valid vertical refresh rates (or vertical synchronization frequencies) for your monitor, in Hz. Like `HorizSync` this can be a range or a list of discrete values; your monitor manual should list them.

`Bandwidth`, `HorizSync`, and `VertRefresh` are used only to double-check that the monitor resolutions that you specify are in valid ranges. This is to reduce the chance that you will damage your monitor by attempting to drive it at a frequency for which it was not designed.

The `ModeLine` directive is used to specify a single resolution mode for your monitor. The format of `ModeLine` is

```
ModeLine ⟨name⟩ ⟨clock⟩ ⟨horiz-values⟩ ⟨vert-values⟩
```

⟨name⟩ is an arbitrary string, which you will use to refer to the resolution mode later in the file. ⟨dot-clock⟩ is the driving clock frequency, or "dot clock" associated with the resolution mode. A dot clock is usually specified in MHz, and is the rate at which the video card must send pixels to the monitor at this resolution. ⟨horiz-values⟩ and ⟨vert-values⟩ are four numbers each which specify when the electron gun of the monitor should fire, and when the horizontal and vertical sync pulses fire during a sweep.

How can you determine the **ModeLine** values for your monitor? The file **VideoModes.doc**, included with the XFree86 distribution, describes in detail how to determine these values for each resolution mode that your monitor supports. First of all, ⟨*clock*⟩ must correspond to one of the dot clock values that your video card can produce. Later in the **XF86Config** file you will specify these clocks; you can only use video modes which have a ⟨*clock*⟩ value supported by your video card.

There are two files included in the XFree86 distribution which may include **ModeLine** data for your monitor. These files are **modeDB.txt** and **Monitors**, both of which are found in **/usr/X11R6/lib/X11/doc**.

You should start with **ModeLine** values for the VESA standard monitor timings, which most monitors support. **modeDB.txt** includes timing values for VESA standard resolutions. In that file, you will see entries such as

```
# 640x480@60Hz Non-Interlaced mode
# Horizontal Sync = 31.5kHz
# Timing: H=(0.95us, 3.81us, 1.59us), V=(0.35ms, 0.064ms, 1.02ms)
#
# name        clock   horizontal timing     vertical timing      flags
  "640x480"   25.175  640  664  760  800    480  491  493  525
```

This is a VESA standard timing for a 640x480 video mode. It uses a dot clock of 25.175, which your video card must support to use this mode (more on this later). To include this entry in the **XF86Config** file, you'd use the line

```
ModeLine "640x480" 25.175  640 664 760 800  480 491 493 525
```

Note that the ⟨*name*⟩ argument to **ModeLine** (in this case **"640x480"**) is an arbitrary string— the convention is to name the mode after the resolution, but ⟨*name*⟩ can technically be anything descriptive which describes the mode to you.

For each **ModeLine** used the server will check that the specifications for the mode fall within the range of values specified with **Bandwidth**, **HorizSync** and **VertRefresh**. If they do not, the server will complain when you attempt to start up X (more on this later). For one thing, the dot clock used by the mode should not be greater than the value used for **Bandwidth**. (However, in many cases it is safe to use modes with a slightly higher bandwidth than your monitor can support.)

If the VESA standard timings do not work for you (you'll know after trying to use them later) then the files **modeDB.txt** and **Monitors** include specific mode values for many monitor types. You can create **ModeLine** entries from the values found in those two files as well. Be sure to only use values for the specific model of monitor that you have. Note that many 14 and 15-inch monitors cannot support higher resolution modes, and often resolutions of 1024x768 at low dot clocks. This means that if you can't find high resolution modes for your monitor in these files, then your monitor probably does not support those resolution modes.

If you are completely at a loss, and can't find working **ModeLine** values for your monitor, you can follow the instructions in the **VideoModes.doc** file included in the XFree86 distribution to generate **ModeLine** values from the specifications listed in your monitor's manual. While your mileage will certainly vary when attempting to generate **ModeLine** values by hand, this is a good place to look if you can't find the values that you need. **VideoModes.doc** also describes the format of the **ModeLine** directive and other aspects of the XFree86 server in gory detail.

Lastly, if you do obtain **ModeLine** values which are almost, but not quite, right, then it may be possible to simply modify the values slightly to obtain the desired result. For example, if while running XFree86 the image on the monitor is shifted slightly, or seems to "roll", you can follow the instructions in the **VideoModes.doc** file to try to fix these values. Also, be sure to check the knobs and controls on the monitor itself! In many cases it is necessary to change the horizontal or vertical size of the display after starting up XFree86 in order for the image to be centered and be of the appropriate size. Having these controls on the front of the monitor can certainly make life easier.

◇   You shouldn't use monitor timing values or **ModeLine** values for monitors other than the model that you own. If you attempt to drive the monitor at a frequency for which it was not designed, you can damage or even destroy it.

The next section of the **XF86Config** file is **Device**, which specifies parameters for your video card. Here is an example.

```
Section "Device"
        Identifier "#9 GXE 64"

        # Nothing yet; we fill in these values later.

EndSection
```

This section defines properties for a particular video card. **Identifier** is an arbitrary string describing the card; you will use this string to refer to the card later.

Initially, you don't need to include anything in the **Device** section, except for **Identifier**. This is because we will be using the X server itself to probe for the properties of the video card, and entering them into the **Device** section later. The XFree86 server is capable of probing for the video chipset, clocks, RAMDAC, and amount of video RAM on the board.

Before we do this, however, we need to finish writing the **XF86Config** file. The next section is **Screen**, which specifies the monitor/video card combination to use for a particular server.

```
Section "Screen"
        Driver     "Accel"
        Device     "#9 GXE 64"
```

```
Monitor     "CTX 5468 NI"
Subsection "Display"
     Depth       16
     Modes       "1024x768" "800x600" "640x480"
     ViewPort    0 0
     Virtual     1024 768
EndSubsection
EndSection
```

The **Driver** line specifies the X server that you will be using. The value values for **Driver** are:

- **Accel:** For the **XF86_S3**, **XF86_Mach32**, **XF86_Mach8**, **XF86_8514**, **XF86_P9000**, **XF86_AGX**, and **XF86_W32** servers;

- **SVGA:** For the **XF86_SVGA** server;

- **VGA16:** For the **XF86_VGA16** server;

- **VGA2:** For the **XF86_Mono** server;

- **Mono:** For the non-VGA monochrome drivers in the **XF86_Mono** and **XF86_VGA16** servers.

You should be sure that **/usr/X11R6/bin/X** is a symbolic link to the server that you are using.

The **Device** line specifies the **Identifier** of the **Device** section corresponding to the video card to use for this server. Above, we created a **Device** section with the line

```
Identifier "#9 GXE 64"
```

Therefore, we use **"#9 GXE 64"** on the **Device** line here.

Similarly, the **Monitor** line specifies the name of the **Monitor** section to be used with this server. Here, **"CTX 5468 NI"** is the **Identifier** used in the **Monitor** section described above.

Subsection "Display" defines several properties of the XFree86 server corresponding to your monitor/video card combination. The **XF86Config** file describes all of these options in detail; most of them are icing on the cake and not necessary to get the system working.

The options that you should know about are:

- **Depth.** Defines the number of color planes—the number of bits per pixel. Usually, **Depth** is set to 8. For the **VGA16** server, you would use a depth of 4, and for the monochrome server a depth of 1. If you are using an accelerated video card with enough memory to support more bits per pixel, you can set **Depth** to 16, 24, or 32. If

you have problems with depths higher than 8, set it back to 8 and attempt to debug
the problem later.

- **Modes**. This is the list of video mode names which have been defined using the
  ModeLine directive in the **Monitor** section. In the above section, we used **ModeLines**
  named **"1024x768"**, **"800x600"**, and **"640x48"0**. Therefore, we use a **Modes** line of

  Modes   "1024x768" "800x600" "640x480"

  The first mode listed on this line will be the default when XFree86 starts up. After
  XFree86 is running, you can switch between the modes listed here using the keys
  ctrl ┤ alt ┤ numeric + and ctrl ┤ alt ┤ numeric - .
  It might be best, when initially configuring XFree86, to use lower resolution video
  modes, such as 640x480, which tend to work on most systems. Once you have the
  basic configuration working you can modify **XF86Config** to support higher resolutions.

- **Virtual**. Sets the virtual desktop size. XFree86 has the ability to use any additional
  memory on your video card to extend the size of your desktop. When you move the
  mouse pointer to the edge of the display, the desktop will scroll, bringing the additional
  space into view. Therefore, even if you are running at a lower video resolution such
  as 800x600, you can set **Virtual** to the total resolution which your video card can
  support (a 1-megabyte video card can support 1024x768 at a depth of 8 bits per pixel;
  a 2-megabyte card 1280x1024 at depth 8, or 1024x768 at depth 16). Of course, the
  entire area will not be visible at once, but it can still be used.

  The **Virtual** feature is a nice way to utilize the memory of your video card, but it
  is rather limited. If you want to use a true virtual desktop, we suggest using **fvwm**,
  or a similar window manager, instead. **fvwm** allows you to have rather large virtual
  desktops (implemented by hiding windows, and so forth, instead of actually storing
  the entire desktop in video memory at once). See the man pages for **fvwm** for more
  details about this; most Linux systems use **fvwm** by default.

- **ViewPort**. If you are using the **Virtual** option described above, **ViewPort** sets the
  coordinates of the upper-left-hand corner of the virtual desktop when XFree86 starts
  up. **Virtual 0 0** is often used; if this is unspecified then the desktop is centered on
  the virtual desktop display (which may be undesirable to you).

Many other options for this section exist; see the **XF86Config** man page for a complete description. In practice these other options are not necessary to get XFree86 initially
working.

5.1.4   Filling in video card information

Your **XF86Config** file is now ready to go, with the exception of complete information on
the video card. What we're going to do is use the X server to probe for the rest of this
information, and fill it into **XF86Config**.

Instead of probing for this information with the X server, the `XF86Config` values for many cards are listed in the files `modeDB.txt`, `AccelCards`, and `Devices`. These files are all found in `/usr/X11R6/lib/X11/doc`. In addition, there are various `README` files for certain chipsets. You should look in these files for information on your video card, and use that information (the clock values, chipset type, and any options) in the `XF86Config` file. If any information is missing, you can probe for it as described here.

In these examples we will demonstrate configuration for a #9 GXE 64 video card, which uses the `XF86_S3` chipset. This card happens to be the one which the author uses, but the discussion here applies to any video card.

The first thing to do is to determine the video chipset used on the card. Running `SuperProbe` (found in `/usr/X11R6/bin`) will tell you this information, but you need to know the chipset name as it is known to the X server.

To do this, run the command

```
X -showconfig
```

This will give the chipset names known to your X server. (The man pages for each X server list these as well.) For example, with the accelerated `XF86_S3` server, we obtain:

```
XFree86 Version 3.1 / X Window System
(protocol Version 11, revision 0, vendor release 6000)
Operating System: Linux
Configured drivers:
  S3: accelerated server for S3 graphics adaptors (Patchlevel 0)
      mmio_928, s3_generic
```

The valid chipset names for this server are `mmio_928` and `s3_generic`. The `XF86_S3` man page describes these chipsets and which videocards use them. In the case of the #9 GXE 64 video card, `s3_generic` is appropriate.

If you don't know which chipset to use, the X server can probe it for you. To do this, run the command

```
X -probeonly > /tmp/x.out 2>&1
```

if you use `bash` as your shell. If you use `csh`, try:

```
X -probeonly &> /tmp/x.out
```

You should run this command while the system is unloaded, that is, while no other activity is occurring on the system. This command will also probe for your video card dot clocks (as seen below), and system load can throw off this calculation.

The output from the above (in `/tmp/x.out` should contain lines such as the following:

```
XFree86 Version 3.1 / X Window System
(protocol Version 11, revision 0, vendor release 6000)
Operating System: Linux
Configured drivers:
   S3: accelerated server for S3 graphics adaptors (Patchlevel 0)
       mmio_928, s3_generic
Several lines deleted...
(--) S3: card type: 386/486 localbus
(--) S3: chipset:   864 rev. 0
(--) S3: chipset driver: s3_generic
```

Here, we see that the two valid chipsets for this server (in this case, XF86_S3) are mmio_928 and s3_generic. The server probed for and found a video card using the s3_generic chipset.

In the Device section of the XF86Config file, add a Chipset line, containing the name of the chipset as determined above. For example,

```
Section "Device"
        # We already had Identifier here...
        Identifier "#9 GXE 64"
        # Add this line:
        Chipset "s3_generic"
EndSection
```

Now we need to determine the driving clock frequencies used by the video card. A driving clock frequency, or dot clock, is simply a rate at which the video card can send pixels to the monitor. As we have seen, each monitor resolution has a dot clock associated with it. Now we need to determine which dot clocks are made available by the video card.

First you should look into the files (modeDB.txt, and so forth) mentioned above and see if your card's clocks are listed there. The dot clocks will usually be a list of 8 or 16 values, all of which are in MHz. For example, when looking at modeDB.txt we see an entry for the Cardinal ET4000 video board, which looks like this:

```
# chip    ram   virtual   clocks                      default-mode  flags
ET4000    1024  1024 768   25  28  38  36  40  45  32   0  "1024x768"
```

As we can see, the dot clocks for this card are 25, 28, 38, 36, 40, 45, 32, and 0 MHz.

In the Devices section of the XF86Config file, you should add a Clocks line containing the list of dot clocks for your card. For example, for the clocks above, we would add the line

```
Clocks 25 28 38 36 40 45 32 0
```

to the Devices section of the file, after Chipset. Note that the order of the clocks is important! Don't resort the list of clocks or remove duplicates.

If you cannot find the dot clocks associated with your card, the X server can probe for these as well. Using the **X -probeonly** command described above, the output should contain lines which look like the following:

```
(--) S3: clocks:  25.18  28.32  38.02  36.15  40.33  45.32  32.00  00.00
```

We could then add a **Clocks** line containing all of these values, as printed. You can use more than one **Clocks** line in **XF86Config** should all of the values (sometimes there are more than 8 clock values printed) not fit onto one line. Again, be sure to keep the list of clocks in order as they are printed.

Be sure that there is no **Clocks** line (or that it is commented out) in the **Devices** section of the file when using **X -probeonly** to probe for the clocks. If there is a **Clocks** line present, the server will *not* probe for the clocks—it will use the values given in **XF86Config**.

Note that some accelerated video boards use a programmable clock chip. (See the **XF86_Accel** man page for details; this generally applies to S3, AGX, and XGA-2 boards.) This chip essentially allows the X server to tell the card which dot clocks to use. If this is the case, then you may not find a list of dot clocks for the card in any of the above files. Or, the list of dot clocks printed when using **X -probeonly** will only contain one or two discrete clock values, with the rest being duplicates or zero.

For boards which use a programmable clock chip, you would use a **ClockChip** line, instead of a **Clocks** line, in your **XF86Config** file. **ClockChip** gives the name of the clock chip as used by the video card; the man pages for each server describe what these are. For example, in the file **README.S3**, we see that several S3-864 video cards use an "ICD2061A" clock chip, and that we should use the line

```
ClockChip "icd2061a"
```

instead of **Clocks** in the **XF86Config** file. As with **Clocks**, this line should go in the **Devices** section, after **Chipset**.

Similarly, some accelerated cards require you to specify the RAMDAC chip type in the **XF86Config** file, using a **Ramdac** line. The **XF86_Accel** man page describes this option. Usually, the X server will correctly probe for the RAMDAC.

Some video card types require you to specify several options in the **Devices** section of **XF86Config**. These options will be described in the man page for your server, as well as in the various files (such as **README.cirrus** or **README.S3**. These options are enabled using the **Option** line. For example, the #9 GXE 64 card requires two options:

```
Option "number_nine"
Option "dac_8_bit"
```

Usually, the X server will work without these options, but they are necessary to obtain the best performance. There are too many such options to list here, and they each depend on the particular video card being used. If you must use one of these options, fear not—the X server man pages and various files in /usr/X11R6/lib/X11/doc will tell you what they are.

So, when you're finished, you should end up with a Devices section which looks something like this:

```
Section "Device"
        # Device section for the #9 GXE 64 only !
        Identifier "#9 GXE 64"
        Chipset "s3_generic"
        ClockChip "icd2061a"
        Option "number_nine"
        Option "dac_8_bit"
EndSection
```

Most video cards will require a Clocks line, instead of ClockChip, as described above. The above Device entry is only valid for a particular video card, the #9 GXE 64. It is given here only as an example.

There are other options that you can include in the Devices entry. Check the X server man pages for the gritty details, but the above should suffice for most systems.

5.1.5   Running XFree86

With your XF86Config file configured, you're ready to fire up the X server and give it a spin. First, be sure that /usr/X11R6/bin is on your path.

The command to start up XFree86 is

```
startx
```

This is a front-end to xinit (in case you're used to using xinit on other UNIX systems).

This command will start the X server and run the commands found in the file .xinitrc in your home directory. .xinitrc is just a shell script containing X clients to run. If this file does not exist, the system default /usr/X11R6/lib/X11/xinit/xinitrc will be used.

A standard .xinitrc file looks like this:

```
#!/bin/sh

xterm -fn 7x13bold -geometry 80x32+10+50 &
xterm -fn 9x15bold -geometry 80x34+30-10 &
oclock -geometry 70x70-7+7 &
xsetroot -solid midnightblue &

exec twm
```

This script will start up two **xterm** clients, an **oclock**, and set the root window (background) color to **midnightblue**. It will then start up **twm**, the window manager. Note that **twm** is executed with the shell's **exec** statement; this causes the **xinit** process to be replaced with **twm**. Once the **twm** process exits, the X server will shut down. You can cause **twm** to exit by using the root menus: depress mouse button 1 on the desktop background—this will display a pop up menu which will allow you to **Exit Twm**.

Be sure that the last command in **.xinitrc** is started with **exec**, and that it is not placed into the background (no ampersand on the end of the line). Otherwise the X server will shut down as soon as it has started the clients in the **.xinitrc** file.

Alternately, you can exit X by pressing <kbd>ctrl</kbd>-<kbd>alt</kbd>-<kbd>backspace</kbd> in combination. This will kill the X server directly, exiting the window system.

The above is a very, very simple desktop configuration. Many wonderful programs and configurations are available with a bit of work on your **.xinitrc** file. For example, the **fvwm** window manager will provide a virtual desktop, and you can customize colors, fonts, window sizes and positions, and so forth to your heart's content. Although the X Window System might appear to be simplistic at first, it is extremely powerful once you customize it for yourself.

If you are new to the X Window System environment, we strongly suggest picking up a book such as *The X Window System: A User's Guide*. Using and configuring X is far too in-depth to cover here. See the man pages for **xterm**, **oclock**, and **twm** for clues on getting started.

5.1.6 Running into trouble

Often, something will not be quite right when you initially fire up the X server. This is almost always caused by a problem in your **XF86Config** file. Usually, the monitor timing values are off, or the video card dot clocks set incorrectly. If your display seems to roll, or the edges are fuzzy, this is a clear indication that the monitor timing values or dot clocks are wrong. Also be sure that you are correctly specifying your video card chipset, as well as other options for the **Device** section of **XF86Config**. Be absolutely certain that you are using the right X server and that **/usr/X11R6/bin/X** is a symbolic link to this server.

If all else fails, try to start X "bare"; that is, use a command such as:

```
X > /tmp/x.out 2>&1
```

You can then kill the X server (using the <kbd>ctrl</kbd>-<kbd>alt</kbd>-<kbd>backspace</kbd> key combination) and examine the contents of **/tmp/x.out**. The X server will report any warnings or errors—for example, if your video card doesn't have a dot clock corresponding to a mode supported by your monitor.

The file **VideoModes.doc** included in the XFree86 distribution contains many hints for tweaking the values in your **XF86Config** file.

Remember that you can use $\boxed{\texttt{ctrl}}$ $\boxed{\texttt{alt}}$ $\boxed{\texttt{numeric +}}$ and $\boxed{\texttt{ctrl}}$ $\boxed{\texttt{alt}}$ $\boxed{\texttt{numeric -}}$ to switch between the video modes listed on the **Modes** line of the **Screen** section of **XF86Config**. If the highest resolution mode doesn't look right, try switching to lower resolutions. This will let you know, at least, that those parts of your X configuration are working correctly.

Also, check the vertical and horizontal size/hold knobs on your monitor. In many cases it is necessary to adjust these when starting up X. For example, if the display seems to be shifted slightly to one side, you can usually correct this using the monitor controls.

The USENET newsgroup **comp.windows.x.i386unix** is devoted to discussions about XFree86. It might be a good idea to watch that newsgroup for postings relating to your video configuration—you might run across someone with the same problems as your own.

5.2   Accessing MS-DOS Files

If, for some twisted and bizarre reason, you would have need to access files from MS-DOS, it's quite easily done under Linux.

The usual way to access MS-DOS files is to mount an MS-DOS partition or floppy under Linux, allowing you to access the files directly through the filesystem. For example, if you have an MS-DOS floppy in **/dev/fd0**, the command

> # *mount -t msdos /dev/fd0 /mnt*

will mount it under **/mnt**. See Section 4.6.2 for more information on mounting floppies.

You can also mount an MS-DOS partition of your hard drive for access under Linux. If you have an MS-DOS partition on **/dev/hda1**, the command

> # *mount -t msdos /dev/hda1 /mnt*

will mount it. Be sure to **umount** the partition when you're done using it. You can have your MS-DOS partitions automatically mounted at boot time if you include entries for them in **/etc/fstab**; see Section 4.8 for details. For example, the following line in **/etc/fstab** will mount an MS-DOS partition on **/dev/hda1** on the directory **/dos**.

```
/dev/hda1      /dos      msdos      defaults
```

The **Mtools** software may also be used to access MS-DOS files. For example, the commands **mcd**, **mdir**, and **mcopy** all behave as their MS-DOS counterparts. If you installed **Mtools**, there should be man pages available for these commands.

Accessing MS-DOS files is one thing; running MS-DOS programs from Linux is another. There is an MS-DOS Emulator under development for Linux; it is widely available, and even distributed with SLS. It can be retrieved from a number of locations, including the various

Linux FTP sites (see Appendix C for details). The MS-DOS Emulator is reportedly powerful enough to run a number of applications, including Wordperfect, from Linux. However, Linux and MS-DOS are vastly different operating systems. The power of any MS-DOS emulator under UNIX is somewhat limited.

In addition, work is underway on a Microsoft Windows emulator to run under X Windows. Watch the newsgroups and FTP sites for more information.

5.3 Networking with TCP/IP

Linux supports a full implementation of the TCP/IP (Transport Control Protocol/Internet Protocol) networking protocols. TCP/IP has become the most successful mechanism for networking computers worldwide. With Linux and an Ethernet card, you can network your machine to a local area network, or (with the proper network connections), to the Internet—the worldwide TCP/IP network.

Hooking up a small LAN of UNIX machines is easy. It simply requires an Ethernet controller in each machine and the appropriate Ethernet cables and other hardware. Or, if your business or university provides access to the Internet, you can easily add your Linux machine to this network.

The current implementation of TCP/IP and related protocols for Linux is called "NET-2". This has no relationship to the so-called NET-2 release of BSD UNIX; instead, "NET-2" in this context means the second implementation of TCP/IP for Linux.

Linux NET-2 also supports SLIP—Serial Line Internet Protocol. SLIP allows you to have dialup Internet access using a modem. If your business or university provides SLIP access, you can dial in to the SLIP server and put your machine on the Internet over the phone line. Alternately, if your Linux machine also has Ethernet access to the Internet, you can set up your Linux box as a SLIP server.

For complete information on setting up TCP/IP under Linux, we encourage you to read the Linux NET-2 HOWTO, available via anonymous FTP from `sunsite.unc.edu`. The NET-2 HOWTO is a complete guide to configuring TCP/IP, including Ethernet and SLIP connections, under Linux. The Linux Ethernet HOWTO is a related document that describes configuration of various Ethernet card drivers for Linux. The *Linux Network Administrator's Guide*, from the Linux Documentation Project, is also available. See Appendix A for more information on these documents.

Also of interest is the book *TCP/IP Network Administration*, by Craig Hunt. It contains complete information on using and configuring TCP/IP on UNIX systems.

5.3.1   Hardware Requirements

You can use Linux TCP/IP without any networking hardware at all—configuring "loopback" mode allows you to talk to yourself. This is necessary for some applications and games which use the "loopback" network device.

However, if you want to use Linux with an Ethernet TCP/IP network, you need one of the following Ethernet cards: 3com 3c503, 3c503/16; Novell NE1000, NE2000; Western Digital WD8003, WD8013; Hewlett Packard HP27245, HP27247, HP27250.

The following clones are reported to work: WD-80x3 clones: LANNET LEC-45; NE2000 clones: Alta Combo, Artisoft LANtastic AE-2, Asante Etherpak 2001/2003, D-Link Ethernet II, LTC E-NET/16 P/N 8300-200-002, Network Solutions HE-203, SVEC 4 Dimension Ethernet, 4-Dimension FD0490 EtherBoard 16, and D-Link DE-600, SMC Elite 16.

See the Linux Ethernet HOWTO for a more complete discussion of Linux Ethernet hardware compatibility.

Linux also supports SLIP, which allows you to use a modem to access the Internet over the phone line. In this case, you'll need a modem compatible with your SLIP server—most servers require a 14.4bps V.32bis modem.

5.3.2   Configuring TCP/IP on your system

In this section we're going to discuss how to configure an Ethernet TCP/IP connection on your system. Note that this method should work for many systems, but certainly not all. This discussion should be enough to get you on the right path to configuring the network parameters of your machine, but there are numerous caveats and fine details not mentioned here. We direct you to the *Linux Network Administrators' Guide* and the NET-2-HOWTO for more information.[3]

First of all, we assume that you have a Linux system that has the TCP/IP software installed. This includes basic clients such as **telnet** and **ftp**, system administration commands such as **ifconfig** and **route** (usually found in /etc), and networking configuration files (such as /etc/hosts). The other Linux-related networking documents described above explain how to go about installing the Linux networking software if you do not have it already.

We also assume that your kernel has been configured and compiled with TCP/IP support enabled. See Section 4.7 for information on compiling your kernel. To enable networking, you must answer "yes" to the appropriate questions during the **make config** step, and rebuild the kernel.

Once this has been done, you must modify a number of configuration files used by NET-2. For the most part this is a simple procedure. Unfortunately, however, there is wide

---

[3] Some of this information is adapted from the NET-2-HOWTO by Terry Dawson and Matt Welsh.

disagreement between Linux distributions as to where the various TCP/IP configuration files and support programs should go. Much of the time, they can be found in /etc, but in other cases may be found in /usr/etc, /usr/etc/inet, or other bizarre locations. In the worst case you'll have to use the find command to locate the files on your system. Also note that not all distributions keep the NET-2 configuration files and software in the same location—they may be spread across several directories.

The following information applies primarily to Ethernet connections. If you're planning to use SLIP, read this section to understand the concepts, and follow the SLIP-specific instructions in the following section.

5.3.2.1 Your network configuration

Before you can configure TCP/IP, you need to determine the following information about your network setup. In most cases, your local network administrator can provide you with this information.

- IP address. This is the unique machine address in dotted-decimal format. An example is 128.253.153.54. Your network admins will provide you with this number.

  If you're only configuring loopback mode (i.e. no SLIP, no ethernet card, just TCP/IP connections to your own machine) then your IP address is 127.0.0.1.

- Your network mask ("netmask"). This is a dotted quad, similar to the IP address, which determines which portion of the IP address specifies the subnetwork number, and which portion specifies the host on that subnet. (If you're shaky on these TCP/IP networking terms, we suggest reading some introductory material on network administration.) The network mask is a pattern of bits, which when overlayed onto an address on your network, will tell you which subnet that address lives on. This is very important for routing, and if you find, for example, that you can happily talk to people outside your network, but not to some people within your network, there is a good chance that you have an incorrect mask specified.

  Your network administrators will have chosen the netmask when the network was designed, and therefore they should be able to supply you with the correct mask to use. Most networks are class C subnetworks which use 255.255.255.0 as their netmask. Other Class B networks use 255.255.0.0. The NET-2 code will automatically select a mask that assumes no subnetting as a default if you do not specify one.

  This applies as well to the loopback port. Since the loopback port's address is always 127.0.0.1, the netmask for this port is always 255.0.0.0. You can either specify this explicitly or rely on the default mask.

- Your network address. This is your IP address masked bitwise-ANDed the netmask. For example, if your netmask is 255.255.255.0, and your IP address is 128.253.154.32, your network address is 128.253.154.0. With a netmask of 255.255.0.0, this would be 128.253.0.0.

If you're only using loopback, you don't have a network address.

- Your broadcast address. The broadcast address is used to broadcast packets to every machine on your subnet. Therefore, if the host number of machines on your subnet is given by the last byte of the IP address (netmask 255.255.255.0), your broadcast address will be your network address ORed with 0.0.0.255.

  For example, if your IP address is 128.253.154.32, and your netmask is 255.255.255.0, your broadcast address is 128.253.154.255.

  Note that for historical reasons, some networks are setup to use the network address as the broadcast address, if you have any doubt, check with your network administrators. (In many cases, it will suffice to duplicate the network configuration of other machines on your subnet, substituting your own IP address, of course.)

  If you're only using loopback, you don't have a broadcast address.

- Your gateway address. This is the address of the machine which is your "gateway" to the outside world (i.e. machines not on your subnet). In many cases the gateway machine has an IP address identical to yours but with a ".1" as its host address; e.g., if your IP address is 128.253.154.32, your gateway might be 128.253.154.1. Your network admins will provide you with the IP address of your gateway.

  In fact, you may have multiple gateways. A *gateway* is simply a machine that lives on two different networks (has IP addresses on different subnets), and routes packets between them. Many networks have a single gateway to "the outside world" (the network directly adjacent to your own), but in some cases you will have multiple gateways—one for each adjacent network.

  If you're only using loopback, you don't have a gateway address. The same is true if your network is isolated from all others.

- Your nameserver address. Most machines on the net have a name server which translates hostnames into IP addresses for them. Your network admins will tell you the address of your name server. You can also run a server on your own machine by running **named**, in which case the nameserver address is 127.0.0.1. Unless you absolutely *must* run your own name server, we suggest using the one provided to you on the network (if any). Configuration of **named** is another issue altogether; our priority at this point is to get you talking to the network. You can deal with name resolution issues later.

  If you're only using loopback, you don't have a nameserver address.

SLIP users: You may or may not require any of the above information, except for a nameserver address. When using SLIP, your IP address is usually determined in one of two ways: Either (a) you have a "static" IP address, which is the same every time you connect to the network, or (b) you have a "dynamic" IP address, which is allocated from a pool available addresses when you connect to the server. In the following section on SLIP configuration this is covered in more detail.

NET-2 supports full routing, multiple routes, subnetworking (at this stage on byte boundaries only), the whole nine yards. The above describes most basic TCP/IP configurations. Yours may be quite different: when in doubt, consult your local network gurus and check out the man pages for **route** and **ifconfig**. Configuring TCP/IP networks is very much beyond the scope of this book; the above should be enough to get most people started.

5.3.2.2 The networking rc files

rc files are systemwide configuration scripts executed at boot time by **init**, which start up all of the basic system daemons (such as **sendmail**, **cron**, etc.) and configure things such as the network parameters, system hostname, and so on. **rc** files are usually found in the directory **/etc/rc.d** but on other systems may be in **/etc**.

Here, we're going to describe the **rc** files used to configure TCP/IP. There are two of them: **rc.inet1** and **rc.inet2**. **rc.inet1** is used to configure the basic network parameters (such as IP addresses and routing information) and **rc.inet2** fires up the TCP/IP daemons (**telnetd**, **ftpd**, and so forth).

Many systems combine these two files into one, usually called **rc.inet** or **rc.net**. The names given to your **rc** files doesn't matter, as long as they perform the correct functions and are executed at boot time by **init**. To ensure this, you may need to edit **/etc/inittab** and uncomment lines to execute the appropriate **rc** file(s). In the worst case you will have to create the **rc.inet1** and **rc.inet2** files from scratch and add entries for them to **/etc/inittab**.

As we said, **rc.inet1** configures the basic network interface. This includes your IP and network address, and the routing table information for your network. The routing tables are used to route outgoing (and incoming) network datagrams to other machines. On most simple configurations, you have three routes: One for sending packets to your own machine, another for sending packets to other machines on your network, and another for sending packets to machines outside of your network (through the gateway machine). Two programs are used to configure these parameters: **ifconfig** and **route**. Both of these are usually found in **/etc**.

ifconfig is used for configuring the network device interface with the parameters that it requires to function, such as the IP address, network mask, broadcast address and the like. **route** is used to create and modify entries in the routing table.

For most configurations, an **rc.inet1** file that looks like the following should work. You will, of course, have to edit this for your own system. Do *not* use the sample IP and network addresses listed here for your own system; they correspond to an actual machine on the Internet.

```
#!/bin/sh
# This is /etc/rc.d/rc.inet1 -- Configure the TCP/IP interfaces
```

```
# First, configure the loopback device

HOSTNAME=`hostname`

/etc/ifconfig lo 127.0.0.1        # uses default netmask 255.0.0.0
/etc/route add 127.0.0.1          # a route to point to the loopback device

# Next, configure the ethernet device. If you're only using loopback or
# SLIP, comment out the rest of these lines.

# Edit for your setup.
IPADDR="128.253.154.32"           # REPLACE with YOUR IP address
NETMASK="255.255.255.0"           # REPLACE with YOUR netmask
NETWORK="128.253.154.0"           # REPLACE with YOUR network address
BROADCAST="128.253.154.255"       # REPLACE with YOUR broadcast address, if you
                                  # have one. If not, leave blank and edit below.
GATEWAY="128.253.154.1"           # REPLACE with YOUR gateway address!

/etc/ifconfig eth0 ${IPADDR} netmask ${NETMASK} broadcast ${BROADCAST}

# If you don't have a broadcast address, change the above line to just:
# /etc/ifconfig eth0 ${IPADDR} netmask ${NETMASK}

/etc/route add ${NETWORK}

# The following is only necessary if you have a gateway; that is, your
# network is connected to the outside world.
/etc/route add default gw ${GATEWAY} metric 1

# End of Ethernet Configuration
```

Again, you may have to tweak this file somewhat to get it to work. The above should be sufficient for the majority of simple network configurations, but certainly not all.

rc.inet2 starts up various servers used by the TCP/IP suite. The most important of these is inetd. inetd sits in the background and listens to various network ports. When a machine tries to make a connection to a certain port (for example, the incoming telnet port), inetd forks off a copy of the appropriate daemon for that port (in the case of the telnet port, inetd starts in.telnetd). This is simpler than running many separate, standalone daemons (e.g., individual copies of telnetd, ftpd, and so forth)—inetd starts up the daemons only when they are needed.

syslogd is the system logging daemon—it accumulates log messages from various applications and stores them into log files based on the configuration information in /etc/syslogd.conf. routed is a server used to maintain dynamic routing information. When your system attempts to send packets to another network, it may require additional routing table entries in order to do so. `routed` takes care of manipulating the routing table without the need for user intervention.

Our example `rc.inet2`, below, only starts up the bare minimum of servers. There are many other servers as well—many of which have to do with NFS configuration. When attempting to setup TCP/IP on your system, it's usually best to start with a minimal configuration and add more complex pieces (such as NFS) when you have things working.

Note that in the below file, we assume that all of the network daemons are held in `/etc`. As usual, edit this for your own configuration.

```
#! /bin/sh
# Sample /etc/rc.d/rc.inet2

# Start syslogd
if [ -f /etc/syslogd ]
then
        /etc/syslogd
fi

# Start inetd
if [ -f /etc/inetd ]
then
        /etc/inetd
fi

# Start routed
if [ -f /etc/routed ]
then
        /etc/routed -q
fi

# Done!
```

Among the various additional servers that you may want to start in `rc.inet2` is **named**. **named** is a name server—it is responsible for translating (local) IP addresses to names, and vice versa. If you don't have a nameserver elsewhere on the network, or want to provide local machine names to other machines in your domain, it may be necessary to run **named**. (For most configurations it is not necessary, however.) **named** configuration is somewhat complex and requires planning; we refer interested readers to a good book on TCP/IP network administration.

5.3.2.3 /etc/hosts

`/etc/hosts` contains a list of IP addresses and the hostnames that they correspond to. In general, `/etc/hosts` only contains entries for your local machine, and perhaps other "important" machines (such as your nameserver or gateway). Your local name server will provide address-to-name mappings for other machines on the network, transparently.

For example, if your machine is **loomer.vpizza.com** with the IP address 128.253.154.32, your **/etc/hosts** would look like:

```
127.0.0.1               localhost
128.253.154.32          loomer.vpizza.com loomer
```

If you're only using loopback, the only line in **/etc/hosts** should be for 127.0.0.1, with both **localhost** and your hostname after it.

5.3.2.4   /etc/networks

The **/etc/networks** file lists the names and addresses of your own, and other, networks. It is used by the **route** command, and allows you to specify a network by name, should you so desire.

Every network you wish to add a route to using the **route** command (generally called from **rc.inet1**—see above) *must* have an entry in **/etc/networks**.

As an example,

```
default 0.0.0.0 # default route   - mandatory
loopnet 127.0.0.0 # loopback network - mandatory
mynet 128.253.154.0 # Modify for your own network address
```

5.3.2.5   /etc/host.conf

This file is used to specify how your system will resolve hostnames. It should contain the two lines:

```
order hosts,bind
multi on
```

These lines tell the resolve libraries to first check the **/etc/hosts** file for any names to lookup, and then ask the nameserver (if one is present). The **multi** entry allows you to have multiple IP addresses for a given machine name in **/etc/hosts**.

5.3.2.6   /etc/resolv.conf

This file configures the name resolver, specifying the address of your name server (if any) and your domain name. Your domain name is your fully-qualified hostname (if you're a registered machine on the Internet, for example), with the hostname chopped off. That is, if your full hostname is `loomer.vpizza.com`, your domain name is just `vpizza.com`.

For example, if your machine is `goober.norelco.com`, and has a nameserver at the address 128.253.154.5, your `/etc/resolv.conf` would look like:

```
domain      norelco.com
nameserver  127.253.154.5
```

You can specify more than one nameserver—each must have a **nameserver** line of its own in `resolv.conf`.

5.3.2.7 Setting your hostname

You should set your system hostname with the **hostname** command. This is usually called from `/etc/rc` or `/etc/rc.local`; simply search your system **rc** files to determine where it is invoked. For example, if your (full) hostname is `loomer.vpizza.com`, edit the appropriate **rc** file to execute the command:

```
/bin/hostname loomer.vpizza.com
```

Note that the **hostname** executable may not be found in `/bin` on your system.

5.3.2.8 Trying it out

Once you have all of these files set up, you should be able to reboot your new kernel and attempt to use the network. There are many places where things can go wrong, so it's a good idea to test individual aspects of the network configuration (e.g., it's probably not a good idea to test your network configuration by firing up Mosaic over a network-based X connection).

You can use the **netstat** command to display your routing tables; this is usually the source of the most trouble. The **netstat** man page describes the exact syntax of this command in detail. In order to test network connectivity, we suggest using a client such as **telnet** to connect to machines both on your local subnetwork and external networks. This will help to narrow down the source of the problem. (For example, if you're unable to connect to local machines, but can connect to machines on other networks, more than likely there is a problem with your netmask and routing table configuration). You can also invoke the **route** command directly (as **root**) to play with the entries in your routing table.

You should also test network connectivity by specifying IP addresses directly, instead of hostnames. For example, if you have problems with the command

$ *telnet shoop.vpizza.com*

the cause may be incorrect nameserver configuration. Try using the actual IP address of the machine in question; if that works, then you know that your basic network setup is (more than likely) correct, and the problem lies in your specification of the name server address.

Debugging network configurations can be a difficult task, and we can't begin to cover it here. If you are unable to get help from a local guru we strongly suggest reading the *Linux Network Administrators' Guide* from the LDP.

5.3.3   SLIP Configuration

SLIP (Serial Line Internet Protocol) allows you to use TCP/IP over a serial line, be that a phone line, with a dialup modem, or a leased asynchronous line of some sort. Of course, to use SLIP you'll need access to a dial-in SLIP server in your area. Many universities and businesses provide SLIP access for a modest fee.

There are two major SLIP-related programs available—dip and `slattach`. Both of these programs are used to initiate a SLIP connection over a serial device. It is *necessary* to use one of these programs in order to enable SLIP—it will not suffice to dial up the SLIP server (with a communications program such as **kermit**) and issue **ifconfig** and **route** commands. This is because dip and `slattach` issue a special *ioctl()* system call to seize control of the serial device to be used as a SLIP interface.

dip can be used to dial up a SLIP server, do some handshaking to login to the server (exchanging your username and password, for example) and then initate the SLIP connection over the open serial line. **slattach**, on the other hand, does very little other than grab the serial device for use by SLIP. It is useful if you have a permanent line to your SLIP server and no modem dialup or handshaking is necessary to initiate the connection. Most dialup SLIP users should use dip, on the other hand.

dip can also be used to configure your Linux system as a SLIP server, where other machines can dial into your own and connect to the network through a secondary Ethernet connection on your machine. See the documentation and man pages for dip for more information on this procedure.

SLIP is quite unlike Ethernet, in that there are only two machines on the "network"— the SLIP host (that's you) and the SLIP server. For this reason, SLIP is often referred to as a "point-to-point" connection. A generalization of this idea, known as PPP (Point to Point Protocol) has also been implemented for Linux.

When you initiate a connection to a SLIP server, the SLIP server will give you an IP address based on (usually) one of two methods. Some SLIP servers allocate "static" IP addresses—in which case your IP address will be the same every time you connect to the server. However, many SLIP servers allocate IP addresses dynamically—in which case you receive a different IP address each time you connect. In general, the SLIP server will print the values of your IP and gateway addresses when you connect. dip is capable of reading these values from the output of the SLIP server login session and using them to configure the SLIP device.

Essentially, configuring a SLIP connection is just like configuring for loopback or ethernet. The main differences are discussed below. Read the previous section on configuring the basic TCP/IP files, and apply the changes described below.

5.3.3.1   Static IP address SLIP connections using dip

If you are using a static-allocation SLIP server, you may want to include entries for your IP address and hostname in /etc/hosts. Also, configure these files listed in the above section: rc.inet2, host.conf, and resolv.conf.

Also, configure rc.inet1, as described above. However, you only want to execute ifconfig and route commands for the loopback device. If you use dip to connect to the SLIP server, it will execute the appropriate ifconfig and route commands for the SLIP device for you. (If you're using slattach, on the other hand, you *will* need to include ifconfig/route commands in rc.inet1 for the SLIP device—see below.)

dip *should* configure your routing tables appropriately for the SLIP connection when you connect. In some cases, however, dip's behavior may not be correct for your configuration, and you'll have to run ifconfig or route commands by hand after connecting to the server with dip (this is most easily done from within a shell script that runs dip and immediately executes the appropriate configuration commands). Your gateway is, in most cases, the address of the SLIP server. You may know this address before hand, or the gateway address will be printed by the SLIP server when you connect. Your dip chat script (described below) can obtain this information from the SLIP server.

ifconfig may require use of the pointopoint argument, if dip doesn't configure the interface correctly. For example, if your SLIP server address is 128.253.154.2, and your IP address is 128.253.154.32, you may need to run the command

```
ifconfig sl0 128.253.154.32 pointopoint 128.253.154.2
```

as root, after connecting with dip. The man pages for ifconfig will come in handy.

Note that SLIP device names used with the ifconfig and route commands are sl0, sl1 and so on (as opposed to eth0, eth1, etc. for Ethernet devices).

In Section 5.3.4, below, we explain how to configure dip to connect to the SLIP server.

5.3.3.2   Static IP address SLIP connections using slattach

If you have a leased line or cable running directly to your SLIP server, then there is no need to use dip to initiate a connection. slattach can be used to configure the SLIP device instead.

In this case, your /etc/rc.inet1 file should look something like the following:

```
#!/bin/sh
IPADDR="128.253.154.32"        # Replace with your IP address
REMADDR="128.253.154.2" # Replace with your SLIP server address

# Modify the following for the appropriate serial device for the SLIP
# connection:
slattach -p cslip -s 19200 /dev/ttyS0
/etc/ifconfig sl0 $IPADDR pointopoint $REMADDR up
/etc/route add default gw $REMADDR
```

slattach allocates the first unallocated SLIP device (**sl0**, **sl1**, etc.) to the serial line specified.

Note that the first parameter to **slattach** is the SLIP protocol to use. At present the only valid values are **slip** and **cslip**. **slip** is regular SLIP, as you would expect, and **cslip** is SLIP with datagram header compression. In most cases you should use **cslip**; however, if you seem to be having problems with this, try **slip**.

If you have more than one SLIP interface then you will have routing considerations to make. You will have to decide what routes to add, and those decisions can only be made on the basis of the actual layout of your network connections. A book on TCP/IP network configuration, as well as the man pages to **route**, will be of use.

5.3.3.3 Dynamic IP address SLIP connections using dip

If your SLIP server allocates an IP address dynamically, then you certainly don't know your address in advance—therefore, you can't include an entry for it in **/etc/hosts**. (You should, however, include an entry for your host with the loopback address, 127.0.0.1.)

Many SLIP servers print your IP address (as well as the server's address) when you connect. For example, one type of SLIP server prints a string such as,

```
Your IP address is 128.253.154.44.
Server address is 128.253.154.2.
```

dip can capture these numbers from the output of the server and use them to configure the SLIP device.

See Section 5.3.3.1, above, for information on configuring your various TCP/IP files for use with SLIP. Below, we explain how to configure **dip** to connect to the SLIP server.

5.3.4 Using dip

dip can simplify the process of connecting to a SLIP server, logging in, and configuring the SLIP device. Unless you have a leased line running to your SLIP server, **dip** is the way to go.

To use **dip**, you'll need to write a "chat script" which contains a list of commands used to communicate with the SLIP server at login time. These commands can automatically send your username/password to the server, as well as get information on your IP address from the server.

Here is an example **dip** chat script, for use with a dynamic IP address server. For static servers, you will need to set the variables **$local** and **$remote** to the values of your local IP address and server IP address, respectively, at the top of the script. See the **dip** man page for details.

```
main:
  # Set Maximum Transfer Unit. This is the maximum size of packets
  # transmitted on the SLIP device. Many SLIP servers use either 1500 or
  # 1006; check with your network admins when in doubt.
  get $mtu 1500

  # Make the SLIP route the default route on your system.
  default

  # Set the desired serial port and speed.
  port cua03
  speed 38400

  # Reset the modem and terminal line. If this causes trouble for you,
  # comment it out.
  reset

  # Prepare for dialing. Replace the following with your
  # modem initialization string.
  send ATT&C1&D2\\N3&Q5%M3%C1N1W1L1S48=7\r
  wait OK 2
  if $errlvl != 0 goto error
  # Dial the SLIP server
  dial 2546000
  if $errlvl != 0 goto error
  wait CONNECT 60
  if $errlvl != 0 goto error

  # We are connected. Login to the system.
login:
  sleep 3
  send \r\n\r\n
  # Wait for the login prompt
  wait login: 10
  if $errlvl != 0 goto error

  # Send your username
```

```
send USERNAME\n

# Wait for password prompt
wait ord: 5
if $errlvl != 0 goto error

# Send password.
send PASSWORD\n

# Wait for SLIP server ready prompt
wait annex: 30
if $errlvl != 0 goto error

# Send commands to SLIP server to initate connection.
send slip\n
wait Annex 30

# Get the remote IP address from the SLIP server. The 'get...remote'
# command reads text in the form xxx.xxx.xxx.xxx, and assigns it
# to the variable given as the second argument (here, $remote).
get $remote remote
if $errlvl != 0 goto error
wait Your 30

# Get local IP address from SLIP server, assign to variable $local.
get $local remote
if $errlvl != 0 goto error

# Fire up the SLIP connection
done:
  print CONNECTED to $remote at $rmtip
  print GATEWAY address $rmtip
  print LOCAL address $local
  mode SLIP
  goto exit
error:
  print SLIP to $remote failed.

exit:
```

dip automatically executes **ifconfig** and **route** commands based on the values of the variables `$local` and `$remote`. Here, those variables are assigned using the `get...remote` command, which obtains text from the SLIP server and assigns it to the named variable.

If the **ifconfig** and **route** commands that **dip** runs for you don't work, you can either run the correct commands in a shell script after executing **dip**, or modify the source for **dip** itself. Running **dip** with the **-v** option will print debugging information while the connection is being set up, which should help you to determine where things might be going awry.

Now, in order to run **dip** and open the SLIP connection, you can use a command such as:

```
/etc/dip/dip -v /etc/dip/mychat 2>&1
```

Where the various **dip** files, and the chat script (**mychat.dip**), are stored in **/etc/dip**.

The above discussion should be enough to get you well on your way to talking to the network, either via Ethernet or SLIP. Again, we strongly suggest looking into a book on TCP/IP network configuration, especially if your network has any special routing considerations, other than those mentioned here.

5.4 Networking with UUCP

UUCP (UNIX-to-UNIX Copy) is an older mechanism used to transfer information between UNIX systems. Using UUCP, UNIX systems dial each other up (using a modem) and transfer mail messages, news articles, files, and so on. If you don't have TCP/IP or SLIP access, you can use UUCP to communicate with the world. Most of the mail and news software (see Sections 5.5 and 5.6) can be configured to use UUCP to transfer information to other machines. In fact, if there is an Internet site nearby, you can arrange to have Internet mail sent to your Linux machine via UUCP from that site.

The *Linux Network Administrator's Guide* contains complete information on configuring and using UUCP under Linux. Also, the Linux UUCP HOWTO, available via anonymous FTP from **sunsite.unc.edu**, should be of help. Another source of information on UUCP is the book *Managing UUCP and USENET*, by Tim O'Reilly and Grace Todino. See Appendix A for more information.

5.5 Electronic Mail

Like most UNIX systems, Linux provides a number of software packages for using electronic mail. E-mail on your system can either be local (that is, you only mail other users on your system), or networked (that is, you mail, using either TCP/IP or UUCP, users on other machines on a network). E-mail software usually consists of two parts: a *mailer* and a *transport*. The mailer is the user-level software which is used to actually compose and read e-mail messages. Popular mailers include **elm** and **mailx**. The transport is the low-level software which actually takes care of delivering the mail, either locally or remotely. The user never sees the transport software; they only interact with the mailer. However, as the system administrator, it is important to understand the concepts behind the transport software and how to configure it.

The most popular transport software for Linux is `Smail`. This software is easy to configure, and is able to send both local and remote TCP/IP and UUCP e-mail. The more powerful `sendmail` transport is used on most UNIX systems, however, because of its complicated setup mechanism, many Linux systems don't use it.

The Linux Mail HOWTO gives more information on the available mail software for Linux and how to configure it on your system. If you plan to send mail remotely, you'll need to understand either TCP/IP or UUCP, depending on how your machine is networked (see Sections 5.3 and 5.4). The UUCP and TCP/IP documents listed in Appendix A should be of help there.

Most of the Linux mail software can be retrieved via anonymous FTP from `sunsite.unc.edu` in the directory `/pub/Linux/system/Mail`.

5.6   News and USENET

Linux also provides a number of facilities for managing electronic news. You may choose to set up a local news server on your system, which will allow users to post "articles" to various "newsgroups" on the system. . . a lively form of discussion. However, if you have access to a TCP/IP or UUCP network, then you will be able to participate in USENET—a worldwide network news service.

There are two parts to the news software—the *server* and the *client*. The news server is the software which controls the newsgroups and handles delivering articles to other machines (if you are on a network). The news client, or *newsreader*, is the software which connects to the server to allow users to read and post news.

There are several forms of news servers available for Linux. They all follow the same basic protocols and design. The two primary versions are "C News" and "INN". There are many types of newsreaders, as well, such as `rn` and `tin`. The choice of newsreader is more or less a matter of taste; all newsreaders should work equally well with different versions of the server software. That is, the newsreader is independent of the server software, and vice versa.

If you only want to run news locally (that is, not as part of USENET), then you will need to run a server on your system, as well as install a newsreader for the users. The news server will store the articles in a directory such as `/usr/spool/news`, and the newsreader will be compiled to look in this directory for news articles.

However, if you wish to run news over the network, there are several options open to you. TCP/IP network-based news uses a protocol known as NNTP (Network News Transmission Protocol). NNTP allows a newsreader to read news over the network, on a remote machine. NNTP also allows news servers to send articles to each other over the network—this is the software upon which USENET is based. Most businesses and universities have one or more NNTP servers set up to handle all of the USENET news for that site. Every other machine at the site runs an NNTP-based newsreader to read and post news over the network via the

NNTP server. This means that only the NNTP server actually stores the news articles on disk.

Here are some possible scenarios for news configuration.

- You run news locally. That is, you have no network connection, or no desire to run news over the network. In this case, you need to run C News or INN on your machine, and install a newsreader to read the news locally.

- You have access to a TCP/IP network and an NNTP server. If your organization has an NNTP news server set up, you can read and post news from your Linux machine by simply installing an NNTP-based newsreader. (Most newsreaders available can be configured to run locally or use NNTP). In this case, you do not need to install a news server or store news articles on your system. The newsreader will take care of reading and posting news over the network. Of course, you will need to have TCP/IP configured and have access to the network (see Section 5.3).

- You have access to a TCP/IP network but have no NNTP server. In this case, you can run an NNTP news server on your Linux system. You can install either a local or an NNTP-based newsreader, and the server will store news articles on your system. In addition, you can configure the server to communicate with other NNTP news servers to transfer news articles.

- You want to transfer news using UUCP. If you have UUCP access (see Section 5.4), you can participate in USENET as well. You will need to install a (local) news server and a news reader. In addition, you will need to configure your UUCP software to periodically transfer news articles to another nearby UUCP machine (known as your "news feed"). UUCP does not use NNTP to transfer news; simply, UUCP provides its own mechanism for transferring news articles.

The one downside of most news server and newsreader software is that it must be compiled by hand. Most of the news software does not use configuration files; instead, configuration options are determined at compile time.

Most of the "standard" news software (available via anonymous FTP from `ftp.uu.net` in the directory `/news`) will compile out-of-the box on Linux. Necessary patches can be found on `sunsite.unc.edu` in `/pub/Linux/system/Mail` (which is, incidentally, also where mail software for Linux is found). Other news binaries for Linux may be found in this directory as well.

For more information, refer to the Linux News HOWTO from `sunsite.unc.edu` in `/pub/Linux/docs/HOWTO`. Also, the LDP's *Linux Network Administrator's Guide* contains complete information on configuring news software for Linux. The book *Managing UUCP and Usenet*, by Tim O'Reilly and Grace Todino, is an excellent guide to setting up UUCP and news software. Also of interest is the USENET document "How to become a USENET site," available from `ftp.uu.net`, in the directory `/usenet/news.announce.newusers`.

Appendix A

Sources of Linux Information

This appendix contains information on various sources of Linux information, such as online documents, books, and more. Many of these documents are available either in printed form, or electronically from the Internet or BBS systems. Many Linux distributions also include much of this documentation in the distribution itself, so after you have installed Linux these files may be present on your system.

A.1 Online Documents

These documents should be available on any of the Linux FTP archive sites (see Appendix C for a list). If you do not have direct access to FTP, you may be able to locate these documents on other online services (such as CompuServe, local BBS's, and so on). If you have access to Internet mail, you can use the `ftpmail` service to receive these docucments. See Appendix C for more information.

In particular, the following documents may be found on `sunsite.unc.edu` in the directory `/pub/Linux/docs`. Many sites mirror this directory; however, if you're unable to locate a mirror site near you, this is a good one to fall back on.

You can also access Linux files and documentation using `gopher`. Just point your `gopher` client to port 70 on `sunsite.unc.edu`, and follow the menus to the Linux archive. This is a good way to browse Linux documentation interactively.

The Linux Frequently Asked Questions List

    The Linux Frequently Asked Questions list, or "FAQ", is a list of common questions (and answers!) about Linux. This document is meant to provide a general source of information about Linux, common problems and solutions, and a list of other sources of information. Every new Linux user should read this document. It is available in a number of formats, including plain ASCII, PostScript, and Lout typesetter format. The Linux FAQ is maintained by Ian Jackson, `ijackson@nyx.cs.du.edu`.

The Linux META-FAQ

The META-FAQ is a collection of "metaquestions" about Linux; that is, sources of information about the Linux system, and other general topics. It is a good starting place for the Internet user wishing to find more information about the system. It is maintained by Michael K. Johnson, `johnsonm@sunsite.unc.edu`.

The Linux INFO-SHEET

The Linux INFO-SHEET is a technical introduction to the Linux system. It gives an overview of the system's features and available software, and also provides a list of other sources of Linux information. The format and content is similar in nature to the META-FAQ; incidentally, it is also maintained by Michael K. Johnson.

The Linux Software Map

The Linux Software Map is a list of many applications available for Linux, where to get them, who maintains them, and so forth. It is far from complete—to compile a complete list of Linux software would be nearly impossible. However, it does include many of the most popular Linux software packages. If you can't find a particular application to suit your needs, the LSM is a good place to start. It is maintained by Lars Wirzenius, `lars.wirzenius@helsinki.fi`.

The Linux HOWTO Index

The Linux HOWTOs are a collection of "how to" documents, each describing in detail a certain aspect of the Linux system. They are maintained by Matt Welsh, `mdw@sunsite.unc.edu`. The HOWTO Index lists the HOWTO documents which are available (several of which are listed below).

The Linux Installation HOWTO

The Linux Installation HOWTO describes how to obtain and install a distribution of Linux, similar to the information presented in Chapter 2.

The Linux Distribution HOWTO

This document is a list of Linux distributions available via mail order and anonymous FTP. It also includes information on other Linux-related goodies and services. Appendix B contains a list of Linux vendors, many of which are listed in the *Distribution HOWTO*.

The Linux XFree86 HOWTO

This document describes how to install and configure the X Window System software for Linux. See the section "5.1" for more about the X Window System.

The Linux Mail, News, and UUCP HOWTOs

These three HOWTO documents describe configuration and setup of electronic mail, news, and UUCP communications on a Linux system. Because these three subjects are often intertwined, you may wish to read all three of these HOWTOs together.

The Linux Hardware HOWTO

This HOWTO contains an extensive list of hardware supported by Linux. While this list is far from complete, it should give you a general picture of which hardware devices should be supported by the system.

The Linux SCSI HOWTO

The Linux SCSI HOWTO is a complete guide to configuration and usage of SCSI devices under Linux, such as hard drives, tape drives and CD-ROM.

The Linux NET-2-HOWTO

The Linux NET-2-HOWTO describes installation, setup, and configuration of the "NET-2" TCP/IP software under Linux, including SLIP. If you want to use TCP/IP on your Linux system, this document is a must read.

The Linux Ethernet HOWTO

Closely related to the NET-2-HOWTO, the Ethernet HOWTO describes the various Ethernet devices supported by Linux, and explains how to configure each of them for use by the Linux TCP/IP software.

The Linux Printing HOWTO

This document describes how to configure printing software under Linux, such as `lpr`. Configuration of printers and printing software under UNIX can be very confusing at times; this document sheds some light on the subject.

Other online documents

If you browse the **docs** subdirectory of any Linux FTP site, you'll see many other documents which are not listed here: A slew of FAQ's, interesting tidbits, and other important information. This miscellany is difficult to categorize here; if you don't see what you're looking for on the list above, just take a look at one of the Linux archive sites listed in Appendix C.

A.2　Linux Documentation Project Manuals

The Linux Documentation Project is working on developing a set of manuals and other documentation for Linux, including man pages. These manuals are in various stages of development, and any help revising and updating them is greatly appreciated. If you have questions about the LDP, please contact Matt Welsh (`mdw@sunsite.unc.edu`).

These books are available via anonymous FTP from a number of Linux archive sites, including `sunsite.unc.edu` in the directory `/pub/Linux/docs/LDP`. A number of commercial distributors are selling printed copies of these books; in the future, you may be able to find the LDP manuals on the shelves of your local bookstore.

Linux Installation and Getting Started, by Matt Welsh
> A new user's guide for Linux, covering everything the new user needs to know to get started. You happen to hold this book in your hands.

The Linux System Administrators' Guide, by Lars Wirzenius
> This is a complete guide to running and configuring a Linux system. There are many issues relating to systems administration which are specific to Linux, such as needs for supporting a user community, filesystem maintenance, backups, and more. This guide covers them all.

The Linux Network Administrators' Guide, by Olaf Kirch
> An extensive and complete guide to networking under Linux, including TCP/IP, UUCP, SLIP, and more. This book is a very good read; it contains a wealth of information on many subjects, clarifying the many confusing aspects of network configuration.

The Linux Kernel Hackers' Guide, by Michael Johnson
> The gritty details of kernel hacking and development under Linux. Linux is unique in that the complete kernel source is available. This book opens the doors to developers who wish to add or modify features within the kernel. This guide also contains comprehensive coverage of kernel concepts and conventions used by Linux.

A.3　Books and Other Published Works

Linux Journal is a monthly magazine for and about the Linux community, written and produced by a number of Linux developers and enthusiasts. It is distributed worldwide, and is an excellent way to keep in touch with the dynamics of the Linux world, especially if you don't have access to USENET news.

At the time of this writing, subscriptions to *Linux Journal* are US\$19/year in the United

States, US$24 in Canada, and US$29 elsewhere. To subscribe, or for more information, write to Linux Journal, PO Box 85867, Seattle, WA, 98145-1867, USA, or call +1 206 527-3385. Their FAX number is +1 206 527-2806, and e-mail address is `linux@ssc.com`. You can also find a *Linux Journal* FAQ and sample articles via anonymous FTP on `sunsite.unc.edu` in `/pub/Linux/docs/linux-journal`.

As we have said, not many books have been published dealing with Linux specifically. However, if you are new to the world of UNIX, or want more information than is presented here, we suggest that you take a look at the following books which are available.

A.3.1 Using UNIX

Title:	*Learning the UNIX Operating System*
Author:	Grace Todino & John Strang
Publisher:	O'Reilly and Associates, 1987
ISBN:	0-937175-16-1, $9.00

A good introductory book on learning the UNIX operating system. Most of the information should be applicable to Linux as well. I suggest reading this book if you're new to UNIX and really want to get started with using your new system.

Title:	*Learning the* **vi** *Editor*
Author:	Linda Lamb
Publisher:	O'Reilly and Associates, 1990
ISBN:	0-937175-67-6, $21.95

This is a book about the **vi** editor, a powerful text editor found on every UNIX system in the world. It's often important to know and be able to use **vi**, because you won't always have access to a "real" editor such as Emacs.

A.3.2 Systems Administration

Title:	*Essential System Administration*
Author:	Æleen Frisch
Publisher:	O'Reilly and Associates, 1991
ISBN:	0-937175-80-3, $29.95

From the O'Reilly and Associates Catalog, "Like any other multi-user system,

UNIX requires some care and feeding. *Essential System Administration* tells you how. This book strips away the myth and confusion surrounding this important topic and provides a compact, manageable introduction to the tasks faced by anyone responsible for a UNIX system." I couldn't have said it better myself.

Title:	*TCP/IP Network Administration*
Author:	Craig Hunt
Publisher:	O'Reilly and Associates, 1990
ISBN:	0-937175-82-X, $24.95

A complete guide to setting up and running a TCP/IP network. While this book is not Linux-specific, roughly 90% of it is applicable to Linux. Coupled with the Linux NET-2-HOWTO and *Linux Network Administrator's Guide*, this is a great book discussing the concepts and technical details of managing TCP/IP.

Title:	*Managing UUCP and Usenet*
Author:	Tim O'Reilly and Grace Todino
Publisher:	O'Reilly and Associates, 1991
ISBN:	0-937175-93-5, $24.95

This book covers how to install and configure UUCP networking software, including configuration for USENET news. If you're at all interested in using UUCP or accessing USENET news on your system, this book is a must-read.

A.3.3   The X Window System

Title:	*The X Window System: A User's Guide*
Author:	Niall Mansfield
Publisher:	Addison-Wesley
ISBN:	0-201-51341-2, ??

A complete tutorial and reference guide to using the X Window System. If you installed X windows on your Linux system, and want to know how to get the most out of it, you should read this book. Unlike some windowing systems, a lot of the power provided by X is not obvious at first sight.

A.3.4 Programming

Title:	*The C Programming Language*
Author:	Brian Kernighan and Dennis Ritchie
Publisher:	Prentice-Hall, 1988
ISBN:	0-13-110362-8, $25.00

This book is a must-have for anyone wishing to do C programming on a UNIX system. (Or any system, for that matter.) While this book is not obstensibly UNIX-specific, it is quite applicable to programming C under UNIX.

Title:	*The Unix Programming Environment*
Author:	Brian Kernighan and Bob Pike
Publisher:	Prentice-Hall, 1984
ISBN:	0-13-937681-X, ??

An overview to programming under the UNIX system. Covers all of the tools of the trade; a good read to get acquainted with the somewhat amorphous UNIX programming world.

Title:	*Advanced Programming in the UNIX Environment*
Author:	W. Richard Stevens
Publisher:	Addison-Wesley
ISBN:	0-201-56317-7, $50.00

This mighty tome contains everything that you need to know to program UNIX at the system level—file I/O, process control, interprocess communication, signals, terminal I/O, the works. This book focuses on various UNI standards, including POSIX.1, which Linux mostly adheres to.

A.3.5 Kernel Hacking

Title:	*The Design of the UNIX Operating System*
Author:	Maurice J. Bach
Publisher:	Prentice-Hall, 1986
ISBN:	0-13-201799-7, ??

This book covers the algorithms and internals of the UNIX kernel. It is not specific to any particular kernel, although it does lean towards System V-isms. This is the best place to start if you want to understand the inner tickings of the Linux system.

Title:	*The Magic Garden Explained*
Author:	Berny Goodheart and James Cox
Publisher:	Prentice-Hall, 1994
ISBN:	0-13-098138-9, ??

This book describes the System V R4 kernel in detail. Unlike Bach's book, which concentrates heavily on the algorithms which make the kernel tick, this book presents the SVR4 implementation on a more technical level. Although Linux and SVR4 are distant cousins, this book can give you much insight into the workings of an actual UNIX kernel implementation. This is also a very modern book on the UNIX kernel—published in 1994.

Appendix B

Linux Vendor List

This appendix lists contact information for a number of vendors which sell Linux on diskette, tape, and CD-ROM. Many of them provide Linux documentation, support, and other services as well. This is by no means a complete listing; if you purchased this book in printed form, it's very possible that the vendor or publishing company also provides Linux software and services.

The author makes no guarantee as to the accuracy of any of the information listed in this Appendix. This information is included here only as a service to readers, not as an advertisement for any particular organization.

Fintronic Linux Systems
1360 Willow Rd., Suite 205
Menlo Park, CA 94025 USA
Tel: +1 415 325-4474
Fax: +1 415 325-4908
linux@fintronic.com

InfoMagic, Inc.
PO Box 30370
Flagstaff, AZ 86003-0370 USA
Tel: +1 800 800-6613, +1 602 526-9565
Fax: +1 602 526-9573
Orders@InfoMagic.com

Lasermoon Ltd
2a Beaconsfield Road, Fareham,
Hants, England. PO16 0QB.
Tel: +44 (0) 329 826444.

Fax: +44 (0) 329 825936.
info@lasermoon.co.uk

Linux Journal
P.O. Box 85867
Seattle, WA 98145-1867 USA
Tel: +1 206 527-3385
Fax: +1 206 527-2806
linux@ssc.com

Linux Systems Labs
18300 Tara Drive
Clinton Twp, MI 48036 USA
Tel: +1 313 954-2829, +1 800 432-0556
Fax: +1 313 954-2806
info@lsl.com

Morse Telecommunication, Inc.
26 East Park Avenue, Suite 240
Long Beach, NY 11561 USA
Tel: +1 800 60-MORSE
Fax: +1 516 889-8665
Linux@morse.net

Nascent Technology
Linux from Nascent CDROM
P.O. Box 60669
Sunnyvale CA 94088-0669 USA
Tel: +1 408 737-9500
Fax: +1 408 241-9390
nascent@netcom.com

Red Hat Software
P.O. Box 4325
Chapel Hill, NC 27515 USA
Tel: +1 919 309-9560
redhat@redhat.com

SW Technology
251 West Renner Suite 229
Richardson, TX 75080 USA
Tel: +1 214 907-0871
swt@netcom.com

Takelap Systems Ltd.
The Reddings, Court Robin Lane,
Llangwm, Usk, Gwent, United Kingdom NP5 1ET.
Tel: +44 (0)291 650357
Fax: +44 (0)291 650500
`info@ddrive.demon.co.uk`

Trans-Ameritech Enterprises, Inc.
2342A Walsh Ave
Santa Clara, CA 95051 USA
Tel: +1 408 727-3883
`roman@trans-ameritech.com`

Unifix Software GmbH
Postfach 4918
D-38039 Braunschweig
Germany
Tel: +49 (0)531 515161
Fax: +49 (0)531 515162

Yggdrasil Computing, Incorporated
4880 Stevens Creek Blvd., Suite 205
San Jose, CA 95129-1034 USA
Tel: +1 800 261-6630, +1 408 261-6630
Fax: +1 408 261-6631
`info@yggdrasil.com`

Appendix C

FTP Tutorial and Site List

FTP ("File Transfer Protocol") is the set of programs that are used for transferring files between systems on the Internet. Most UNIX, VMS, and MS-DOS systems on the Internet have a program called **ftp** which you use to transfer these files, and if you have Internet access, the best way to download the Linux software is by using **ftp**. This appendix covers basic **ftp** usage—of course, there are many more functions and uses of **ftp** than are given here.

At the end of this appendix there is a listing of FTP sites where Linux software can be found. Also, if you don't have direct Internet access but are able to exchange electronic mail with the Internet, information on using the **ftpmail** service is included below.

If you're using an MS-DOS, UNIX, or VMS system to download files from the Internet, then **ftp** is a command-driven program. However, there are other implementations of **ftp** out there, such as the Macintosh version (called **Fetch**) with a nice menu-driven interface, which is quite self-explanatory. Even if you're not using the command-driven version of **ftp**, the information given here should help.

ftp can be used to both upload (send) or download (receive) files from other Internet sites. In most situations, you're going to be downloading software. On the Internet there are a large number of publicly-available **FTP archive sites**, machines which allow anyone to **ftp** to them and download free software. One such archive site is **sunsite.unc.edu**, which has a lot of Sun Microsystems software, and acts as one of the main Linux sites. In addition, FTP archive sites **mirror** software to each other—that is, software uploaded to one site will be automatically copied over to a number of other sites. So don't be surprised if you see the exact same files on many different archive sites.

C.1   Starting `ftp`

Note that in the example "screens" printed below I'm only showing the most important information, and what you see may differ. Also, commands in *italics* represent commands that you type; everything else is screen output.

To start **ftp** and connect to a site, simply use the command

```
ftp ⟨hostname⟩
```

where ⟨*hostname*⟩ is the name of the site you are connecting to. For example, to connect to the mythical site **shoop.vpizza.com** we can use the command

```
ftp shoop.vpizza.com
```

C.2   Logging In

When **ftp** starts up we should see something like

```
Connected to shoop.vpizza.com.
220 Shoop.vpizza.com FTPD ready at 15 Dec 1992 08:20:42 EDT
Name (shoop.vpizza.com:mdw):
```

Here, **ftp** is asking us to give the username that we want to login as on **shoop.vpizza.com**. The default here is **mdw**, which is my username on the system I'm using FTP from. Since I don't have an account on **shoop.vpizza.com** I can't login as myself. Instead, to access publicly-available software on an FTP site you login as **anonymous**, and give your Internet e-mail address (if you have one) as the password. So, we would type

```
Name (shoop.vpizza.com:mdw):  anonymous
331-Guest login ok, send e-mail address as password.
Password:  mdw@sunsite.unc.edu
230- Welcome to shoop.vpizza.com.
230- Virtual Pizza Delivery[tm]:  Download pizza in 30 cycles or less
230- or you get it FREE!
ftp>
```

Of course, you should give your e-mail address, instead of mine, and it won't echo to the screen as you're typing it (since it's technically a "password"). **ftp** should allow us to login and we'll be ready to download software.

C.3   Poking Around

Okay, we're in. **ftp>** is our prompt, and the **ftp** program is waiting for commands. There are a few basic commands you need to know about. First, the commands

>   ls ⟨*file*⟩

and

>   dir ⟨*file*⟩

both give file listings (where ⟨*file*⟩ is an optional argument specifying a particular filename to list). The difference is that **ls** usually gives a short listing and **dir** gives a longer listing (that is, with more information on the sizes of the files, dates of modification, and so on).

The command

>   cd ⟨*directory*⟩

will move to the given directory (just like the **cd** command on UNIX or MS-DOS systems). You can use the command

>   cdup

to change to the parent directory[1].

The command

>   help ⟨*command*⟩

will give help on the given **ftp** ⟨*command*⟩ (such as **ls** or **cd**). If no command is specified, **ftp** will list all of the available commands.

If we type **dir** at this point we'll see an initial directory listing of where we are.

```
ftp> dir
200 PORT command successful.
150 Opening ASCII mode data connection for /bin/ls.
total 1337


dr-xr-xr-x  2 root     wheel       512 Aug 13 13:55 bin
drwxr-xr-x  2 root     wheel       512 Aug 13 13:58 dev
drwxr-xr-x  2 root     wheel       512 Jan 25 17:35 etc
drwxr-xr-x 19 root     wheel      1024 Jan 27 21:39 pub
drwxrwx-wx  4 root     ftp-admi   1024 Feb  6 22:10 uploads
drwxr-xr-x  3 root     wheel       512 Mar 11  1992 usr
```

---

[1] The directory above the current one.

```
226 Transfer complete.
921 bytes received in 0.24 seconds (3.7 Kbytes/s)
ftp>
```

Each of these entries is a directory, not an individual file which we can download (specified by the **d** in the first column of the listing). On most FTP archive sites, the publicly available software is under the directory **/pub**, so let's go there.

```
ftp> cd pub
ftp> dir
200 PORT command successful.
150 ASCII data connection for /bin/ls (128.84.181.1,4525) (0 bytes).
total 846
```

```
-rw-r--r--   1 root     staff        1433 Jul 12  1988 README
-r--r--r--   1 3807     staff       15586 May 13  1991 US-DOMAIN.TXT.2
-rw-r--r--   1 539      staff       52664 Feb 20  1991 altenergy.avail
-r--r--r--   1 65534    65534       56456 Dec 17  1990 ataxx.tar.Z
-rw-r--r--   1 root     other     2013041 Jul  3  1991 gesyps.tar.Z
-rw-r--r--   1 432      staff       41831 Jan 30  1989 gnexe.arc
-rw-rw-rw-   1 615      staff       50315 Apr 16  1992 linpack.tar.Z
-r--r--r--   1 root     wheel       12168 Dec 25  1990 localtime.o
-rw-r--r--   1 root     staff        7035 Aug 27  1986 manualslist.tblms
drwxr-xr-x   2 2195     staff         512 Mar 10 00:48 mdw
-rw-r--r--   1 root     staff        5593 Jul 19  1988 t.out.h
```

```
226 ASCII Transfer complete.
2443 bytes received in 0.35 seconds (6.8 Kbytes/s)
ftp>
```

Here we can see a number of (interesting?) files, one of which is called **README**, which we should download (most FTP sites have a **README** file in the **/pub** directory).

C.4   Downloading files

Before downloading files, there are a few things that you need to take care of.

- **Turn on hash mark printing.** *Hash marks* are printed to the screen as files are being transferred; they let you know how far along the transfer is, and that your connection hasn't hung up (so you don't sit for 20 minutes, thinking that you're still downloading a file). In general, a hash mark appears as a pound sign (**#**), and one is printed for every 1024 or 8192 bytes transferred, depending on your system.

  To turn on hash mark printing, give the command **hash**.

```
ftp> hash
Hash mark printing on (8192 bytes/hash mark).
ftp>
```

- **Determine the type of file which you are downloading.** As far as FTP is concerned, files come in two flavors: *binary* and *text*. Most of the files which you'll be downloading are binary files: that is, programs, compressed files, archive files, and so on. However, many files (such as README s and so on) are text files.

  Why does the file type matter? Only because on some systems (such as MS-DOS systems), certain characters in a text file, such as carriage returns, need to be converted so that the file will be readable. While transferring in binary mode, no conversion is done—the file is simply transferred byte after byte.

  The commands **bin** and **ascii** set the transfer mode to binary and text, respectively. *When in doubt, always use binary mode to transfer files.* If you try to transfer a binary file in text mode, you'll corrupt the file and it will be unusable. (This is one of the most common mistakes made when using FTP.) However, you can use text mode for plain text files (whose filenames often end in .txt).

  For our example, we're downloading the file **README**, which is most likely a text file, so we use the command

```
ftp> ascii
200 Type set to A.
ftp>
```

- **Set your local directory.** Your *local directory* is the directory on your system where you want the downloaded files to end up. Whereas the **cd** command changes the remote directory (on the remote machine which you're FTPing to), the **lcd** command changes the local directory.

  For example, to set the local directory to **/home/db/mdw/tmp**, use the command

```
ftp> lcd /home/db/mdw/tmp
Local directory now /home/db/mdw/tmp
ftp>
```

Now you're ready to actually download the file. The command

```
get ⟨remote-name⟩ ⟨local-name⟩
```

is used for this, where ⟨remote-name⟩ is the name of the file on the remote machine, and ⟨local-name⟩ is the name that you wish to give the file on your local machine. The ⟨local-name⟩ argument is optional; by default, the local filename is the same as the remote one. However, if for example you're downloading the file **README**, and you already have a **README** in your local directory, you'll want to give a different ⟨local-filename⟩ so that the first one isn't overwritten.

For our example, to download the file **README**, we simply use

```
ftp> get README
200 PORT command successful.
150 ASCII data connection for README (128.84.181.1,4527) (1433 bytes).
#
226 ASCII Transfer complete.
local:  README remote:  README
1493 bytes received in 0.03 seconds (49 Kbytes/s)
ftp>
```

C.5   Quitting FTP

To end your FTP session, simply use the command

```
quit
```

The command

```
close
```

can be used to close the connection with the current remote FTP site; the **open** command
can then be used to start a session with another site (without quitting the FTP program
altogether).

```
ftp> close
221 Goodbye.
ftp> quit
```

C.6   Using `ftpmail`

`ftpmail` is a service which allows you to obtain files from FTP archive sites via Internet
electronic mail. If you don't have direct Internet access, but are able to send mail to the
Internet (from a service such as CompuServe, for example), `ftpmail` is a good way to get
files from FTP archive sites. Unfortunately, `ftpmail` can be slow, especially when sending
large jobs. Before attempting to download large amounts of software using `ftpmail`, be sure
that your mail spool will be able to handle the incoming traffic. Many systems keep quotas
on incoming electronic mail, and may delete your account if your mail exceeds this quota.
Just use common sense.

`sunsite.unc.edu`, one of the major Linux FTP archive sites, is home to an `ftpmail`
server. To use this service, send electronic mail to

    ftpmail@sunsite.unc.edu

with a message body containing only the word:

    help

This will send you back a list of **ftpmail** commands and a brief tutorial on using the system.

For example, to get a listing of Linux files found on **sunsite.unc.edu**, send mail to the above address containing the text

    open sunsite.unc.edu
    cd /pub/Linux
    dir
    quit

You may use the **ftpmail** service to connect to any FTP archive site; you are not limited to **sunsite.unc.edu**. The next section lists a number of Linux FTP archives.

C.7 Linux FTP Site List

Table C.1 is a listing of the most well-known FTP archive sites which carry the Linux software. Keep in mind that many other sites mirror these, and more than likely you'll run into Linux on a number of sites not on this list.

tsx-11.mit.edu, **sunsite.unc.edu**, and **nic.funet.fi** are the "home sites" for the Linux software, where most of the new software is uploaded. Most of the other sites on the list mirror some combination of these three. To reduce network traffic, choose a site that is geographically closest to you.

Site name	IP Address	Directory
tsx-11.mit.edu	18.172.1.2	/pub/linux
sunsite.unc.edu	152.2.22.81	/pub/Linux
nic.funet.fi	128.214.6.100	/pub/OS/Linux
ftp.mcc.ac.uk	130.88.200.7	/pub/linux
fgb1.fgb.mw.tu-muenchen.de	129.187.200.1	/pub/linux
ftp.informatik.tu-muenchen.de	131.159.0.110	/pub/Linux
ftp.dfv.rwth-aachen.de	137.226.4.105	/pub/linux
ftp.informatik.rwth-aachen.de	137.226.112.172	/pub/Linux
ftp.ibp.fr	132.227.60.2	/pub/linux
kirk.bu.oz.au	131.244.1.1	/pub/OS/Linux
ftp.uu.net	137.39.1.9	/systems/unix/linux
wuarchive.wustl.edu	128.252.135.4	/systems/linux
ftp.win.tue.nl	131.155.70.100	/pub/linux
ftp.ibr.cs.tu-bs.de	134.169.34.15	/pub/os/linux
ftp.denet.dk	129.142.6.74	/pub/OS/linux

Table C.1: Linux FTP Sites

Appendix D

Linux BBS List

Printed here is a list of bulletin board systems (BBS) which carry Linux software. Zane Healy (`healyzh@holonet.net`) maintains this list. If you know of or run a BBS which provides Linux software which isn't on this list, you should get in touch with him.

The Linux community is no longer an Internet-only society. In fact, it is now estimated that the majority of Linux users don't have Internet access. Therefore, it is especially important that BBSs continue to provide and support Linux to users worldwide.

D.1 United States

Citrus Grove Public Access, 916-381-5822. ZyXEL 16.8/14.4 Sacramento, CA. Internet: `citrus.sac.ca.us`
Higher Powered BBS, 408-737-7040. ? CA. RIME ->HIGHER
hip-hop, 408-773-0768. 19.2k Sunnyvale, CA. USENET access
hip-hop, 408-773-0768. 38.4k Sunnyvale, CA.
Unix Online, 707-765-4631. 9600 Petaluma, CA. USENET access
The Outer Rim, 805-252-6342. Santa Clarita, CA.
Programmer's Exchange, 818-444-3507. El Monte, CA. Fidonet
Programmer's Exchange, 818-579-9711. El Monte, CA.
Micro Oasis, 510-895-5985. 14.4k San Leandro, CA.
Test Engineering, 916-928-0504. Sacramento, CA.
Slut Club, 813-975-2603. USR/DS 16.8k HST/14.4K Tampa, FL. Fidonet 1:377/42
Lost City Atlantis, 904-727-9334. 14.4k Jacksonville, FL. FidoNet
Aquired Knowledge, 305-720-3669. 14.4k v.32bis Ft. Lauderdale, FL. Internet, UUCP
The Computer Mechanic, 813-544-9345. 14.4k v.32bis St. Petersburg, FL. Fidonet, Sailnet, MXBBSnet
AVSync, 404-320-6202. Atlanta, GA.

Information Overload, 404-471-1549. 19.2k ZyXEL Atlanta, GA. Fidonet 1:133/308

Atlanta Radio Club, 404-850-0546. 9600 Atlanta, GA.

Rebel BBS, 208-887-3937. 9600 Boise, ID.

Rocky Mountain HUB, 208-232-3405. 38.4k Pocatello, ID. Fionet, SLNet, CinemaNet

EchoMania, 618-233-1659. 14.4k HST Belleville, IL. Fidonet 1:2250/1, f'req LINUX

UNIX USER, 708-879-8633. 14.4k Batavia, IL. USENET, Internet mail

PBS BBS, 309-663-7675. 2400 Bloomington, IL.

Third World, 217-356-9512. 9600 v.32 IL.

Digital Underground, 812-941-9427. 14.4k v.32bis IN. USENET

The OA Southern Star, 504-885-5928. New Orleans, LA. Fidonet 1:396/1

Channel One, 617-354-8873. Boston, MA. RIME ->CHANNEL

VWIS Linux Support BBS, 508-793-1570. 9600 Worcester, MA.

WayStar BBS, 508-481-7147. 14.4k V.32bis USR/HST Marlborough, MA. Fidonet 1:333/14

WayStar BBS, 508-481-7293. 14.4k V.32bis USR/HST Marlborough, MA. Fidonet 1:333/15

WayStar BBS, 508-480-8371. 9600 V.32bis or 14.4k USR/HST Marlborough, MA. Fidonet 1:333/16

Programmer's Center, 301-596-1180. 9600 Columbia, MD. RIME

Brodmann's Place, 301-843-5732. 14.4k Waldorf, MD. RIME ->BRODMANN, Fidonet

Main Frame, 301-654-2554. 9600 Gaithersburg, MD. RIME ->MAINFRAME

1 Zero Cybernet BBS, 301-589-4064. MD.

WaterDeep BBS, 410-614-2190. 9600 v.32 Baltimore, MD.

Harbor Heights BBS, 207-663-0391. 14.4k Boothbay Harbor, ME.

Part-Time BBS, 612-544-5552. 14.4k v.32bis Plymouth, MN.

The Sole Survivor, 314-846-2702. 14.4k v.32bis St. Louis, MO. WWIVnet, WWIVlink, etc

MAC's Place, 919-891-1111. 16.8k, DS modem Dunn, NC. RIME ->MAC

Digital Designs, 919-423-4216. 14.4k, 2400 Hope Mills, NC.

Flite Line, 402-421-2434. Lincoln, NE. RIME ->FLITE, DS modem

Legend, 402-438-2433. Lincoln, NE. DS modem

MegaByte Mansion, 402-551-8681. 14.4 V,32bis Omaha, NE.

Mycroft QNX, 201-858-3429. 14.4k NJ.

Steve Leon's, 201-886-8041. 14.4k Cliffside Park, NJ.

Dwight-Englewood BBS, 201-569-3543. 9600 v.42 Englewood, NJ. USENET

The Mothership Cnection, 908-940-1012. 38.4k Franklin Park, NJ.

The Laboratory, 212-927-4980. 16.8k HST, 14.4k v.32bis NY. FidoNet 1:278/707

Valhalla, 516-321-6819. 14.4k HST v.32 Babylon, NY. Fidonet (1:107/255), UseNet (die.linet.org)

Intermittent Connection, 503-344-9838. 14.4k HST v.32bis Eugene, OR. 1:152/35

Horizon Systems, 216-899-1086. USR v.32 Westlake, OH.

Horizon Systems, 216-899-1293. 2400 Westlake, OH.

Centre Programmers Unit, 814-353-0566. 14.4k V.32bis/HST Bellefonte, PA.

Allentown Technical, 215-432-5699. 9600 v.32/v.42bis Allentown, PA. WWIVNet 2578

Tactical-Operations, 814-861-7637. 14.4k V32bis/V42bis State College, PA. Fidonet 1:129/226, tac_ops.UUCP
North Shore BBS, 713-251-9757. Houston, TX.
The Annex, 512-575-1188. 9600 HST TX. Fidonet 1:3802/217
The Annex, 512-575-0667. 2400 TX. Fidonet 1:3802/216
Walt Fairs, 713-947-9866. Houston, TX. FidoNet 1:106/18
CyberVille, 817-249-6261. 9600 TX. FidoNet 1:130/78
splat-ooh, 512-578-2720. 14.4k Victoria, TX.
splat-ooh, 512-578-5436. 14.4k Victoria, TX.
alaree, 512-575-5554. 14.4k Victoria, TX.
Ronin BBS, 214-938-2840. 14.4 HST/DS Waxahachie (Dallas), TX. RIME, Intelec, Smartnet, etc.
VTBBS, 703-231-7498. Blacksburg, VA.
MBT, 703-953-0640. Blacksburg, VA.
NOVA, 703-323-3321. 9600 Annandale, VA. Fidonet 1:109/305
Rem-Jem, 703-503-9410. 9600 Fairfax, VA.
Enlightend, 703-370-9528. 14.4k Alexandria, VA. Fidonet 1:109/615
My UnKnown BBS, 703-690-0669. 14.4k V.32bis VA. Fidonet 1:109/370
Georgia Peach BBS, 804-727-0399. 14.4k Newport News, VA.
Top Hat BBS, 206-244-9661. 14.4k WA. Fidonet 1:343/40
victrola.sea.wa.us, 206-838-7456. 19.2k Federal Way, WA. USENET

D.2 Outside of the United States

Galaktische Archive, 0043-2228303804. 16.8 ZYX Wien, Austria. Fidonet 2:310/77 (19:00-7:00)
Linux-Support-Oz, +61-2-418-8750. v.32bis 14.4k Sydney, NSW, Austrailia. Internet/Usenet, E-Mail/News
500cc Formula 1 BBS, +61-2-550-4317. V.32bis Sydney, NSW, Australia.
Magic BBS, 403-569-2882. 14.4k HST/Telebit/MNP Calgary, AB, Canada. Internet/Usenet
Logical Solutions, 299-9900 through 9911. 2400 AB, Canada.
Logical Solutions, 299-9912, 299-9913. 14.4k Canada.
Logical Solutions, 299-9914 through 9917. 16.8k v.32bis Canada.
V.A.L.I.S., 403-478-1281. 14.4k v.32bis Edmonton, AB, Canada. USENET
The Windsor Download, (519)-973-9330. v32bis 14.4 ON, Canada.
r-node, 416-249-5366. 2400 Toronto, ON, Canada. USENET
Synapse, 819-246-2344. 819-561-5268 Gatineau, QC, Canada. RIME->SYNAPSE
Radio Free Nyongwa, 514-524-0829. v.32bis ZyXEL Montreal, QC, Canada. USENET, Fidonet
DataComm1, +49.531.132-16. 14.4 HST Braunschweig, NDS, Germany. Fido 2:240/550,

LinuxNet

DataComm2, +49.531.132-17. 14.4 HST Braunschweig, NDS, Germany. Fido 2:240/551, LinuxNet

Linux Server /Braukmann, +49.441.592-963. 16.8 ZYX Oldenburg, NDS, Germany. Fido 2:241/2012, LinuxNet

MM's Spielebox, +49.5323.3515. 14.4 ZYX Clausthal-Zfd., NDS, Germany. Fido 2:241/3420

MM's Spielebox, +49.5323.3516. 16.8 ZYX Clausthal-Zfd., NDS, Germany. Fido 2:241/3421

MM's Spielebox, +49.5323.3540. 9600 Clausthal-Zfd., NDS, Germany. Fido 2:241/3422

Bit-Company / J. Bartz, +49.5323.2539. 16.8 ZYX MO Clausthal-Zfd., NDS, Germany. Fido 2:241/3430

Fractal Zone BBS /Maass, +49.721.863-066. 16.8 ZYX Karlsruhe, BW, Germany. Fido 2:241/7462

Hipposoft /M. Junius, +49.241.875-090. 14.4 HST Aachen, NRW, Germany. Fido 2:242/6, 4:30-7,8-23:30

UB-HOFF /A. Hoffmann, +49.203.584-155. 19.2 ZYX+ Duisburg, Germany. Fido 2:242/37

FORMEL-Box, +49.4191.2846. 16.8 ZYX Kaltenkirchen, SHL, Germany. Fido 2:242/329, LinuxNet (6:00-20:00)

BOX/2, +49.89.601-96-77. 16.8 ZYX Muenchen, BAY, Germany. Fido 2:246/147, info magic: LINUX (22-24,0:30-2,5-8)

Die Box Passau 2+1, +49.851.555-96. 14.4 V32b Passau, BAY, Germany. Fido 2:246/200 (8:00-3:30)

Die Box Passau Line 1, +49.851.753-789. 16.8 ZYX Passau, BAY, Germany. Fido 2:246/2000 (8:00-3:30)

Die Box Passau Line 3, +49.851.732-73. 14.4 HST Passau, BAY, Germany. Fido 2:246/202 (5:00-3:30)

Die Box Passau ISDN, +49.851.950-464. 38.4/64k V.110/X.75 Passau, BAY, Germany. Fido 2:246/201 (8:00-24:00,1:00-3:30)

Public Domain Kiste, +49.30.686-62-50. 16.8 ZYX BLN, Germany. Fido 2:2403/17

CS-Port / C. Schmidt, +49.30.491-34-18. 19.2 Z19 Berlin, BLN, Germany. Fido 2:2403/13

BigBrother / R. Gmelch, +49.30.335-63-28. 16.8 Z16 Berlin, BLN, Germany. Fido 2:2403/36.4 (16-23:00)

CRYSTAL BBS, +49.7152.240-86. 14.4 HST Leonberg, BW, Germany. Fido 2:2407/3, LinuxNet

Echoblaster BBS #1, +49.7142.213-92. HST/V32b Bietigheim, BW, Germany. Fido 2:2407/4, LinuxNet (7-19,23-01h)

Echoblaster BBS #2, +49.7142.212-35. V32b Bietigheim, BW, Germany. Fido 2:2407/40, LinuxNet (20h-6h)

LinuxServer / P. Berger, +49.711.756-275. 16.8 HST Stuttgart, BW, Germany. Fido 2:2407/34, LinuxNet (8:3-17:5,19-2)

Rising Sun BBS, +49.7147.3845. 16.8 ZYX Sachsenheim, BW, Germany. Fido 2:2407/41,

LinuxNet (5:30-2:30)

bakunin.north.de, +49.421.870-532. 14.4 D 2800 Bremen, HB, Germany.
`kraehe@bakunin.north.de`

oytix.north.de, +49.421.396-57-62. ZYX HB, Germany. `mike@oytix.north.de`, login as gast

Fiffis Inn BBS, +49-89-5701353. 14.4-19.2 Munich, Germany. FidoNet 2:246/69,Internet,USENET,LinuxNet

The Field of Inverse Chaos, +358 0 506 1836. 14.4k v32bis/HST Helsinki, Finland. USENET; ichaos.nullnet.fi

Modula BBS, +33-1 4043 0124. HST 14.4 v.32bis Paris, France.

Modula BBS, +33-1 4530 1248. HST 14.4 V.32bis Paris, France.

STDIN BBS, +33-72375139. v.32bis Lyon, Laurent Cas, France. FidoNet 2:323/8

Le Lien, +33-72089879. HST 14.4/V32bis Lyon, Pascal Valette, France. FidoNet 2:323/5

Basil, +33-1-44670844. v.32bis Paris, Laurent Chemla, France.

Cafard Naum, +33-51701632. v.32bis Nantes, Yann Dupont, France.

DUBBS, +353-1-6789000. 19.2 ZyXEL Dublin, Ireland. Fidonet 2:263/167

Galway Online, +353-91-27454. 14.4k v32b Galway, Ireland. RIME, `@iol.ie`

Nemesis' Dungeon, +353-1-324755 or 326900. 14.4k v32bis Dublin, Ireland. Fidonet 2:263/150

nonsolosoftware, +39 51 6140772. v.32bis, v.42bis Italy. Fidonet 2:332/407

nonsolosoftware, +39 51 432904. ZyXEL 19.2k Italy. Fidonet 2:332/417

Advanced Systems, +64-9-379-3365. ZyXEL 16.8k Auckland, New Zealand. Singet, INTLnet, Fidonet

Thunderball Cave, 472567018. Norway. RIME ->CAVE

DownTown BBS Lelystad, +31-3200-48852. 14.4k Lelystad, Netherlands. Fido 2:512/155, UUCP

MUGNET Intl-Cistron BBS, +31-1720-42580. 38.4k Alphen a/d Rijn, Netherlands. UUCP

The Controversy, (65)560-6040. 14.4k V.32bis/HST Singapore. Fidonet 6:600/201

Pats System, +27-12-333-2049. 14.4k v.32bis/HST Pretoria, South Africa. Fidonet 5:71-1/36

Gunship BBS, +46-31-693306. 14.4k HST DS Gothenburg Sweden.

Baboon BBS, +41-62-511726. 19.2k Switzerland. Fido 2:301/580 and /581

The Purple Tentacle, +44-734-590990. HST/V32bis Reading, UK. Fidonet 2:252/305

A6 BBS, +44-582-460273. 14.4k Herts, UK. Fidonet 2:440/111

On the Beach, +444-273-600996. 14.4k/16.8k Brighton, UK. Fidonet 2:441/122

Appendix E

The GNU General Public License

Printed below is the GNU General Public License (the *GPL* or *copyleft*), under which Linux is licensed. It is reproduced here to clear up some of the confusion about Linux's copyright status—Linux is *not* shareware, and it is *not* in the public domain. The bulk of the Linux kernel is copyright ©1993 by Linus Torvalds, and other software and parts of the kernel are copyrighted by their authors. Thus, Linux *is* copyrighted, however, you may redistribute it under the terms of the GPL printed below.

GNU GENERAL PUBLIC LICENSE
Version 2, June 1991

Copyright ©1989, 1991 Free Software Foundation, Inc. 675 Mass Ave, Cambridge, MA 02139, USA Everyone is permitted to copy and distribute verbatim copies of this license document, but changing it is not allowed.

E.1   Preamble

The licenses for most software are designed to take away your freedom to share and change it. By contrast, the GNU General Public License is intended to guarantee your freedom to share and change free software–to make sure the software is free for all its users. This General Public License applies to most of the Free Software Foundation's software and to any other program whose authors commit to using it. (Some other Free Software Foundation software is covered by the GNU Library General Public License instead.) You can apply it to your programs, too.

When we speak of free software, we are referring to freedom, not price. Our General Public Licenses are designed to make sure that you have the freedom to distribute copies of free software (and charge for this service if you wish), that you receive source code or can get it if you want it, that you can change the software or use pieces of it in new free programs; and that you know you can do these things.

To protect your rights, we need to make restrictions that forbid anyone to deny you these rights or to ask you to surrender the rights. These restrictions translate to certain responsibilities for you if you distribute copies of the software, or if you modify it.

For example, if you distribute copies of such a program, whether gratis or for a fee, you must give the recipients all the rights that you have. You must make sure that they, too, receive or can get the source code. And you must show them these terms so they know their rights.

We protect your rights with two steps: (1) copyright the software, and (2) offer you this license which gives you legal permission to copy, distribute and/or modify the software.

Also, for each author's protection and ours, we want to make certain that everyone understands that there is no warranty for this free software. If the software is modified by someone else and passed on, we want its recipients to know that what they have is not the original, so that any problems introduced by others will not reflect on the original authors' reputations.

Finally, any free program is threatened constantly by software patents. We wish to avoid the danger that redistributors of a free program will individually obtain patent licenses, in effect making the program proprietary. To prevent this, we have made it clear that any patent must be licensed for everyone's free use or not licensed at all.

The precise terms and conditions for copying, distribution and modification follow.

E.2   Terms and Conditions for Copying, Distribution, and Modification

0. This License applies to any program or other work which contains a notice placed by the copyright holder saying it may be distributed under the terms of this General Public License. The "Program", below, refers to any such program or work, and a "work based on the Program" means either the Program or any derivative work under copyright law: that is to say, a work containing the Program or a portion of it, either verbatim or with modifications and/or translated into another language. (Hereinafter, translation is included without limitation in the term "modification".) Each licensee is addressed as "you".

   Activities other than copying, distribution and modification are not covered by this License; they are outside its scope. The act of running the Program is not restricted, and the output from the Program is covered only if its contents constitute a work based on the Program (independent of having been made by running the Program). Whether that is true depends on what the Program does.

1. You may copy and distribute verbatim copies of the Program's source code as you receive it, in any medium, provided that you conspicuously and appropriately publish on each copy an appropriate copyright notice and disclaimer of warranty; keep intact all the notices that refer to this License and to the absence of any warranty; and give any other recipients of the Program a copy of this License along with the Program.

   You may charge a fee for the physical act of transferring a copy, and you may at your option offer warranty protection in exchange for a fee.

2. You may modify your copy or copies of the Program or any portion of it, thus forming a work based on the Program, and copy and distribute such modifications or work under the terms of Section 1 above, provided that you also meet all of these conditions:

   a. You must cause the modified files to carry prominent notices stating that you changed the files and the date of any change.

   b. You must cause any work that you distribute or publish, that in whole or in part contains or is derived from the Program or any part thereof, to be licensed as a whole at no charge to all third parties under the terms of this License.

   c. If the modified program normally reads commands interactively when run, you must cause it, when started running for such interactive use in the most ordinary way, to print or display an announcement including an appropriate copyright notice and a notice that there is no warranty (or else, saying that you provide a warranty) and that users may redistribute the program under these conditions, and telling the user how to view a copy of this License. (Exception: if the Program itself is interactive but does not normally print such an announcement, your work based on the Program is not required to print an announcement.)

These requirements apply to the modified work as a whole. If identifiable sections of that work are not derived from the Program, and can be reasonably considered independent and separate works in themselves, then this License, and its terms, do not apply to those sections when you distribute them as separate works. But when you distribute the same sections as part of a whole which is a work based on the Program, the distribution of the whole must be on the terms of this License, whose permissions for other licensees extend to the entire whole, and thus to each and every part regardless of who wrote it.

Thus, it is not the intent of this section to claim rights or contest your rights to work written entirely by you; rather, the intent is to exercise the right to control the distribution of derivative or collective works based on the Program.

In addition, mere aggregation of another work not based on the Program with the Program (or with a work based on the Program) on a volume of a storage or distribution medium does not bring the other work under the scope of this License.

3. You may copy and distribute the Program (or a work based on it, under Section 2) in object code or executable form under the terms of Sections 1 and 2 above provided that you also do one of the following:

    a. Accompany it with the complete corresponding machine-readable source code, which must be distributed under the terms of Sections 1 and 2 above on a medium customarily used for software interchange; or,

    b. Accompany it with a written offer, valid for at least three years, to give any third party, for a charge no more than your cost of physically performing source distribution, a complete machine-readable copy of the corresponding source code, to be distributed under the terms of Sections 1 and 2 above on a medium customarily used for software interchange; or,

    c. Accompany it with the information you received as to the offer to distribute corresponding source code. (This alternative is allowed only for noncommercial distribution and only if you received the program in object code or executable form with such an offer, in accord with Subsection b above.)

The source code for a work means the preferred form of the work for making modifications to it. For an executable work, complete source code means all the source code for all modules it contains, plus any associated interface definition files, plus the scripts used to control compilation and installation of the executable. However, as a special exception, the source code distributed need not include anything that is normally distributed (in either source or binary form) with the major components (compiler, kernel, and so on) of the operating system on which the executable runs, unless that component itself accompanies the executable.

If distribution of executable or object code is made by offering access to copy from a designated place, then offering equivalent access to copy the source code from the same place counts as distribution of the source code, even though third parties are not compelled to copy the source along with the object code.

4. You may not copy, modify, sublicense, or distribute the Program except as expressly provided under this License. Any attempt otherwise to copy, modify, sublicense or distribute the Program is void, and will automatically terminate your rights under this License. However, parties who have received copies, or rights, from you under this License will not have their licenses terminated so long as such parties remain in full compliance.

5. You are not required to accept this License, since you have not signed it. However, nothing else grants you permission to modify or distribute the Program or its derivative works. These actions are prohibited by law if you do not accept this License. Therefore, by modifying or distributing the Program (or any work based on the Program), you indicate your acceptance of this License to do so, and all its terms and conditions for copying, distributing or modifying the Program or works based on it.

6. Each time you redistribute the Program (or any work based on the Program), the recipient automatically receives a license from the original licensor to copy, distribute or modify the Program subject to these terms and conditions. You may not impose any further restrictions on the recipients' exercise of the rights granted herein. You are not responsible for enforcing compliance by third parties to this License.

7. If, as a consequence of a court judgment or allegation of patent infringement or for any other reason (not limited to patent issues), conditions are imposed on you (whether by court order, agreement or otherwise) that contradict the conditions of this License, they do not excuse you from the conditions of this License. If you cannot distribute so as to satisfy simultaneously your obligations under this License and any other pertinent obligations, then as a consequence you may not distribute the Program at all. For example, if a patent license would not permit royalty-free redistribution of the Program by all those who receive copies directly or indirectly through you, then the only way you could satisfy both it and this License would be to refrain entirely from distribution of the Program.

   If any portion of this section is held invalid or unenforceable under any particular circumstance, the balance of the section is intended to apply and the section as a whole is intended to apply in other circumstances.

   It is not the purpose of this section to induce you to infringe any patents or other property right claims or to contest validity of any such claims; this section has the sole purpose of protecting the integrity of the free software distribution system, which is implemented by public license practices. Many people have made generous contributions to the wide range of software distributed through that system in reliance on consistent application of that system; it is up to the author/donor to decide if he or she is willing to distribute software through any other system and a licensee cannot impose that choice.

   This section is intended to make thoroughly clear what is believed to be a consequence of the rest of this License.

8. If the distribution and/or use of the Program is restricted in certain countries either by patents or by copyrighted interfaces, the original copyright holder who places the Program under this License may add an explicit geographical distribution limitation excluding those countries, so that distribution is permitted only in or among countries not thus excluded. In such case, this License incorporates the limitation as if written in the body of this License.

9. The Free Software Foundation may publish revised and/or new versions of the General Public License from time to time. Such new versions will be similar in spirit to the present version, but may differ in detail to address new problems or concerns.

   Each version is given a distinguishing version number. If the Program specifies a version number of this License which applies to it and "any later version", you have the option of following the terms and conditions either of that version or of any later version published by the Free Software Foundation. If the Program does not specify a version number of this License, you may choose any version ever published by the Free Software Foundation.

10. If you wish to incorporate parts of the Program into other free programs whose distribution conditions are different, write to the author to ask for permission. For software which is copyrighted by the Free Software Foundation, write to the Free Software Foundation; we sometimes make exceptions for this. Our decision will be guided by the two goals of preserving the free status of all derivatives of our free software and of promoting the sharing and reuse of software generally.

NO WARRANTY

11. BECAUSE THE PROGRAM IS LICENSED FREE OF CHARGE, THERE IS NO WARRANTY FOR THE PROGRAM, TO THE EXTENT PERMITTED BY APPLICABLE LAW. EXCEPT WHEN OTHERWISE STATED IN WRITING THE COPYRIGHT HOLDERS AND/OR OTHER PARTIES PROVIDE THE PROGRAM "AS IS" WITHOUT WARRANTY OF ANY KIND, EITHER EXPRESSED OR IMPLIED, INCLUDING, BUT NOT LIMITED TO, THE IMPLIED WARRANTIES OF MERCHANTABILITY AND FITNESS FOR A PARTICULAR PURPOSE. THE ENTIRE RISK AS TO THE QUALITY AND PERFORMANCE OF THE PROGRAM IS WITH YOU. SHOULD THE PROGRAM PROVE DEFECTIVE, YOU ASSUME THE COST OF ALL NECESSARY SERVICING, REPAIR OR CORRECTION.

12. IN NO EVENT UNLESS REQUIRED BY APPLICABLE LAW OR AGREED TO IN WRITING WILL ANY COPYRIGHT HOLDER, OR ANY OTHER PARTY WHO MAY MODIFY AND/OR REDISTRIBUTE THE PROGRAM AS PERMITTED ABOVE, BE LIABLE TO YOU FOR DAMAGES, INCLUDING ANY GENERAL, SPECIAL, INCIDENTAL OR CONSEQUENTIAL DAMAGES ARISING OUT OF THE USE OR INABILITY TO USE THE PROGRAM (INCLUDING BUT NOT LIMITED TO LOSS OF DATA OR DATA BEING RENDERED INACCURATE OR LOSSES SUSTAINED BY YOU OR THIRD PARTIES OR A FAILURE OF THE PROGRAM TO OPERATE WITH ANY OTHER PROGRAMS), EVEN IF SUCH HOLDER OR OTHER PARTY HAS BEEN ADVISED OF THE POSSIBILITY OF SUCH DAMAGES.

END OF TERMS AND CONDITIONS

E.3 Appendix: How to Apply These Terms to Your New Programs

If you develop a new program, and you want it to be of the greatest possible use to the public, the best way to achieve this is to make it free software which everyone can redistribute and change under these terms.

To do so, attach the following notices to the program. It is safest to attach them to the start of each source file to most effectively convey the exclusion of warranty; and each file should have at least the "copyright" line and a pointer to where the full notice is found.

⟨*one line to give the program's name and a brief idea of what it does.*⟩ Copyright ©19yy ⟨*name of author*⟩

This program is free software; you can redistribute it and/or modify it under the terms of the GNU General Public License as published by the Free Software Foundation; either version 2 of the License, or (at your option) any later version.

This program is distributed in the hope that it will be useful, but WITHOUT ANY WARRANTY; without even the implied warranty of MERCHANTABILITY or FITNESS FOR A PARTICULAR PURPOSE. See the GNU General Public License for more details.

You should have received a copy of the GNU General Public License along with this program; if not, write to the Free Software Foundation, Inc., 675 Mass Ave, Cambridge, MA 02139, USA.

Also add information on how to contact you by electronic and paper mail.

If the program is interactive, make it output a short notice like this when it starts in an interactive mode:

```
Gnomovision version 69, Copyright (C) 19yy name of author Gnomovision
comes with ABSOLUTELY NO WARRANTY; for details type 'show w'. This is
free software, and you are welcome to redistribute it under certain
conditions; type 'show c' for details.
```

The hypothetical commands 'show w' and 'show c' should show the appropriate parts of the General Public License. Of course, the commands you use may be called something other than 'show w' and 'show c'; they could even be mouse-clicks or menu items–whatever suits your program.

You should also get your employer (if you work as a programmer) or your school, if any, to sign a "copyright disclaimer" for the program, if necessary. Here is a sample; alter the names:

Yoyodyne, Inc., hereby disclaims all copyright interest in the program 'Gnomovision' (which makes passes at compilers) written by James Hacker.

⟨*signature of Ty Coon*⟩, 1 April 1989
Ty Coon, President of Vice

This General Public License does not permit incorporating your program into proprietary programs. If your program is a subroutine library, you may consider it more useful to permit linking proprietary applications with the library. If this is what you want to do, use the GNU Library General Public License instead of this License.

Index